Selected
Hotels & Inns
EAST COAST
NORTH AMERICA

FEATURED ON FRONT COVER:
Ripplecove Inn, Quebec
Newcastle Inn, Maine
Woodstock Inn & Resort, Vermont
Inn at Ormsby Hill, Vermont
Tides Inn, Virginia

Copyright © U.S. Welcome Ltd.

All rights reserved.
No part of this book may be reproduced in any manner whatsoever without the written permission of the publishers.

ISBN 0 9522508 2 9
First edition January 1997

Editor:
Marilyn Messik

Editorial Team:
Caroline Marcuse, Carole Bernholt, Andree Curtis, Estelle Hilsum, Dani Messik.

Whilst every possible care has been taken in the compilation of this directory, the publishers cannot accept responsibility for any inaccuracies or changes since going to press, or for consequential loss arising from such changes or inaccuracies, or for any other loss, direct or consequential arising in connection with information describing properties in this publication.

Published in the UK by
U.S Welcome Directories
A Division of U.S. Welcome Ltd.,
PO Box 116, Northwood, England HA6 3BH
Tel (0) 1923 821469. Fax (0) 1923 827157
http://www.uswelcome.com
100127.2706@compuserve.com
Freephone in the U.S. 1-888 INN VISIT

Design & Reproduction: Triffik Technology Ltd.
Printing: The Really Reliable Company Ltd.

This book is dedicated to those hundreds of travellers who have given me invaluable feedback; to the hoteliers, innkeepers and professional associations who have shared their acquired wisdom so generously with me and to the saintly crew in my office. Grateful thanks also to my intrepid research team of inspectors who must, of necessity, remain anonymous, but who leave no stone unturned in their search for excellence.

MARILYN MESSIK

Selected Hotels & Inns

EAST COAST NORTH AMERICA

For PEOPLE WHO PREFER TO BE MORE THAN JUST A ROOM NUMBER.

Our aim in putting together this book is to offer a range of accommodation choices to suit all tastes, from luxury hotels and resorts to cosy country inns. Each of the properties we select for the Directory is independently owned and run and, although no two are the same, what they all have in common is their standard of excellence and a commitment to work with **U.S. Welcome**, to ensure that every guest has a wonderful visit.

Choice matters...

International Associations

U.S. Welcome is proud to be associated with those who share the same philosophy of hospitality in Great Britain, Ireland and South Africa
(see pages 215, 216 & 217)

Meeting your expectations

We believe that the definition of a good holiday or business trip is one where expectations are met (and hopefully exceeded!). When making your plans, it is important to consider the differences between full-service hotels or resorts, country inns and small bed & breakfasts. How you make your choices will depend entirely on your own personal preferences.

Whilst the charm of smaller establishments is their size and informality, bear in mind that some services and facilities are not automatically available. There may be no-one to help with luggage at check-in, rooms do not always have tv and phone and there isn't usually 24-hour room service. If you have a heavy case and a bad back, need to be in constant touch with the outside world and are subject to food cravings in the middle of the night, this will not be the right place for you! On the other hand, if you travel light, loathe tv, never want to hear from the office again, and can struggle through from a cordon bleu five-course candlelit dinner to a gourmet breakfast, without a midnight snack – you'll be in heaven!

Small inns often offer wonderful opportunities for guests to socialise; over breakfast or pre-dinner drinks, or perhaps dining family-style with everyone seated around one table. This can be a highlight of the holiday, a chance to meet and mix with interesting folk you might never normally come across and to forge friendships that may last long beyond the holiday. If, however, you are going away for peace and solitude and want to commune with nothing more than nature, each other and some excellent food, then you might prefer a slightly larger inn.

continued...

Meeting your expectations

If you have special dietary requirements, do mention this when making a reservation so that you can be reassured you will have no problems when you arrive. The same applies to any pet hates or phobias – too late, when greeted enthusiastically by an inn's Great Dane, to point out that you can't stand dogs.

Some inns and resorts cater for children, some don't; do take note and not offence at this, telling you in advance is just as much for your benefit as the innkeeper's. Few parents amongst us can relax while a boisterous toddler wreaks havoc with the antiques and throws-up the gourmet cuisine!

We do strongly suggest that you book ahead at peak times such as foliage season in New England. Nothing spoils a holiday more than arriving at an inn or hotel after a long drive, only to be told that they are full. Even the most even-tempered of couples can be reduced to exchanging recriminations at this point!

Although we shouldn't generalise, hoteliers and innkeepers are a warm, professional, friendly and helpful bunch of people - if they weren't they wouldn't still be in business! They want you to enjoy your trip as much as you do. So, before booking, take the time to ask as many questions as you need - the first sign of a good hotel or inn is their willingness to give you all the answers and information you require. Alternatively you can call our FREE Booking Service on 01923 821469 in the U.K. or 1-888-INN-VISIT in the U.S. we are always happy to offer you as much help as we can.

Terms used in the Directory

We're not great believers in using symbols - in our experience they can lead to confusion and a migraine! You will find information about each property set out as follows:

✻ **ROOM RATES** are quoted per room, per night, for two people, unless stated otherwise.
Children are often welcome to stay free in a room with their parents, but there is usually an additional charge made for teenagers or another adult.

✻ **EUROPEAN PLAN (EP)** indicates that no meals are included in the rate.

✻ **BED & BREAKFAST (B&B)** can range from a simple coffee and Danish, to a cooked country breakfast that will set you up for the day and beyond!

✻ **MODIFIED AMERICAN PLAN (MAP)** means that breakfast and dinner are both included in the quoted rate.

✻ **AMERICAN PLAN (AP)** is still offered by a few of the traditional family resorts and this covers three meals a day.

✻ **PRICE RANGES** reflect the size, views or facilities of the room. At off-season periods, prices may be lower and it is always worth asking if there are any Special Rates available. For example, city hotels may offer a reduction on some week-ends, while resort hotels often have a special rate for longer stays, or to include sports facilities and tuition. Rates are quoted, in most cases, exclusive of tax, which varies from state to state.

✻ **SUITES, APARTMENTS, COTTAGES OR CONDOMINIUMS**. As a general rule anything that is defined as self-contained has its own entrance. A condominium is a property that is privately owned but rented out and managed by a hotel, inn or resort complex.
Cottages, apartments or houses usually have fully equipped kitchens, whereas this is not always the case with suites. If you are unsure, always check with US Welcome's Booking Service or with the individual establishment.

✻ **SERVICE CHARGE.** Some properties include a service charge in their rate, others leave gratuities to the discretion of guests. N.B. Tipping is more formalised in America and ranges between 15-20%.

DO MENTION the **Welcome Directory** when you make a booking directly with a hotel or inn - it may get you a better deal!

PERPETUAL CALENDAR

ITINERARY

FLIGHT DETAILS

Departure date/times ....

Homeward date/times ....

Car hire details ....

....

....

Holiday insurance ....

ACCOMMODATION DETAILS

Hotel/Inn	Check in date	Check out date	No. of nights	Cost per night	Total cost	Deposit paid

Don't forget - call U.S. Welcome for free booking service
01923 821469.

EAST COAST

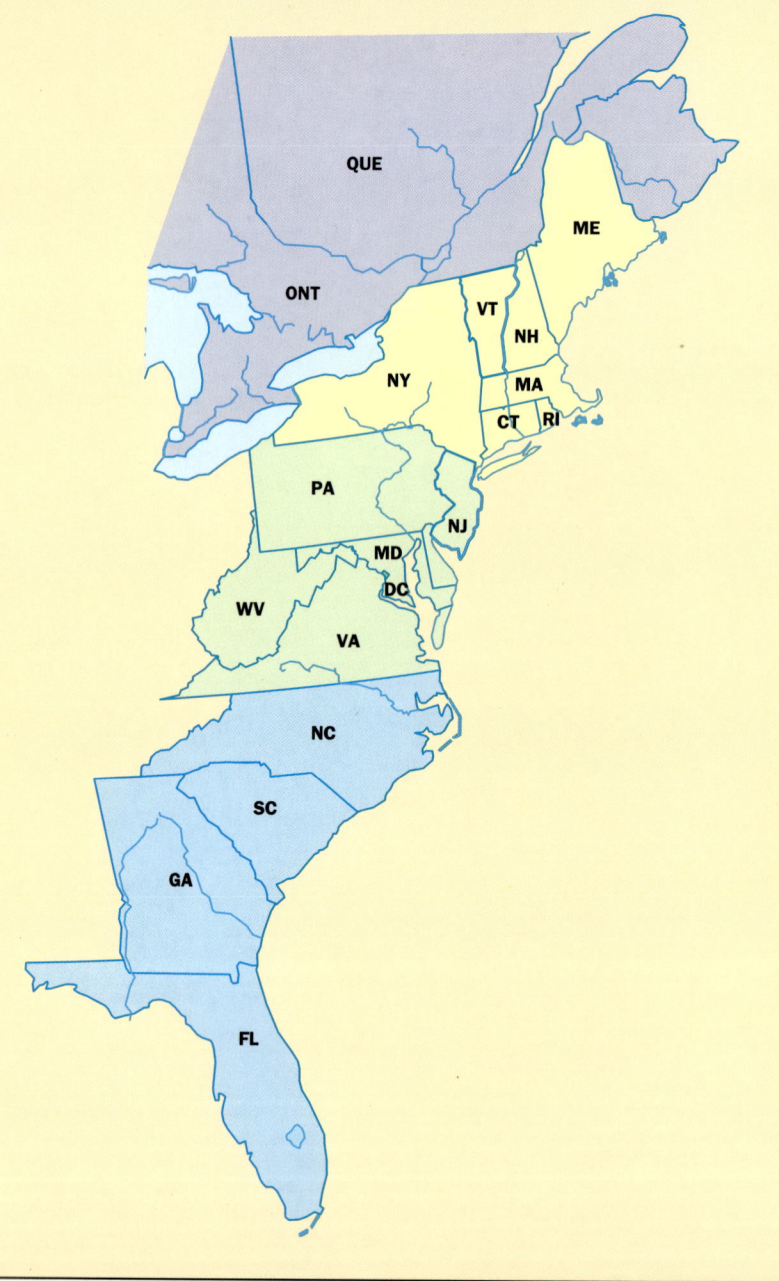

NOTES

Contents

EASTERN CANADA
Eastern Canada Map — 16

ONTARIO
Briars — 17
Little Inn of Bayfield — 18
Millcroft Inn — 19

QUEBEC
Auberge des Sablons — 20
Auberge Handfield — 21
Auberge Saint-Antoine — 22
Ripplecove Inn — 23

NEW ENGLAND

CONNECTICUT
Connecticut Map — 24
Bee & Thistle Inn — 25
Boulders — 26
Homestead Inn (Greenwich) — 27
Inn at National Hall — 28
Norwich Inn & Spa — 29
Brigadoon — 30
Griswold Inn — 30
Homestead Inn (New Milford) — 31
Manor House — 31
Old Mystic Inn — 32
Riverwind Inn — 32
White Hart Inn — 33

MAINE
Maine Map — 34
Bar Harbor Hotel-Bluenose Inn — 35
Bayview Hotel — 36
Black Point Inn — 37
Captain Daniel Stone Inn — 38
Captain Lord Mansion — 39
Gorges Grant Hotel — 40
Harraseeket Inn — 41
Inn By The Sea — 42
Spruce Point Inn — 43
Stage Neck Inn — 44
Sugarloaf — 45
Andrews Lodging — 46
Bagley House — 46
Blue Harbor House — 47
Blue Hill Inn — 47
Captain Lindsay House Inn — 48
Dockside Guest Quarters — 48
Greenville Inn — 49
Kennebunkport Inn — 49
Lawnmeer Inn — 50
Lodge at Moosehead Lake — 50
Maine Stay Inn — 51
Maine Stay Inn & Cottages — 51
Mira Monte Inn — 52
Newcastle Inn — 52
Ocean Gate — 53
Ocean Point Inn — 53
York Harbor Inn — 54

MASSACHUSETTS
Massachusetts Map — 56
Blantyre — 58
Boston Harbor Hotel — 59
Captain's House Inn of Chatham — 60
Charles Hotel — 61
Chatham Bars Inn — 62
Colonnade Hotel — 63
Dan'l Webster Inn — 64
Deerfield Inn — 65
Harbor Light Inn — 66
Jared Coffin House — 67
Lenox Hotel — 68
Ocean Edge Resort & Golf Club — 69
Publick House Historic Inn — 70
Red Lion Inn — 72
Salem Inn — 73
Thorncroft Inn — 74
Whalewalk Inn — 75
Yankee Clipper Inn — 76
Bradford Inn — 78
Cambridge House — 78
Captain Nickerson Inn — 79
Corner House Inn — 79
Diamond District Inn — 80
Hawthorne Inn — 80
Inn at Stockbridge — 81
Isaiah Hall — 81
Isaiah Jones Homestead — 82
John Carver Inn — 83
Lighthouse Inn — 83
Longfellow's Wayside Inn — 84
Marlborough — 84
Mary Prentiss — 85
Mostly Hall — 85
Onset Pointe Inn — 86
Pleasant Bay Village Resort — 86
Queen Anne Inn — 87
Rocky Shores Inn & Cottages — 87
Sharon Inn — 88
Village Green Inn — 88
Village Inn — 89
Weathervane Inn — 89
Wedgewood Inn — 90
Wildflower Inn — 90

Contents

NEW HAMPSHIRE

New Hampshire Map	92
Chesterfield Inn	93
Inns at Mills Falls & Bay Point	94
Inn at Thorn Hill	95
Inn of Exeter	96
Manor on Golden Pond	97
Sise Inn	98
Snowvillage Inn	99
Waterville Estates Resort	100
Buttonwood Inn	101
Colby Hill Inn	101
Dexter's Inn & Tennis Club	102
Ellis River House	102
Forest, A Country Inn	103
Foxglove	103
Franconia Inn	104
Hancock Inn	104
New London Inn	105
Notchland Inn	105
Olde Orchard Inn	106
Sugar Hill Inn	106
Village House	107

RHODE ISLAND

Rhode Island Map	108
Block Island Resorts	109
Cliffside Inn	110
Bed & Breakfast on the Point	111
Grandview	111
Larchwood Inn	112
Villa	112

VERMONT

Vermont Map	114
Basin Harbor Club	117
Cornucopia of Dorset	118
Cortina Inn	119
Equinox	120
Four Columns Inn	121
Golden Eagle Resort	122
Hawk Inn & Resort	123
Inn at Essex	124
Inn at Ormsby Hill	125
Inn on the Common	126
Mountain Road Resort	127
Old Tavern at Grafton	128
Rabbit Hill Inn	129
Sugarbush Inn & Resort	130
Windham Hill Inn	131
Woodstock Inn & Resort	132
Ardmore Inn	134
Barrows House	134
Blueberry Hill Inn	135

Brandon Inn	135
Castle	136
Churchill House Inn	136
Deerhill Inn	137
Gables	137
Hamilton House	138
Inn at the Brass Lantern	138
Inn at the Round Barn Farm	139
Inn at West View Farm	139
Landgrove Inn	140
Lareau Farm Country Inn	140
Maple Leaf Inn	141
Middlebury Inn	141
October Country Inn	142
Quechee Bed & Breakfast	142
Shire Inn	143
Siebeness	143
Sugartree	144
Sugar Lodge	144
Tucker Hill Lodge	145
Vermont Inn	145
Village Country Inn	146
West Hill House	146
West Mountain Inn	147
Woods	147

MID-ATLANTIC

Mid-Atlantic Map	150

MARYLAND

Antrim 1844	152
Harbor Court Hotel	153
Inn at Perry Cabin	154
Historic Inns of Annapolis	155
Kent Manor Inn	155
Mr. Mole	156
Wades Point Inn on the Bay	156

NEW JERSEY

Bernards Inn	157
Chimney Hill Farm	158
Inn at Millrace Pond	158

NEW YORK STATE

Copperfield Inn	159
Craftsman Inn	160
Geneva-on-the-Lake	161
Manhattan East Suites Hotels	162
Roycroft Inn	163
Sagamore on Lake George	164
Bird & Bottle	165
Halsey House	165
Rose Inn	166
Sedgwick Inn	166

Contents

PENNSYLVANIA

Baladerry Inn	167
Barleysheaf Inn	167
Boxwood Inn	168
Carnegie House	168
Doneckers	169
Evermay on the Delaware	169
French Manor	170
Historic Smithton Inn	170
King's Cottage	171
Pineapple Hill	171
Settlers Inn	172
Sterling Inn	172
Wedgwood Inn of New Hope	173

VIRGINIA

Bailiwick Inn	174
Berkeley Hotel	175
Boar's Head Inn	176
Keswick Hall	177
L'Auberge Provencale	178
Morrison House	179
Staunton Hill Country Inn	180
Tides Inn	181
Applewood Colonial	182
Chester House	182
Clifton	183
Colonial Capital	183
Frederick House	184
Henry Clay Inn	184
Homestay	185
Hummingbird Inn	185
Inn at Gristmill Square	186
Inn at Meander Plantation	186
Inn at Narrow Passage	187
Llewellyn Lodge	187
Manor at Taylor's Store	188
Oaks	188
Steeles Tavern Manor	189
Trillium House	189

WASHINGTON DC

George Washington University Inn	190
Embassy Inn	191
Normandy Inn	191
Windsor Inn	192

WEST VIRGINIA

Country Inn	193
Hillbrook Inn	194

SOUTHERN STATES

Southern States Map	195

FLORIDA

Amelia Island Plantation	196
Elizabeth Pointe Lodge	197
Heron House	198
Lakeside Inn	199
Chalet Suzanne	200
Darst Victorian Manor	200
Hibiscus House	201
Verona House	201

GEORGIA

Little St. Simon's Island	202
Glen-Ella Springs	203

NORTH CAROLINA

First Colony Inn	204
Swag Country Inn	205

SOUTH CAROLINA

Fulton Lane Inn	206
Planters Inn	207
Ashley Inn	208
Cannonboro Inn	208

TASTERS

Tasters Map	210
Empress of Little Rock	210
Southwest Inn at Sedona	211
Laburnum Cottage	211
Camellia Inn	211
Campbell Ranch Inn	211
Cheshire Cat Inn	211
Goose & Turrets	211
Inn at Union Square	212
Two Angels Inn	212
Abriendo Inn	212
Alpine Inn	212
Castle Marne	212
Queen Anne Inn	212
Woodland Inn	213
Chalet Kilauea	213
Shipman House	213
Bear Creek Lodge	213
Channel House	213
Columbia Gorge Hotel	213
Peacock Hill	214
Brown Pelican	214
Mariposa Ranch	214
Rosevine Inn	214
Shelburne Inn	214
Mansion Hill Inn	214
E-mail & Web site index	218

DISCOVER
...some of the finest scenery in the world.

Unspoiled forests, lakes, rivers and sandy beaches are the backdrop for a wonderful resort escape to beautiful Ontario, Canada. Whether you're looking for your own rustic cabin and fireplace or the ultimate in luxury and amenities, you'll find the experience you were searching for.

The Great Escapes Guide is a colourful catalogue of over 220 Ontario resorts with photos, descriptions and pertinent contact information.

Just telephone, fax, write or e-mail and ask for your free copy.

Tel: 705-325-9115   Fax: 705-325-7999
E-mail: escapes@resorts-ontario.com
Internet: http://www.resorts-ontario.com
P.O. Box 2148, Orillia, Ontario, Canada L3V 6S1

Eastern Canada

QUEBEC
1. Auberge Des Sablons — 20
2. Auberge Handfield — 21
3. Auberge Saint-Antoine — 22
4. Ripplecove Inn — 23

ONTARIO
5. Briars — 17
6. Little Inn of Bayfield — 18
7. Millcroft Inn — 19

ONTARIO

THE BRIARS
JACKSON'S POINT

This magnificent 200-acre Lake Simcoe estate is less than an hour from Toronto and its many attractions, theatres and shopping, but provides so many recreation, sporting and entertainment diversions that guests simply don't want to leave. Here, guests return year after year to fifth generation Sibbald family hospitality.

This idyllic setting inspires romantic strolls among expansive gardens and towering trees, along sweeping shoreline reflecting fluffy clouds, or amid marked nature trails that provide sanctuary to you and over 140 species of birds.

Of course, The Briars experience also includes attentive service, fine country dining and charming accommodations in the Manor House, adjoining wings, lakeside and woodland cottages.

It's another world. You'll be glad you came.

55 Hedge Road, RR1
Jackson's Point,
Ontario L0E 1L0
•
Tel 905 722 3271
Fax 905 722 9698
Freephone in US & Canada
800 465 2376
•
Owner & Manager:
John D. Sibbald
•
80 rooms plus 12 one and two bedroom cottages and suites

Doubles, suites and cottages
$290 - $390 (Can.$) AP
Tax 12% s.c. 15%
•
Indoor and outdoor pools,
whirlpool, sauna, tennis,
golf, sailing, cruises,
cycling, summer theatre,
fitness centre, childrens'
programmes, skiing,
skating, conference facilities
•
Children welcome
•
VS • MC • Amex

ONTARIO

LITTLE INN OF BAYFIELD
BAYFIELD

This AAA Four Diamond Award winner has been welcoming guests to its two-storey gingerbread embellished porch, comfortably shaded by an old willow tree, since the 1830s. With the beaches of beautiful Lake Huron for boating and water sports nearby, the picturesque village of Bayfield is ideally located for Ontario explorations whilst in Fall and Winter the Little Inn is a popular destination for hikers, cross-country skiers and snowshoers.

Guest rooms are individually and thoughtfully decorated, many with double whirlpools and a few with fireplaces. Dining at the Little Inn, which has just achieved the accolade of the Wine Spectator Award of Excellence, is an experience not to be missed - an imaginative menu full of fresh local produce, beautifully presented and topped by one of the Inn's superb desserts for which they are justifiably famed.

Within comfortable driving distances are three theatre festivals, or drive a little further to the Mennonite communities around Elmira and hike through dramatic Elora Gorge.

Main Street,
P.O. Box 100,
Bayfield,
Ontario N0M 1G0

•

Tel 519 565 2611
Fax 519 565 5474
Freephone in US
800 565 1832

•

General Manager:
Richard Fitoussi

•

30 rooms & suites

•

Doubles $99 - $215
(Can $.)B&B

Tax 12%
•
Conference facilities, beach.
•
Nearby: Outdoor pool, tennis, golf, riding, cycling, sailing, water skiing, cross-country skiing, snowshoeing
•
Children welcome.
•
Non-smoking
•
VS • MC • Amex
Diners • En Route

ONTARIO

MILLCROFT INN
ALTON

Nestled in the rolling Caledon Hills, only 40 minutes from Toronto, the Millcroft Inn's understated elegance and charm is a balm for the soul.

The award-winning, Four Diamond Millcroft Inn is a beautifully restored 19th century knitting mill, set serenely on the Credit River. Warm hospitality, luxurious accommodations decorated in period antiques and four diamond cuisine are just a few of the reasons for you to pay a visit. Savour delicious meals in the historic dining room, on the outdoor patio overlooking the peaceful millpond or in the glass dining area spectacularly suspended over the falls. For extra privacy you may choose to stay in one of the Crofts, two storey chalet type accommodations with outdoor hot tub.

The 100 acre woodland property offers wonderful hiking and cycling or simply drift over the countryside in a hot air balloon.

55 John Street, Alton,
Ontario L0N 1A0

•

Tel 519 941 8111
Fax 519 941 9192
Freephone in Ontario
800 383 3976

•

Innkeeper
Wolfgang Stichnothe

•

52 rooms

•

Doubles $175 - $250
(Can.$) B&B

Tax 15%

•

Outdoor pool, sauna, tennis, hiking, biking, cross-country skiing, fly fishing.

•

Nearby downhill skiing, golf, horseriding, hot air ballooning

•

Children welcome

•

VS • MC
Amex • Diners

19

QUEBEC

AUBERGE DES SABLONS
ST-IRÉNÉE

"Villa des Sablons" was built in 1902 by Joseph Lavergne, an Ottawa District Superior Court judge. As a lawyer, he was an associate and close friend of Sir Wilfrid Laurier, the first French Canadian to be elected Prime Minister.

In 1983, the house was renovated and became l'Auberge des Sablons. Each of its rooms is decorated artfully, inspired by the countryside, some rooms have fireplaces, others have a balcony from which guests can experience the unparalleled scenery of this breathtaking area. Your hosts and innkeepers, Marielle and Jean-Guy Alain, are known for their special way of welcoming guests as friends. Enjoy a peaceful retreat in an intimate setting, and a traditional fine cuisine considered to be among the best in the area.

Located in the magnificent Charlevoix region of Quebec, Auberge des Sablons is just 1½ hours of beautiful scenery Northeast of Quebec City.

223 Chemin les Bains,
St-Irénée,
Quebec, GOT 1VO
•
Tel 418 452 3594
Fax 418 452 3240
Freephone in US & Canada
800 267 3594
•
Owner/Innkeeper:
Jean-Guy Alain
•
15 rooms, 13 of which
have private baths.
1 one bedroom suite
4 apartments with fireplaces

Doubles $158 - $268
(Can $) MAP
Suites and apartments
$198 - $248 EP
•
Tax 13.5%
•
Conference facilities.
Nearby: golf courses, riding,
sailing, water skiing, down-
hill & cross-country skiing
Children over 12 welcome.
•
Non-smoking
•
VS • MC
Amex • Diners

QUEBEC

AUBERGE HANDFIELD
ST-MARC-SUR-RICHELIEU

In an historic French-Canadian village on the Richelieu River, 30 minutes north of Montreal, enjoy the atmosphere, rustic decor and country crafted furnishings of a venerable, 160 year old mansion.

The warm and cosy log cabin style dining room serves outstanding cuisine and opens to a sunny converted glassed-in porch. All rooms have colour cable tv, phones and private baths with the deluxe Laflamme Pavillon located right by the river and offering extra facilities such as balcony, fireplace and whirlpool bath.

A marina, and resort facilities including an extremely well equipped health club and spa and the attentions of professional staff to administer luxurious treatments, complete the pleasure of your stay at the Auberge Handfield.

555 Chemin du Prince,
St-Marc-Sur-Richelieu,
Quebec J0L 2E0

•

Tel 514 584 2226
Fax 514 584 3650
Freephone in US & Canada
800 667 1087

•

General Manager:
Pierre Handfield

•

Owner: Conrad Handfield

•

53 rooms
3 one-bedroom suites

1 two-bedroom suite

•

Doubles $65 - $110
(Can $) EP
Suites $145 - $160

•

Tax 13.96%

•

Outdoor pool,
fitness center, spa,
conference facilities

•

Children welcome

•

VS • MC
Amex • Diners

21

QUEBEC

AUBERGE SAINT-ANTOINE
QUEBEC

Auberge Saint-Antoine is unquestionably one of the most captivating inns within Quebec City. Every thought has been given to making our guests feel at home. The living room, has a quiet relaxing atmosphere with its stone walls, wooden beams, subdued lighting and furniture upholstered with warmly coloured fabrics. In the winter, sit by the windows and daydream while watching the drifting ice on the St. Lawrence River, in summer watch the cruising and sailing boats.

Guest rooms are unique and beautifully appointed, offering amenities usually reserved for the most luxurious hotels. For social and business functions, the personnel of the Auberge Saint-Antoine guarantees the success of each of your initiatives. In short, many say that the Auberge Saint-Antoine is a small paradise nestled in a heavenly city!

Museums, antiques, art galleries and boutiques are minutes away, and the area is rich with restaurants and cafes, from the charming to the very sophisticated.

10 rue Saint-Antoine,
Quebec City,
Quebec G1K 4C9
•
Tel 418 692 2211
Fax 418 692 1177
Freephone in US
888 692 2211
•
General Manager:
Julie Leclerc
•
31 rooms
including 5 one bedroom
suites, 2 two bedroom suites

Doubles $169 - $439
(Can $) B&B
Suites $199 - $439
•
Tax 13.5%
•
Conference facilities
Nearby: swimming, tennis,
golf, riding, sailing, skiing
•
Free parking available
•
Children welcome.
•
Non-smoking

VS • MC • Amex • Diners

QUEBEC

RIPPLECOVE INN
AYER'S CLIFF

On a beautifully landscaped, 12 acre lakeside estate, 75 minutes east of Montreal and just three hours north of Boston, stands the Ripplecove Inn. Recipient of the coveted Four Diamond Award every year since 1987, this establishment has grown to be one of Canada's most prestigious and luxurious Country Inns.

In Winter enjoy 35 km of groomed and tracked ski trails, ice fishing and skating, or excellent downhill skiing at five nearby mountains. In Summer we offer a fully equipped waterfront facility, with private beaches, heated pool, lake cruises, sailing and waterskiing.

Rooms and suites are beautifully decorated, many with whirlpool baths, balconies and fireplaces to add to your comfort and enjoyment. Award-winning French cuisine is served in the Victorian style dining room and lakeside terrace and Pub. Our pristine rural setting, together with luxurious accommodations and friendly bilingual service, makes Ripplecove Inn a must when visiting the beautiful province of Quebec.

700 Ripplecove Road,
Ayer's Cliff, Quebec,
J0B 1C0
•
Tel 819 838 4296
Fax 819 838 5541
•
Innkeeper/Owners:
Jeff & Debra Stafford
•
25 rooms
5 one bedroom suites
3-bedroom log cabin
with private beach,
porch, fireplace

Doubles $184 - $350
(Can $) MAP
Suites/cottage $310 - $420
•
Tax 14%
•
Outdoor pool, sailing, waterskiing, canoeing, windsurfing, conference facilities. Nearby: golf, horseriding, spa
•
Best meets the needs of children over age 4
•
VS • MC • Amex

Connecticut

❶	Bee & Thistle	25
❷	Boulders	26
❸	Brigadoon	30
❹	Griswold Inn	30
❺	Homestead Inn (Greenwich)	27
❻	Homestead Inn (New Milford)	31
❼	Inn at National Hall	28
❽	Manor House	31
❾	Norwich Inn & Spa	29
❿	Old Mystic Inn	32
⓫	Riverwind Inn	32
⓬	White Hart Inn	33

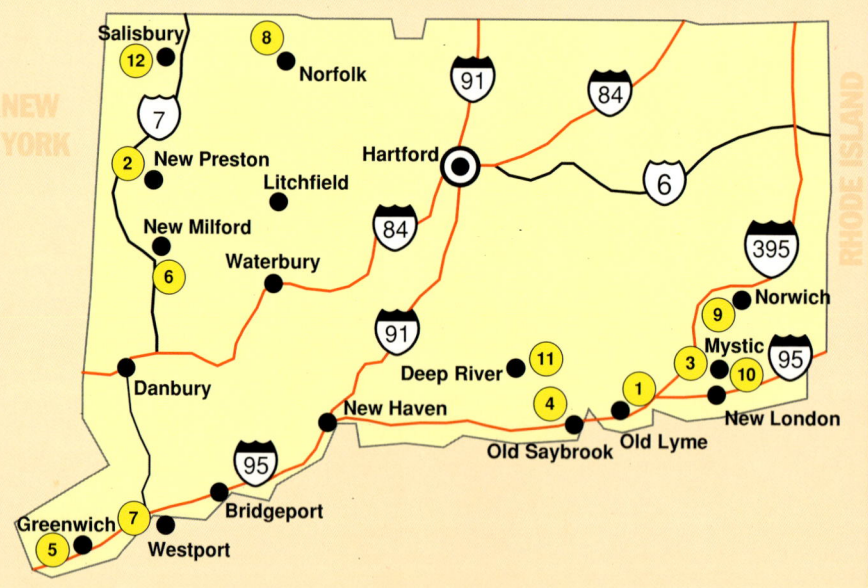

CONNECTICUT

BEE & THISTLE INN
OLD LYME

The Bee & Thistle Inn, built in 1756, and described as the "Quintessential American Inn" by the London Financial Times sits on five tree shaded acres along the Lieutenant River in the charming historic district of Old Lyme. It is bordered by stone walls, containing a sunken English perennial garden and is next to the Florence Griswold Museum, the home of American Impressionist art.

Eleven antique filled guest rooms and parlors offer a warm and comfortable place to pause for a moment from today's hectic pace of living. Its three star restaurant has been voted the "Most Romantic" place to dine in Connecticut for eight straight years by the readers of Connecticut Magazine.

An easy two hour drive from New York or Boston, will bring you to the inn. Let us share with you the hospitality and warmth of our home. Truly experience a return to early American gracious living.

100 Lyme Street,
Old Lyme, CT 06371
•
Tel 860 434 1667
Fax 860 434 3402
Freephone in US
800 622 4946
•
Innkeepers:
Bob, Penny,
Lori & Jeff Nelson
•
11 rooms
including
1 one bedroom cottage

Doubles $69 - $140 EP
Cottage $195
•
Tax 12%
•
Nearby: tennis, golf, horseriding, sailing, fitness center, hiking
•
Children over
12 welcome
•
VS • MC
Amex • Diners

CONNECTICUT

THE BOULDERS
NEW PRESTON

Nestled in the Litchfield Hills, the Boulders Inn was built in 1895 as a private residence. This architecturally striking Victorian home combines mansion-like elegance with the warmth of the country. In the 40-plus years of its existence as an inn, it has established an outstanding reputation, receiving countless kudos from respected national publications such as the New York Times, The Wine Spectator, Travel and Leisure Magazine, Country Inns and B&B Magazine etc.

Set at the foot of Pinnacle Mountain, guests can view breathtaking sunsets over Lake Waramaug, while enjoying the renowned cuisine in the glass-enclosed Lake Room, the outdoor terraces or relaxing by a fire. Beach, boats, tennis court and bicycles are available to guests. A hike up Pinnacle Mountain is rewarded with a spectacular vista of the Lake and surrounding mountains.

Dutch born Kees Adema & his German wife Ulla run the inn with relaxed European flair. In 1991 the Boulders received the much coveted "10 Best Country Inns of the Year" award.

East Shore Road,
(Rt 45)
New Preston,
CT 06777
•
Tel 860 868 0541
Fax 860 868 1925
Freephone in US
800 55 Boulders
•
Innkeepers:
Kees & Ulla Adema

15 rooms/guesthouses
including
2 one bedroom suites
•
Doubles $250 – $350
MAP
Suites $285 - $350
•
Tax 9.6%. s.c. 15%
•
Tennis, sailing, hiking
•
VS • MC • Amex

CONNECTICUT

HOMESTEAD INN
GREENWICH

Set among graceful trees and sweeping lawns in exclusive Belle Haven, just 45 minutes from New York City, the Homestead Inn's elegant facade invites the traveller to pause and savour the joys of a simpler time and place.

Each of the bedrooms in our three historic buildings reflects the romance and style of another era, many have canopy beds, and all are decorated in a simple yet elegant manner. Blending in with the many antiques are such civilised amenities as electric blankets, good reading lights, colour tv and clock radios.

A lovely old hydrangea bush drapes the front porch of the Main House, providing a shady nook for a cosy tête-à-tête on blue cushioned, white wicker settees. Fresh lemonade on warm, sunny afternoons encourages relaxation and renewal or enjoy the little Backgammon Room with its softly glowing fireplace in winter and The Chocolate Bar, an exceptionally pleasant spot for a quiet drink.

420 Field Point Road
Greenwich
CT 06830

•

Tel: 203 869 7500
Fax: 203 869 7500

•

Co-owners
Lessie Davison &
Nancy Smith

•

23 rooms
including 6 one
bedroom suites.

Doubles: $127 - $185
B&B
Suites: $160 - $185

•

Tax 12%. s.c. 6%

•

Conference facilities

•

Children welcome.

•

VS • MC
Amex • Diners

CONNECTICUT

INN AT NATIONAL HALL
WESTPORT

Fashioned after Europe's elite Manor Houses, the deluxe Inn at National Hall invites you to journey into the rich heritage of yesteryear. Built in 1873, it displays a delightful mix of whimsy, privacy, and history blended together to create the perfect setting for your Westport visit. The inn is comprised of fifteen individually decorated rooms and suites, a large first class restaurant, awarded a Four Star rating by the New York Times, and a resident's drawing room. The hotel is a member of Relais and Chateaux.

Selected chambers feature soaring two-storey ceilings with loft bedrooms enhanced by expansive windows and sweeping river views.

Westport, an easy drive from New York, offers visitors an abundance of stimulating cultural and recreational activities. Art and antique galleries attract collectors from far and wide, theatre flourishes, and the area's lively calendar bursts with exciting events year round.

Two Post Road West,
Westport,
CT 06880
•
Tel 203 221 1351
Fax 203 221 0276
Freephone in US
800 NAT HALL
•
General Manager:
Nick Carter M.V.O.
•
Non-smoking
•
8 rooms
7 one bedroom suites

Doubles $195 - $395
B&B
Suites $325 - $475
•
Tax 12%
•
Conference facility for
up to 16 people.
•
Nearby: fitness center
and pool
•
VS • MC
Amex • Diners

CONNECTICUT

NORWICH INN & SPA
NORWICH

Set amidst forty acres of lush gardens and woodlands with spring fed ponds, this historic Georgian style inn reflects an era of quiet refinement. From charming inn rooms to private villas accented with Ralph Lauren fabrics and prints, the Norwich Inn & Spa is the perfect New England country retreat.

Superb dining, delicious and satisfying Spa cuisine and a professional and attentive staff devoted to the guests' ultimate pleasure are all part of the experience. Relax and revitalize, set your own pace and indulge body and mind in a selection of fitness classes and pampering spa treatments that will leave you with a fresh outlook on life.

Within easy driving distance from New York City, Boston and Newport and convenient to trains and airline services. Minutes from Old Mystic Seaport, many historic sites, shops, antiques, and gambling at nearby Foxwoods and Mohican Sun Casinos.

607 West Thames St,
Norwich,
CT 06360

•

Tel 860 886 2401
Fax 860 886 9299
Freephone in US
800 275 4772

•

Vice President of
Operations:
Mark Vinchesi

•

30 inn rooms, 70 villas

Doubles $85 - $220 EP
Villas $220 - $245

•

Tax 12%

•

Outdoor & indoor pools,
tennis, golf, conference
facilities

•

Does not meet the
needs of children.

•

Non-smoking

•

VS • MC
Amex • Diners

CONNECTICUT

BRIGADOON
MYSTIC

Experience the relaxed, friendly atmosphere of a 250-year-old Victorian farmhouse just 1.3 miles from town. Enjoy our famous country breakfasts and afternoon tea, served by a roaring fire in winter or in the shade of an old dogwood tree in summer. Relax in our eight air-conditioned bedrooms, all with private baths and king or queen beds. Visit with other guests in our keeping room where complimentary wine is served nightly, or enjoy the large colour tv and vcr, books, games, magazines and movies provided for your pleasure.

Both Kay and Ted are avid travellers and love to compare notes with their guests, who come to Brigadoon from all over the world. They are dedicated to providing comfortable rooms, good food and genuine hospitality.

180 Cow Hill Road, Mystic, CT 06355　Tel 860 536 3033　Fax 860 536 1628	Owners/Innkeepers: Kay & Ted Lucas　8 rooms	Doubles $75 - $140 B&B including afternoon tea and evening beverage	Tax 12% Nearby: outdoor & indoor pools, tennis, golf, riding, sailing,	conference facilities, down-hill skiing, cross-country skiing Children over 5 welcome.	Non-smoking VS • MC • Amex

GRISWOLD INN
ESSEX

The Griswold Inn. More than a country hotel, more than a comfortable bed, an extraordinary meal, or a superb drink, the "Gris" is what Essex is all about. It embodies a spirit understood perhaps only as one warms up to its potbelly stove, or is hypnotized by the magic of a crackling log in one of its many fireplaces. It is a kaleidoscope of nostalgic images: a lovely country place. A myriad of Currier and Ives steamboat prints. A taproom described as the most handsome bar-room in America. A library of fire-arms dating from the 15th century. A group of charming dining rooms from which marvellous aromas and smiling faces flow. An historic collection of Antonio Jacobsen marine art. A gentle smile and a helping hand from a waitress. An affable bartender. A cuisine unmatched for its authenticity and purity.

| 36 Main Street, Essex, CT 06426 | Tel 860 767 1776 Fax 860 767 0381 | Innkeepers: Gregory, Douglas & Geoffrey Paul | 27 rooms including 14 suites Doubles $95 EP Suites $105 - $185 | Tax 12% Conference facilities. Nearby: tennis, golf, sailing, horseriding | Children welcome VS • MC • Amex |

CONNECTICUT

HOMESTEAD INN
NEW MILFORD

Located just off the Village Green in the centre of New Milford, in a restored Victorian home, the Homestead Bed & Breakfast Inn offers comfortable rooms with phones, tv, desks, air conditioning and a warm welcome.

There is a hearty continental buffet breakfast served in the living room, tea and coffee are available on request any time during the day or evening.

Rolf, Peggy and their staff are dedicated to making your stay special. The atmosphere here is friendly, relaxed and homelike with the opportunity to mix with other guests if you choose, but plenty of space to allow privacy if you prefer. The inn holds the AAA Three Diamond rating.

| 5 Elm Street, New Milford, CT 06776 | Tel 860 354 4080 Fax 860 354 7046 | Owner/Innkeepers: Rolf & Peggy Hammer | 14 rooms, in main inn and annexe | Doubles $76 – $99 B&B Tax 12% | Children welcome VS • MC • Amex |

MANOR HOUSE
NORFOLK

Set on a quiet country road, with five acres of flower-filled gardens and a gazebo, the Manor House is within walking distance of the village and within easy reach of sporting activities and cultural events. Individually decorated rooms are special retreats and romantic getaways, amenities include fireplaces, canopy beds and private balconies.

The interior of the Manor has a traditional look with extensive cherry panelling, while the living room with its six foot fireplace and stunning Tiffany windows is the perfect spot to relax with a book from the extensive library or CD collection. Refreshments are available throughout the day. Delights at breakfast include homemade bread, poached egg with lemon-butter-chive sauce, bacon, banana pancakes and honey from the inn's own hives.

| 69 Maple Avenue, PO Box 447, Norfolk, CT 06058 | Tel /Fax 860 542 5690 | Innkeepers: Henry & Diane Tremblay 8 rooms | Doubles $95 – $175 B&B Tax 12% | Nearby: tennis, golf, horseriding, skiing, private lake for swimming | Non-smoking Children over 8 welcome. VS • MC • Amex |

CONNECTICUT

OLD MYSTIC INN
OLD MYSTIC

The warmth of a cosy fire and the aroma of freshly baked cookies welcome guests arriving at this 1784 Inn, built when Mystic was noted for whaling, fishing and ship-building.

Eight guest rooms with queen size beds and private baths, each named after a New England author, all have special touches to make you feel at home. Three rooms have working fireplaces and two have whirlpool tubs. Most rooms are hand-stencilled and many have canopy beds.

A complimentary full country breakfast served each morning in our cheery dining room will be the highlight of your day. Saturday evenings bring good cheer and conversation with complimentary wine and cheese. A wealth of attractions, including Mystic Seaport and Marinelife Aquarium, are minutes from the Inn.

| 52 Main Street, Old Mystic, CT 06372-0634 Tel 860 572 9422 | Innkeepers: Mary & Peter Knight 8 rooms | Doubles $115 - $145 B&B Tax 12% | Nearby: tennis, golf, riding, sailing, conference facilities | Children over 8 welcome. | Non-smoking VS • MC • Amex |

RIVERWIND INN
DEEP RIVER

Relax, step back in time and enjoy a stay amid an enchanting collection of New England and Southern country antiques. With eight delightful guest rooms and numerous common rooms there is ample opportunity for mingling or privacy.
Four of these rooms boast fireplaces, including a breathtaking twelve-foot stone cooking fireplace in the 18th century keeping room.
Opt for a glass of sherry in the front parlour with its piano, choose a game from the trophy room where George, the Inn's resident deer, keeps stately watch over the antique checkerboard, or simply select a book from the library and curl up before the fire in the spacious upstairs study. Wonderfully appointed guest rooms, rambling common areas and informal country atmosphere, mean that Riverwind is more than just a place to stay – it's a destination!

| 209 Main Street, Deep River, CT 06417 | Tel 860 526 2014 Innkeeper/Owners: Barbara Barlow, Bob Bucknall | 8 rooms 1 two bedroom cottage with fully equipped kitchen | Doubles $90 - $155 B&B Cottage $200 - $300 EP | Tax 12% Nearby tennis and golf. | Children welcome in cottage suites VS • MC • Amex |

CONNECTICUT

WHITE HART INN
SALISBURY

Welcome to the White Hart, in a picture perfect New England town at the foothills of the Berkshires. All of the Inn's rooms have been completely redecorated and feature private baths, cable tv, telephones and air-conditioning. We are proud that we have frequently been recognised for our dedication to fine food and wine, including an "excellent" rating from the New York Times. Breakfast, lunch and a light dinner are served in the Garden Room and in the historic tavern. Julie's New American Sea Grill is our showcase restaurant for dinner and Sunday brunch.

A short walk from local shops, with nearby swimming, boating, golf, skiing and hiking. Northwestern Connecticut and the adjacent Berkshires offer a wealth of festivals, Summer theatre and antiquing, as well as Tanglewood and the Jacob's Pillow Dance Festival. Please join us!

The Village Green, (Rt 44) Salisbury, CT 06068	Tel 860 435 0030 Fax 860 435 0040 Freephone in US 800 832 0041	Innkeepers: Terry & Juliet Moore 26 rooms including 3 one bedroom suites.	Doubles $90 - $165 EP Suites $175 - $190	Tax 12% Nearby: tennis, golf, horseriding, sailing, fitness center, hiking	Conference, function and wedding facilities VS • MC Amex • Diners

---

Let us put you IN THE STATE YOU WANT TO BE IN
IN THE STATE YOU WANT TO BE IN

Take advantage of US WELCOME'S *completely free* booking service and our knowledge of the individual properties and areas to help you get the most out of your travels. We can help you plan a trip to exactly suit your taste, budget and individual requirements, just one phone call and we do the rest.

01923 821469
(U.K. OFFICE)

Fax 01923 827157
100127.2706@compuserve.com
Toll free number in US & Canada
1-888-INN VISIT

Maine

ging	46	
	46	
otel-Bluenose Inn	35	
④ Bayview Hotel	36	
⑤ Black Point Inn	37	
⑥ Blue Harbor House	47	
⑦ Blue Hill Inn	47	
⑧ Captain Daniel Stone Inn	38	
⑨ Captain Lindsey House Inn	48	
⑩ Captain Lord Mansion	39	
⑪ Dockside Guest Quarters	48	
⑫ Gorges Grant Hotel	40	
⑬ Greenville Inn	49	
⑭ Harraseeket Inn	41	
⑮ Inn By The Sea	42	
⑯ Kennebunkport Inn	49	
⑰ Lawnmeer Inn	50	
⑱ Lodge at Moosehead Lake	50	
⑲ Maine Stay Inn	51	
⑳ Maine Stay Inn & Cottages	51	
㉑ Mira Monte Inn	52	
㉒ Newcastle Inn	52	
㉓ Ocean Gate	53	
㉔ Ocean Point Inn	53	
㉕ Spruce Point Inn	43	
㉖ Stage Neck Inn	44	
㉗ Sugarloaf	45	
㉘ York Harbor Inn	54	

34

MAINE

BAR HARBOR HOTEL - BLUENOSE INN
BAR HARBOR

Escape to the privacy of America's most beautiful island - Mount Desert. Atop a granite-terraced hillside, the Bar Harbor Hotel-Bluenose Inn offers breathtaking views of sparkling Frenchman Bay and, surrounded by Acadia National Park - a symphony of natural beauty - is only 600 yards to the famed Bluenose Ferry Terminal. Although set aside from bustling Bar Harbor, guests may enjoy a leisurely stroll to its shops, museums, concerts, boat tours, beaches, and mountains.

The Hotel is distinguished by two guest buildings: the Mizzentop and Stenna Nordica feature 97 immaculate rooms and 2-person suites with air conditioning and mini-refrigerator - many with romantic fireplaces. Also featured are the charming Rose Garden Restaurant - distinctive dining, casual attire; the magnificent Great Room & Bar; Raspbeary's Gift Shop; our elegant indoor pool; spa; fitness centre; outdoor heated pool, and rolling garden paths.

We're proud of our long-time AAA Four Diamond Award for Excellence and honoured to be the only resort in Bar Harbor to receive a Four Star rating in the Mobil Travel Guide.

90 Eden Street,
Bar Harbor,
ME 04609
•
Tel 207 288 3348
Fax 207 288 2183
Freephone in US
800 445 4077
•
Owner:
Edward & Judy
Hemmingsen
•
97 rooms
including 30 one bedroom
suites.

Doubles $88 - $248 EP
•
Tax 7%
•
Outdoor & indoor pools,
conference facilities
Nearby: tennis, golf,
riding, sailing
•
Children welcome.
•
Non-smoking
•
VS • MC

35

MAINE

BAYVIEW HOTEL
BAR HARBOR

Down a long winding drive The Bayview offers privacy and serenity with unsurpassed ocean views. The choice of accommodation is varied between the original Bayview Inn, built in 1930 and our modern Hotel and Townhomes built in 1985. All provide the modern luxuries you expect while maintaining the charm of a bygone era. We are small enough to be attentive to your wishes, yet your privacy is always assured.

Enjoy a delicious meal in our gourmet restaurant. Our creative chef prepares exceptional regional cuisine using only the finest ingredients. The restaurant is open daily serving breakfast and dinner.

Our location is convenient to beautiful Acadia National Park and all area attractions. Close by you will find golfing, boating, biking and sightseeing. Spend an afternoon swimming in our oceanfront pool, playing a game of tennis, or just relaxing on our secluded property. The Bayview holds the AAA Four Diamond award and is conveniently located on rt 3, one mile from downtown.

111 Eden Street,
Bar Harbor,
ME 04609
•
Tel 207 288 5861
Fax 207 288 3173
Freephone in US
800 356 5285
•
Manager: Trish Nolan
•
31 rooms
1 one bedroom suite
two and three bedroom townhomes

Doubles $95 - $240 B&B
Suite, townhomes
$135 - $440
•
Tax 7%
•
Indoor and outdoor pools, tennis, hiking.
Nearby: golf, horseriding, sailing
•
Children welcomed in hotel and townhomes
•
VS • MC • Amex • Diners

MAINE

BLACK POINT INN RESORT
SCARBOROUGH

The Black Point Inn is one of America's few remaining resort-inns, and still offers modified or full American meal plan. Awarded Four Diamonds by the AAA, it is unpretentious elegance, recognised the world over.

Accommodations offer spectacular views and vistas. At night you will hear the nearby ocean as waves crash against cliffs or breakers slowly roll across the beaches. A fire crackles in the main lobby.

Fifteen minutes from the centre of Portland, on historic Prout's Neck, come for the unspoiled ocean vistas, rugged cliffs, sheltered sandy beaches and wooded areas fragrant with the smell of pines and balsams.

Enjoy the finest Maine has to offer. Get away from responsibility and routine and let us cater to your every whim. Spend days on white sandy beaches, evenings enjoying gourmet dining. Discover Maine this year!

510 Black Point Road,
Scarborough,
ME 04074
•
Tel 207 883 4126
Fax 207 883 9976
Freephone in US
800 258 0003
•
Owner:
Normand Dugas
•
75 rooms
7 one bedroom suites

Doubles $250 - $375
MAP
Suites $350 - $450
•
Tax 7%. s.c. 15%
•
Indoor and outdoor pools, tennis, golf, sailing, fitness center, bikes available, boat trips. conference facilities
•
Children over 8 welcome
•
VS • MC • Amex

MAINE

CAPTAIN DANIEL STONE INN
BRUNSWICK

This outstanding 1819 Federal-style home built for Captain Daniel Stone and his family and inherited by Miss Narcissa Stone, a prominent figure in Brunswick's history, is now proudly recognized as the Captain Daniel Stone Inn.

All rooms and suites have been tastefully decorated in keeping with the Federal style of the original home. Each has different wall coverings, window treatments, plush carpeting, ceramic tile, museum prints, and fine, Federal-period furniture.

Fine dining is always a pleasure in the intimate dining room and open veranda of the Narcissa Stone Restaurant. For business meetings, functions, banquets and weddings our conference rooms can accommodate up to 150 people.

The coastal town of Brunswick is the home of Bowdoin College, its magnificent campus and art galleries. A summer theatre, several museums, two excellent libraries, many good restaurants and its classic New England architecture complete Brunswick's charming ambiance. Just a ten minute drive north of Freeport, Maine, home of L.L. Bean.

10 Water Street,
Brunswick,
ME 04011
•
Tel 207 725 9898
Fax 207 725 9898
Freephone in US
800 267 0525
•
General Manager:
William Bennett
•
34 rooms
including 4 one bedroom suites

Doubles $109 - $139 EP
Suites $140 - $175
•
Tax 7%
•
Conference facilities.
Nearby: swimming, tennis, riding, sailing, water skiing, down-hill & cross-country skiing
•
Children welcome
•
Non-smoking
•
VS • MC
Amex • Diners

MAINE

CAPTAIN LORD MANSION
KENNEBUNKPORT

The Captain Lord Mansion is an award-winning, intimate country inn overlooking the Kennebunk River from the head of a sweeping lawn. The inn is ideally situated in a quiet, residential neighbourhood but is only four blocks from lively shops and restaurants.

Each bedroom is individually and luxuriously decorated with quality antiques, comfortable seating, good lighting and air conditioning. Many rooms have lace canopy beds and working fireplaces, some also have whirlpool tubs and refrigerators stocked with soft drinks.

A complimentary full breakfast is served.
Free parking passes for area beaches; towels, mats and umbrellas are provided. Free afternoon tea and sweets are offered daily, as is early morning coffee. Maps, tourist information, local menus are always available, together with lots of helpful advice.

Awarded Four Diamonds by the AAA and Four Stars by Mobil, the inn is a member of the Independent Innkeepers Association.

P.O. Box 800,
Kennebunkport,
ME 04046
•
Tel 207 967 3141
Fax 207 967 3172
•
Innkeepers:
Bev Davis &
Rick Litchfield
•
16 rooms

Doubles $149 - $199
B&B
•
Tax 7%
•
Conference room available
to accommodate 16.
Ocean and beaches nearby
•
Not particularly suitable
for children
•
VS • MC • Discover

MAINE

GORGES GRANT HOTEL
OGUNQUIT

Beautiful Gorges Grant Hotel is situated on meticulously manicured grounds in the heart of Ogunquit. Catch the trolley bus in front of the hotel for an easy trip to the village, or wander down to Ogunquit's fabled white sand beach for some sun and surf. Stretch out on our sunning deck and then cool off in our outdoor heated pool or move in out of the sun beside our indoor heated pool, jacuzzi and fitness center.

Treat yourself to fine dining at Raspberri's, our own full-service restaurant open for breakfast and dinner.

You will find your accommodations truly a pleasure. We offer a variety of handsomely appointed guest rooms each with luxurious furnishings, full baths, refrigerators and remote control television with premium movie channel.

We have some connecting units, ideal for families. Indulge yourself at Gorges Grant Hotel where special vacation memories begin.

239 US Rt 1.
PO Box 2240
Ogunquit,
ME 03907
•
Tel 207 646 7003
Fax 207 646 0660
Freephone in US
800 646 5001
•
Innkeeper/Owner:
Karen J. Hanson
•
56 rooms
2 one-bedroom suites

Doubles $129 - $159 EP
Suites $149 - $179
•
Tax 7%
•
Outdoor and indoor pools, spa, fitness center. Nearby: golf, tennis, whale-watching, deep sea fishing, factory outlet shopping
•
Children welcome
•
VS • MC • Amex

MAINE

HARRASEEKET INN
FREEPORT

The Harraseeket is an AAA Four Diamond, 54 room luxury country inn, set on five beautifully landscaped acres of old fashioned gardens in the village of Freeport.

23 bedrooms have fireplaces and jacuzzi tubs. All have private baths and the amenities expected by discerning travellers. An elegant, fine dining restaurant and a casual tavern with award winning wine lists and terrace dining in season await your pleasure. Full breakfast buffet and afternoon tea are included in the room rate.

The inn is located on rt 1, just two blocks north of L.L. Bean and is within easy walking distance of 110 outlet stores for which Freeport is deservedly famous. To drive from Boston takes about 2½ hours.

162 Main Street,
Freeport,
ME 04032
•
Tel 207 865 9377
Fax 207 865 1684
Freephone in US
800 342 6283
•
General Manager:
Nancy D. Gray
•
50 rooms
4 one bedroom suites

Doubles $145 - $195
B&B
Suites $185 - $225
•
Tax 7%
•
Croquet, conference facilities
Nearby: golf, fishing, boating, hiking
•
VS • MC • Amex
Diners • Discover

41

MAINE

INN BY THE SEA
CAPE ELIZABETH

Overlooking the Atlantic, the Inn occupies one of the most splendid locations along Maine's entire 3000 mile coast. In keeping with this incomparable setting the Inn is designed to blend every contemporary amenity with the understated elegance of classic resort architecture.

All accommodations in this AAA Four Diamond resort are one or two-bedroom suites furnished either with period antiques or classic Maine style with wicker and pine. Each suite has fully equipped kitchen, living/dining area and private balcony or deck, complete with rocking chair and garden or ocean views.

The Audubon Restaurant with it's spectacular setting overlooking the water, offers the freshest of local seafood. Evening turndown service features chocolate covered berries or fresh cookies. Amazingly, the city of Portland is only minutes away from the Inn's tranquil setting and you can visit fine museums, enjoy Summer theatre, ballet and concerts, the Old Port shops or take an excursion boat for a cruise of Casco Bay.

40 Bowery Beach Road,
Cape Elizabeth,
ME 04107
•
Tel 207 799 3134
Fax 207 799 4779
Freephone in US
800 888 4287
•
Owner/Innkeeper:
Maureen McQuade
•
25 one-bedroom suites
18 two-bedroom suites

Doubles $110 - $390 EP
•
Tax 7%. s.c. 3%
•
Outdoor pool,
beach, tennis,
jogging trails,
volleyball,
cross-country
skiing
•
VS • MC
Amex • Discover

MAINE

SPRUCE POINT INN
BOOTHBAY HARBOR

This newly renovated Inn, (established 1902), on a tranquil 100 acre peninsula, offers a relaxed yet sophisticated atmosphere, a short distance from the village of Boothbay Harbor; a quaint coastal fishing village. Stonewalls, flowers and well groomed lawns surround the Inn and cottages. Spectacular ocean views and breathtaking sunsets can be enjoyed from most of the accommodations and dining room. All accommodations offer early American furnishings, telephone and cable tv. Recent additions include the Admiral's Quarters executive suite and a group of Downtown suites.

Famous for excellence in dining, the Inn operates the Modified American Plan. During high season a "Traditional Maine Lobster Bake" is on Tuesday evenings and Thursday evening features our "Gourmet Buffet".

There is a heated outdoor freshwater pool and new oceanside saltwater pool along with a heated spa. Tennis, shuffleboard and a putting green are also on site. A stay at the "Spruce Point Inn" is unforgettable.

Atlantic Avenue, Box 237,
Boothbay Harbor ME 04538

•

Tel 207 633 4152
Fax 207 633 7138
Freephone in US
800 553 0289

•

Managers: Angelo Digiulian
& Joseph Paolillo

•

65 rooms
Two and three bedroom
townhouse condominiums

Inn doubles/suites
$190 - $396 MAP for two
Apartments/cottages
$345 - $532 MAP for four
Condominiums
$242 - $532 EP

•

Tax 7%. s.c. 15%

•

2 outdoor pools,
tennis, spa.
Conference room available.

•

Children welcome

•

VS • MC

MAINE

STAGE NECK INN
YORK HARBOR

At the mouth of the York River, where the rocks, beach and ocean meet, you'll find Stage Neck Inn, a small resort which has consistently for twenty years, earned the distinctive AAA Four Diamond Award. Each of the 58 guest rooms offers a balcony or terrace overlooking the beach and ocean. Exceptional accommodations are complemented by full room service, ocean-side pool with restaurant and bar, clay tennis courts, indoor pool/jacuzzi, fitness room with sauna, and membership privileges at a private, 18-hole River-front golf course.

The Inn serves breakfast, lunch and dinner daily. Choose the casual Sandpiper Bar & Grille with outdoor terrace and piano bar or Harbor Porches Café, all of which offer varied menus including appetizers, light fare and creative entrées. Stage Neck Inn is open year-round and features excellent value off-season get-away packages.

"One of the most well-appointed hostelries in the region - dining is either casual or formal, but the fare is consistently excellent - among the best in southern Maine" - Down East Magazine.

PO Box 70,
York Harbor,
ME 03911
•
Tel 207 363 3850
Fax 207 363 2221
Freephone in US
800 222 3238
•
General Manager:
Phoebe Apgar-Pressey
•
58 rooms
•
Doubles $95 - $210

Tax 7%. s.c. 15%
•
Indoor and outdoor pools, tennis, fitness room with sauna.
•
Nearby: golf, horseriding, sailing, water-skiing, hiking.
•
Conference facilities
•
VS • MC
Amex • Discover

MAINE

SUGARLOAF
CARRABASSETT VALLEY

Located in the North Woods, at the foot of Maine's second highest mountain - 2,600 skiable vertical drop - Sugarloaf/USA offers wonderful skiing opportunities. Some of the best snow-making equipment in the East, added to the natural snowfall, ensures that skiing, snowmobiling and snowboarding are available for most of the winter season and right into March and April. There are always excellent all-inclusive prices to cover not only accommodation but also lift tickets and ski hire.

Children are exceptionally well-catered for with programmes specially devised not only for enjoyment but also for education with the result that Sugarloaf has consistently been voted one of the top family ski resorts.

Sugarloaf village is a great community and there are shuttles to take you between various points, whether you choose to stay in the inn, the hotel or in one of the apartments or houses.

RR1 Box 5000
Carrabassett Valley,
ME 04947
•
Tel 207 237 2000
Fax 207 237 2718
Freephone in US
800 THE LOAF (8439623)
•
President
Warren Cook
•
40 inn rooms
900 one to six bedrooms units

Doubles $85 - $120 EP
Suites apartments & homes
$120 - $575
•
Tax 7% s.c. 3%
•
Outdoor and indoor pools, tennis, golf, down-hill & cross-country skiing.
•
Children welcome.
Childrens' programmes available during the winter.
•
VS • MC

45

MAINE

ANDREWS LODGING BED & BREAKFAST
PORTLAND

Situated on one and three quarter acres of beautifully landscaped grounds on the outskirts of the city of Portland, our 250 year old colonial home has been completely renovated for your year-round comfort. We offer modern baths and a completely applianced guest kitchen as well as sitting rooms, solarium and outdoor decks overlooking beautiful gardens in Summer and pristine snow in Winter with an ice skating rink for your enjoyment. Breakfast is served on silver and china in our formal dining room.

Antique furnished bedrooms include quilts and warm comforters for chilly Maine nights. You can expect refreshments in the refrigerator, your bed turned down nightly and warm hospitality from the Andrews family as we share our home with you.

417 Auburn Street,
Portland,
ME 04103
Tel 207 797 9157
Fax 207 797 9040

Owner/innkeeper/
plus everything else!
Elizabeth Andrews

6 rooms, 1 with private bath.
1 suite with bedroom, bathroom and sitting room.

Doubles $68 - $88
B&B
Suite $100 - $150
Tax 7%

Non-smoking
Children over 7 welcome, not ideal for ages 2-6

VS • MC • Amex

BAGLEY HOUSE
DURHAM

Just ten minutes from downtown Freeport situated on six acres of lovely fields and woods the Bagley House offers a comfortable retreat in a peaceful, country setting.

Breakfast is served round an eight-foot antique baker's table in our magnificent country kitchen with its huge brick fireplace, wide pine floors, hand-hewn beams and beehive oven. Handsewn quilts, comforters, individually controlled room heat, thick and thirsty towels and fresh flowers all add to the comfort of our five guest rooms.

We're happy to direct our guests along scenic byways to wonderful little museums, nearby state parks, sparkling clean beaches. On foot you can discover private cross-country ski trails in winter and abundant berry-picking in Summer.

1290 Royalsborough Road
Durham
ME 04222

Tel 207 865 6326
Fax 207 353 5878
Freephone in US
800 765 1772

Owner/Innkeepers:
Suzanne O'Connor &
Susan Backhouse

5 rooms
Doubles $85 - $125
B&B
Tax 7%

Nearby: indoor pool, golf, sailing, beaches, hiking, outlet shopping, summer theatre, country fairs.

Children welcome.
Non-smoking
VS • MC • Amex
Diners • Discover

MAINE

BLUE HARBOR HOUSE
CAMDEN

A classic village inn on the Maine coast, the Blue Harbor House welcomes guests to relax in a restored 1810 Cape home with yesterday's charms blending perfectly with today's comforts.

The beautiful town of Camden, renowned for its spectacular setting, where the mountains meet the sea, is just outside the door. The inn's inviting guest rooms are bright with country antiques and hand-fashioned quilts; several have canopy beds. Breakfasts feature such specialities as lobster quiche, cheese soufflé, and blueberry pancakes with blueberry butter. Dinner, available to guests by reservation, can be a romantic candlelit affair or an old-fashioned Down East lobster feast.

67 Elm Street Camden ME 04843 Tel 207 236 3196 Fax 207 236 6523	Freephone in US 800 243 3196 Innkeeper/Owners: Jody Schmoll & Dennis Hayden	10 rooms including 1 one bedroom suite. 1 two bedroom suite. Doubles $85 - $135 B&B	Suites $135 - $150 Tax 7% Nearby: outdoor & indoor pools, tennis,	golf, riding, sailing, water skiing. Children welcome (kids programme $30 daily)	Non-smoking VS • MC Amex • Diners

BLUE HILL INN
BLUE HILL

Constructed on a scenic part of the dramatic Maine coast 164 years ago, The Blue Hill Inn is set on a one acre perennial garden in the village within walking distance of the harbour, several fine galleries, antique shops, the base of Blue Hill Mountain and easy reach of Acadia National Park. An evening cocktail hour with tempting appetisers including smoked pepper mackerel canapés, assorted French cheeses and fresh lobster on crackers offers a relaxing fireside setting for guests to meet, mingle and exchange sightseeing tips. This is followed by a delicious five-course dinner presented in an intimate many-windowed dining room where service is attentive and friendly and the convivial warmth of the atmosphere is enhanced by the glow from the splendid sixteen candle chandelier. Special Event packages include sailing, chamber music concerts and wine dinners.

PO Box 403, Union Street, Rt 177, Blue Hill, ME 04614	Tel 207 374 2844 Fax 207 374 2829 Innkeepers: Don & Mary Hartley	11 rooms including 1 two- bedroom suite	Doubles $140 - $190 MAP Tax 7%. s.c. 15%	Nearby: Acadia National Park,hiking, birdwatching, kayaking, cycling trails, golf	Children over 13 welcome Non-smoking VS • MC

—47—

MAINE

CAPTAIN LINDSEY HOUSE INN
ROCKLAND

Two relaxing days at the Captain Lindsey House Inn and then a three or six day cruise - let Captains Ken & Ellen Barnes offer you a real taste of Maine. At the inn, a 19th century Sea Captain's home, your stay is enhanced by comfortable beds, inviting bathrooms, a parlour with a softly glowing fire and wonderful meals at the Waterworks pub and restaurant.

The moment you step aboard the 83 foot motor yacht Pauline and relish the mahogany panelled main saloon, the fresh banana bread laid out for tea, the large open air boat-deck and the effortless glide as she leaves the cove, you will know you're in for an unforgettable experience. A longer cruise on the Stephen Taber will have you caught up in the excitement of a voyage on the oldest documented U.S. sailing vessel, as several thousand square feet of canvas unfurl to the waiting breeze.

| 5 Lindsey Street Rockland ME 04841 | Tel 207 596 7950 Fax 207 596 2758 | General Manager: Susan Barnes 9 rooms including 2 one bedroom suites at the Inn. | Doubles $95 - $160 B&B Tax 7% | Nearby: tennis, golf, sailing, water skiing, conference facilities, down-hill skiing, cross-country skiing | Children over 10 welcome. Non-smoking VS • MC • Discover |

DOCKSIDE GUEST QUARTERS
YORK

A small family-run resort situated on a private peninsula in York Harbor, the unsurpassed location provides a panoramic view of ocean and harbour activities. Spacious and meticulously landscaped grounds offer privacy as well as numerous recreational activities.

Accommodations are in the Maine House, a restored seacoast homestead, and modern multi-unit cottages. Most rooms have private balconies or porches with unspoiled views. The Restaurant at the resort is bi-level with floor to ceiling windows affording wonderful water views. Food is equally impressive, offering a varied menu but specialising in Maine seafood.

The York area offers beaches, beautiful scenery, outlet shopping and friendly people, only 1½ hours north of Boston. We hold the Three Diamond AAA rating.

| PO Box 205, York, ME 03909 Tel 207 363 2868 | Innkeepers: The Lusty Family Open all year | 22 rooms, only 2 with shared bath. 7 apartment suites with kitchenettes | Doubles $64 – $107 EP Suites $102 – $153 Tax 7% | Cycling, swimming, motor-boat cruises, canoeing. Nearby: tennis, golf, horseriding, sailing | Children welcome VS • MC |

MAINE

GREENVILLE INN
GREENVILLE

In 1895 a wealthy Lumber Baron, fell in love with the dramatic vista of Moosehead Lake and Squaw Mountain - the elegant Victorian mansion he built is now the Greenville Inn and for ten years, carpenters worked to complete the unique carved embellishments and panelling found throughout. A spruce tree leaded glass window graces the stairway landing, fireplaces are ornamented with carved mantels and mosaics and individually appointed guest rooms and cottages are furnished with equal attention to detail and comfort.

Relish the romantic setting of our lake and mountain view dining rooms whilst enjoying our innovative menus featuring fresh Maine seafood, roast duckling, rack of lamb, steaks and other local specialities. Finish your meal with delicious home-made desserts and pastries.

| Norris Street, PO Box 1194, Greenville, ME 04441 Tel 207 695 2206 Fax 207 695 2206 | Freephone in US 888 695 6000 Innkeepers: Elfi, Michael & Susie Schnetzer | 12 rooms including 1 one bedroom suite & 6 cottages | Doubles $105 - $145 B&B Suites/Cottages $135 - $185 Tax 7% | Nearby: tennis, golf, riding, sailing, water skiing, down-hill skiing, cross-country skiing | Children over 9 welcome. Non-smoking VS • MC • Discover |

KENNEBUNKPORT INN
KENNEBUNKPORT

The Kennebunkport Inn is in Dock Square in the heart of picturesque Kennebunkport. Steps from our door are delightful shops and galleries featuring arts, crafts, clothing and more.

Guest rooms of this elegant 19th Century mansion and the attached River House are thoughtfully and individually decorated with period antiques. All accommodations include colour tv. Take a swim in the pool, lounge on the deck or stroll along beautiful white sandy beaches.

The dining room is renowned for fresh native seafood and Maine lobster, as well as exquisitely prepared regional cuisine. Dinner is served by candlelight in relaxed elegance. For more casual fare try our Martha's Vineyard sidewalk café. Exquisite food, gracious service and charming accommodations – a memorable stay, a truly heartwarming experience. AAA Three Diamond rated.

| One Dock Square, PO Box 111, Kennebunkport, ME 04046 | Tel 207 967 2621 Fax 207 967 3705 Freephone in US 800 248 2621 | Innkeeper: Rick Griffin 34 rooms. 1 apartment with kitchen | Doubles $89 – $234 EP Tax 7% | Outdoor pool. Nearby: tennis, golf, horseriding, sailing, whale-watching. | Children welcome VS • MC • Amex |

MAINE

LAWNMEER INN
WEST BOOTHBAY HARBOR

The only thing we overlook... is the water!
* Old time Maine • Lighthouses • Sea breezes •
• Vivaldi • Rocky coast • Indian Pudding •
• Whales • Clam diggers • Cliffs • Coon Cat •
• Porches • New friends • Schooners • Racoons •
• Serenity • Homemade sausage • Broad lawns •
• Puffins • Key Lime pie • Seals • Blueberries •
• Retreat • Eagles • Homemade ice-cream •
• Fine wines • Lobsters • Lobsters • Lobsters •

Rt 27, Southport Island, ME 04576
(mail PO Box 505, West Boothbay Harbor ME 04575)

Tel 207 633 2544
Freephone in US
800 633 7645

Innkeepers:
Jim & Lee Metzger
32 rooms.,
1 cottage, 1 apartment

Doubles $75 – $130
EP
Cottage etc.
$130 - $170

Off season rates available
Tax 7%
Children welcome

Open mid-May to mid-October
VS • MC

LODGE AT MOOSEHEAD LAKE
GREENVILLE

In a tiny town on a forty mile lake, in the northern reaches of Maine the Lodge at Moosehead Lake can be found. This eight room, AAA Four Diamond Award winning inn with its spectacular lake views, hand-carved four poster beds, fireplaces and whirlpool baths offers you unspoiled serenity and unashamed luxury.

From October to June delicious dinners are included in the rates with tempting items such as apple cider and onion soup, chicken breast sautéed with blueberries and flamed with brandy and, perhaps best of all, Chocolate Moose Maximus! Hearty breakfasts are on offer daily throughout the year and innkeepers Roger & Jennifer Cauchi keep the coffeepot going, the guest pantry stocked with cookies and are always ready with knowledgeable local advice.

Upon Lily Bay Road,
Box 1167
Greenville,
ME 04441
Tel 207 695 4400
Fax 207 695 2181

Owner/Innkeeper:
Roger S. Cauchi
8 rooms
including 3 one bedroom suites

Doubles in season
$135 - $185 B&B
off-season,
weekdays $125 MAP
weekends $160
Tax 7%

Nearby: tennis, golf, riding, down-hill and cross-country skiing
Moose safaris, hiking, dog sledding, snow mobiling, snow shoeing
Does not meet the needs of children

Non-smoking
VS • MC
Amex • Discover

50

MAINE

MAINE STAY INN
CAMDEN

Relaxed, cozy and very friendly, the Maine Stay is a grand old home located in the Historic District of one of America's most beautiful seaside villages. Built in 1802 and situated on two wooded acres, the inn's eight lovely bedrooms, cozy parlours with fireplaces and tv room are tastefully and comfortably decorated with oriental rugs and period furnishings. Guests often gather to gossip round the Queen Atlantic wood and coal stove in the cozy country kitchen.
Breakfasts, delicious, and served at a long harvest table, are designed to set you up for the day and your host, Peter, a former navy captain, is a wonderful source of local knowledge. It is just a two-block walk from the inn, down tree lined streets and through the beautiful harbour park, to the shops and restaurants. This is Down East hospitality at its absolute best!

| 22 High Street
Camden
Maine 04843
Tel 207 236 9636
Fax 207 236 0621 | Owners:
Captain Peter Smith
and the twins, Donny
Smith and Diana
Robson | 8 rooms, (2 do not have private bath). 1 one bedroom suite | Doubles $75 - $95
B&B
Suite $125
Tax 7% | Nearby: tennis, golf, riding, sailing, conference facilities, down-hill & cross-country skiing. | Children over 8 welcome.
Non-smoking
VS • MC • Amex |

MAINE STAY INN & COTTAGES
KENNEBUNKPORT

Beautiful 1860 Victorian-style inn and cottages, located on spacious grounds in the quiet surroundings of Kennebunkport's National Historic District, only a short walk from the delightful shops, galleries and restaurants in Dock Square and Lower Village.

The innkeepers, Carol and Lindsay Copeland and their staff are courteous, attentive and knowledgeable. They are particularly helpful to guests needing assistance in planning activities and itineraries. A full breakfast is served each morning which guests may take in the main inn or have delivered to their cottages. Afternoon tea is a popular time to meet the other guests and exchange travel experiences. The Maine Stay is rated Three Diamonds by the AAA and Three Stars by Mobil

| 4 Maine Street,
PO Box 500 A,
Kennebunkport,
ME 04046
Tel 207 967 2117
Fax 207 967 8757 | Freephone in US
800 950 2117
Owner/Innkeepers:
Carol &
Lindsay Copeland | 6 rooms in the main house, 2 of which are suites,
9 one bedroom cottages with kitchenettes. | 1 two-bedroom cottage with kitchen. (7 rooms have fireplaces) | Doubles $125 - $165
B&B
Cottages $135 – $210
Tax 7%
Non-smoking | 1 mile from beach.
Nearby: golf, horseriding, sailing.
Children welcome.
VS • MC • Amex |

MAINE

MIRA MONTE INN
BAR HARBOR

An 1864 Bar Harbor summer estate graced by porches, balconies and bay windows, the Mira Monte boasts a library, living room, formal dining room and twelve guest rooms with period furnishings, private baths, tv, phones and air conditioning.

Staff here are friendly and helpful and included in the rate is a full buffet breakfast and afternoon refreshments. Located in the historic district, the Inn is set in its own quiet acres, although only an easy walk to shops, restaurant and waterfront and five minutes to the wonders of Acadia National Park.

There is a wealth of activities to choose from, including summer theatre and music, whale watching, guided naturalist walks and sea kayaking.

| 69 Mt Desert Street, Bar Harbor, ME 04609 Tel 207 288 4263 Fax 207 288 3115 | Freephone in US 800 553 5109 Owner: Marian Burns 12 rooms 2 suites with decks and kitchenettes | 1 two bedroom suite sleeps 4 Doubles $115 – $150 B&B Suites $150 – $180 | Two bedroom suite $850 per week. (weekly rate does not include breakfast) Tax 7% | Nearby: tennis, golf, sailing, fitness center, hiking, cycling | Non-smoking Children over 8 welcome VS • MC • Amex |

NEWCASTLE INN
NEWCASTLE

At the Newcastle Inn you find more than a welcome, you find a welcome home! Here, by the broad and salty Damariscotta River, our door is always open. Enjoy our fine small inn and share in our tradition of genuine unpretentious hospitality. At the end of a day's journey – a warm greeting, a comfortable room and an exceptional dinner await you.

Inside, this classic New England dormered colonial offers hand-stenciled floors, beautiful antiques and artwork, an inviting river view and comfortable living rooms for relaxation and conversation.

The three and five course dinners at the inn are nationally acclaimed and have won the restaurant a four star rating. The inn also holds Three Diamonds from the AAA and Three Stars from Mobil.

| RR2 Box 24, River Road, Newcastle, ME 04553 | Tel 207 563 5685 Fax 207 563 6877 Freephone in US 800 832 8669 | Owner/Innkeepers: Howard & Rebecca Levitan 15 rooms including 1 suite | Doubles $167 – $270 MAP $95 – $200 B&B Tax 7% s.c. 15% | Nearby: tennis, golf, swimming, sailing, bird-watching, cycling Non-smoking | Does not meet the needs of children VS • MC • Amex |

MAINE

OCEAN GATE
WEST SOUTHPORT

Escape to 85 wooded waterfront acres on beautiful Southport Island. Relax and watch the boats go by from your private porch. Smoke-free rooms, cottages and efficiencies are available.

A full breakfast and in-room tea and coffee are included in the rate. There is no charge for children under 12 sharing a room with parents. Ocean Gate has a Three Diamond AAA and Three Star Mobil rating and is only five minutes from charming Boothbay Harbor, within easy reach of area attractions.

Cross the bridge to Ocean Gate... your island home.

| Rt 27, PO Box 140, W. Southport, ME 04576 | Tel 207 633 3341 Fax 207 633 7332 Freephone in US 800 221 5924 | General Managers: Ted & Judith Kolva | 67 rooms, plus cottages and efficiencies with kitchenettes | Doubles $80 – $140 B&B Suites from $160 – $190 Tax 7% | Heated swimming pool, fitness center, tennis, boats, outdoor games area. Nearby: golf, fishing VS • MC |

OCEAN POINT INN
EAST BOOTHBAY

Savour the breathtaking view of dark green islands and rock-bound shoreline from the Inn's spectacular setting, across from the Town Pier, near the tip of a peninsula jutting into the vast Gulf of Maine.

Life is easy-going in this area of summer cottages and sea breezes, join us for a relaxing stay in the main inn, lodge or motel and cottage units with colonial or modern decor. All rooms with tv, telephone, fridge, and heating. Ideal for families, the newly renovated Sea Kist Cottage offers spacious accommodation and magnificent views.

Walk run or bike along the Shore Road, watch lobster fishermen at work and sailboats at play in Linekin Bay, visit the lighthouses that beckon from nearby islands. In the evening relax in the cocktail lounge and dining room to watch the sunset and enjoy our varied menu.

| PO Box 409, Shore Road, East Boothbay, ME 04544 | Tel 207 633 4200 Fax 207 633 6040 Freephone in US 800 552 5554 | Managers: David & Beth Dudley 60 rooms, cottages & apartments, some with kitchenette & fireplace (sleep 3 or 4) | Doubles $83 - $128 EP Cottages $78 - $135 per night weekly rates available | Tax 7% Outdoor heated pool Nearby: tennis, golf, sailing, boat excursions, deep sea fishing | Children very welcome VS • MC • Amex |

MAINE

YORK HARBOR INN
YORK HARBOR

Nestled in an historic harbour village, this AAA Three Diamond inn with breathtaking water views, stands as a warm and restful sentinel. At its centre, the immaculate inn has a re-assembled, circa 1637, former fisherman's cabin from the Isles of Shoals. This rustic structure with massive stone fireplace, cosy Oriental rugs and comfortable sofas, offers a uniquely comfortable reading or sitting room.

Imaginative use of floor coverings, wallpaper and fabric create the perfect backdrop for four poster beds, paintings and antiques. Ocean views, fireplaces, classic linens, complimentary toiletries and phones are but a few of the in-room amenities to add to your comfort.

Attention to detail is a matter of pride as is exquisitely prepared cuisine and meticulous service.

PO Box 573, Rt 1A, York Harbor, ME 03911	Tel 207 363 5119 Fax 207 363 3545 ext 295 Freephone in US 800 343 3869	Innkeeper: Garry Dominguez 32 rooms	Doubles $89 – $195 B&B Tax 7%	Tennis, golf, horseriding, sailing, beach, swimming, hot tub	Children welcome VS • MC • Amex

---

FEEDBACK FEEDBACK FEEDBACK FEEDBACK
Your comments are valued!

Please write or call to tell us your opinion of the inns and hotels in which you stayed.
Were your expectations met? Was the welcome warm?
Did you feel you received good value for the money you spent?
Consumer feedback is a vital part of maintaining the standard of **U.S. Welcome Directories** and your input is of great value.
As a small token of thanks, it will be our pleasure to send you a *complimentary copy* of our next book which will reach the bookshops in January 1998.

Please send letters, *no stamp required to:*
U.S. Welcome Directories Ltd.,
FREEPOST (HA4595)
Northwood,
England
HA6 3BR
Telephone : 01923-827157 (U.K.)   888-INN-VISIT (U.S.)

DISTINCTIVE INNS OF NEW ENGLAND

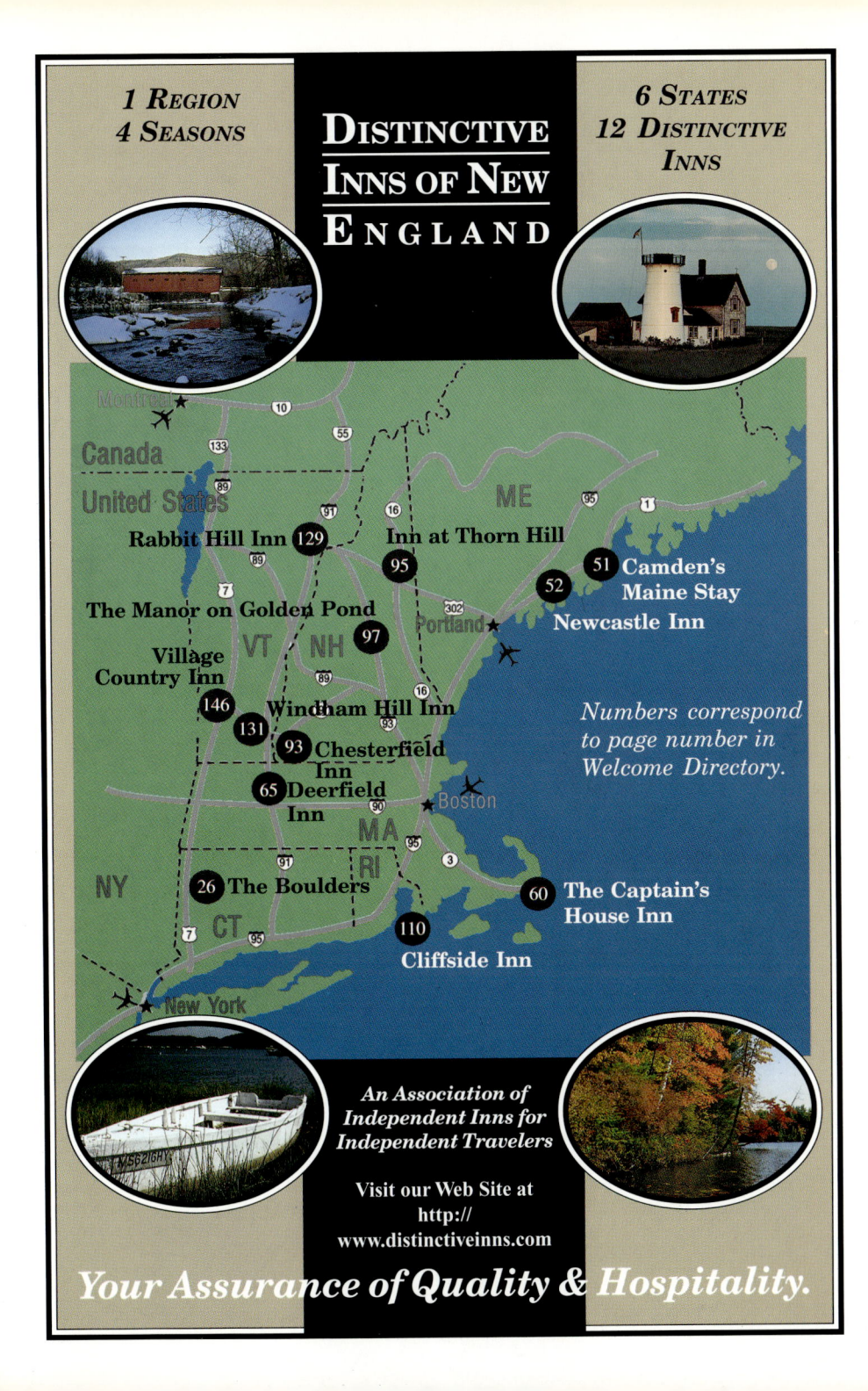

1 REGION
4 SEASONS

6 STATES
12 DISTINCTIVE INNS

- Rabbit Hill Inn 129
- Inn at Thorn Hill 95
- Camden's Maine Stay 51
- Newcastle Inn 52
- The Manor on Golden Pond 97
- Village Country Inn 146
- Windham Hill Inn 131
- Chesterfield Inn 93
- Deerfield Inn 65
- The Boulders 26
- Cliffside Inn 110
- The Captain's House Inn 60

Numbers correspond to page number in Welcome Directory.

An Association of Independent Inns for Independent Travelers

Visit our Web Site at
http://www.distinctiveinns.com

Your Assurance of Quality & Hospitality.

Massachusetts

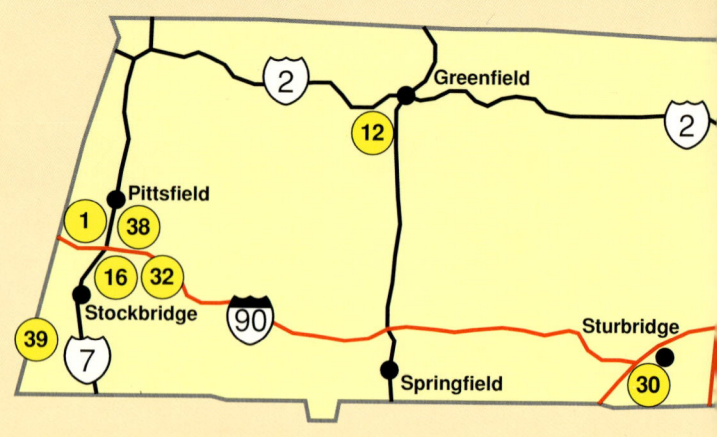

1	Blantyre	58	23	Longfellow's Wayside Inn	84
2	Boston Harbor Hotel	59	24	Marlborough	84
3	Bradford Inn	78	25	Mary Prentiss	85
4	Cambridge House	78	26	Mostly Hall	85
5	Captain Nickerson Inn	79	27	Ocean Edge Resort	69
6	Captain's House Inn	60	28	Onset Pointe Inn	86
7	Charles Hotel	61	29	Pleasant Bay Village Resort	86
8	Chatham Bars Inn	62	30	Publick House	70
9	Colonnade Hotel	63	31	Queen Anne Inn	87
10	Corner House Inn	79	32	Red Lion Inn	72
11	Dan'l Webster Inn	64	33	Rocky Shores Inn	87
12	Deerfield Inn	65	34	Salem Inn	73
13	Diamond District Inn	80	35	Sharon Inn	88
14	Harbor Light Inn	66	36	Thorncroft Inn	74
15	Hawthorne Inn	80	37	Village Green Inn	88
16	Inn at Stockbridge	81	38	Village Inn	89
17	Isaiah Hall	81	39	Weathervane Inn	89
18	Isaiah Jones Homestead	82	40	Wedgewood Inn	90
19	Jared Coffin House	67	41	Whalewalk Inn	75
20	John Carver Inn	83	42	Wildflower Inn	90
21	Lenox Hotel	68	43	Yankee Clipper Inn	76
22	Lighthouse Inn	83			

NEW HAMPSHIRE

Rockport
Lowell
Cambridge
Boston
Provincetown
Plymouth
Sandwich
Chatham
Fall River
New Bedford
Martha's Vineyard
Nantucket

RHODE ISLAND

MASSACHUSETTS

BLANTYRE
LENOX

An impeccably maintained Tudor-style mansion in 85 park-like acres in the Berkshire hills. Enjoy the Boston Symphony Orchestra at Tanglewood, theatre festivals, and attractive shopping villages or visit for the spectacular Fall foliage. Eight exquisite accommodations in the Main House, twelve newly renovated Carriage House rooms and suites, and two cottages. Baronial Great Hall accented by rich panelling, glorious floral displays, heirloom furnishings; also superb formal dining room, glass-enclosed winter garden/conservatory for complimentary continental breakfasts and ornate music salon. Small swimming pool, jacuzzi, sauna, four tennis courts and two croquet lawns all set amid extraordinarily blissful surroundings.

Nearby attractions are the Clark Art Institute, the Norman Rockwell Museum and Chesterwood, home of the sculptor Daniel Chester French. A member of Relais & Chateaux, Blantyre received their prestigious "International Welcome Award" in 1989; currently holds Four Stars from Mobil, and the restaurant has been awarded Four Diamonds from the AAA. Located 2 hours from Boston, 3 hours from New York City.

Rt 20, Lenox,
MA 01240
•
Tel 413 637 3556
(Summer)
413 298 1661
(Winter)
Fax 413 637 4282
•
Managing Director:
Roderick W. Anderson
•
19 rooms
3 one bedroom suites
1 two bedroom suite

Doubles $240 - $450 B&B
Suites $300 - $650
Tax 9.7%. s.c. 10%
•
Outdoor pool, tennis, croquet. Nearby: golf, horseriding, sailing, water skiing, fitness center
•
Conference facilities for up to 25
•
Children over 12 welcome

VS • MC • Amex • Diners

MASSACHUSETTS

BOSTON HARBOR HOTEL
BOSTON

A distinctive twelve story arch greets travellers arriving at Rowes Wharf via water shuttle from Logan Airport. Proximity to Boston's financial District as well as the attractions of Quincy Market and Faneuil Hall, further enhances the location of Boston's only luxury waterfront hotel.

Oversized guest rooms are enhanced by full services and amenities, including a marina, in-house business centre, 24-hour room service, complimentary shoe-shine, overnight valet service, twice daily maid service, complimentary transport to local attractions and shopping, award-winning cuisine and fully equipped health club recognised nationally and internationally as one of the finest hotel health clubs in North America.

The Boston Harbor Hotel, a member of Preferred Hotels and Resorts, holds the Four Diamond award from the AAA and Four Stars from Mobil. Its unbeatable waterfront location amidst Boston's historic district is convenient and exciting with a distinctly Boston character.

70 Rowes Wharf,
Boston,
MA 02110
•
Tel 617 439 7000
Fax 617 330 9450
Freephone in US
800 752 7077
•
Managing Director:
Francois-Laurent Nivaud
•
230 rooms & suites

Doubles $250 - $415 EP
Suites $385 - $1600
•
Tax 9.7%
•
Indoor swimming pool,
fitness center, spa,
children's programmes
available
•
Parking available
•
VS • MC • Amex • Diners
Discover • Carte Blanche

MASSACHUSETTS

CAPTAIN'S HOUSE INN OF CHATHAM
CHATHAM

An authentic captain's house built in 1839, this elegant AAA Four Diamond inn with sixteen bedrooms is situated on two acres of pine trees, shaded lawns and thick hedges. Located ½ mile from Chatham Center and the ocean, The Captain's House provides a romantic and quiet getaway.

The inn consists of three buildings, the Main House, Carriage House and the Captain's Cottage. Each guest room has its own bathroom and is individually stylised with antiques, fine furnishings including four-poster beds with white lace canopies, and woodburning fireplaces in five of the rooms.

Every morning Jan McMaster, an Englishwoman from Bournemouth, and her staff, serve guests an extensive homemade gourmet breakfast. In the afternoon, after a bike ride on one of the inn's courtesy bicycles or a game of croquet on the front lawn, a lovely English tea is served complete with freshly baked scones, jam tarts and cakes. The Captain's House Inn is located off rt 28 in Chatham, about 90 minutes by car from Boston.

369-377 Old Harbor Rd,
Chatham,
MA 02633
•
Tel 508 945 0127
Fax 508 945 0866
•
Owner/Innkeepers:
Jan & Dave McMaster
•
11 rooms
5 one bedroom suites

Doubles $130 - $190
B&B
Suites $185- $225
•
Tax 9.7%
•
Nearby: tennis,
golf, sailing
•
Does not meet the needs
of children
•
VS • MC • Amex

MASSACHUSETTS

CHARLES HOTEL
CAMBRIDGE

Located in Harvard Square, The Charles Hotel is home to the best and the brightest, including visiting business, entertainment and academic leaders. Goosefeather quilts grace each bed and every room offers radio, two line phones with voice mail, PC/fax capabilities and television in bathrooms as well as bedrooms.

The Charles's Four Star Rialto Restaurant, features French, Italian and Spanish cuisine. Boston Magazine's "Best Jazz" can be found at Regattabar, and Henrietta's Table serves fresh from the farm and honest to goodness New England home cooking at breakfast, lunch, supper and Sunday Brunch.

At Charles Square, Le Pli Day Spa and Salon, WellBridge Health & Fitness Center and Spence Center for Women's Health offer a wealth of health, beauty and fitness facilities. Enjoy our simply elegant accommodations as you explore Harvard University and Square, the outdoor cafés, street performers, live theatre, bookstores, museums and boutiques.

In Harvard Square,
One Bennett Street,
Cambridge, MA 02138

•

Tel 617 864 1200
Fax 617 864 5715
Freephone in US
800 882 1818

•

General Manager:
Brian Fitzgerald

•

296 rooms

Doubles $225 - $295 EP

•

Tax 9.7%

•

Indoor pool,
conference facilities

•

Parking available
$18 per day

•

Children welcome.

•

VS • MC • Amex • Diners

MASSACHUSETTS

CHATHAM BARS INN
CHATHAM

Perched gracefully atop a rise overlooking the waters of Chatham Harbor and the open Atlantic beyond, Chatham Bars Inn is Cape Cod's only luxury resort. This beautifully restored 155 room and suite turn-of-the-century resort boasts charming guest rooms located in the Main Inn as well as in 26 surrounding Cape style cottages, and enjoys a reputation for fine food and outstanding service.

Catering to a gracious clientele since 1914, this year-round resort has two award-winning restaurants as well as seasonal beachside dining. Festive beach parties at the Beach House Grill are a cherished summertime tradition. Antique shops, art galleries and boutiques are just minutes away in the delightful seaside village of Chatham. Complimentary children's programme.

A world away..... yet just 90 miles from Boston and easily accessed by major highways. Come and experience a Cape tradition.

Shore Road,
Chatham, MA 02633

•

Tel 508 945 0096
Fax 508 945 5491
Freephone in US
800 527 4884

•

General Manager:
Christopher Diego

•

135 rooms
including 20 luxury suites

•

Doubles $170 - $385 EP
Suites/Cottages $360 - $1,300

Tax 9.7%.
s.c. 17% on food &
beverages only

•

Private beach, outdoor
pool, tennis, golf,
horseback riding, sailing,
watersports, hiking.

•

Children welcome
Childrens Programmes
available during
July and August

•

VS • MC • Amex • Diners

MASSACHUSETTS

COLONNADE HOTEL
BOSTON

The Colonnade Hotel is a 285 room independently owned, luxury hotel that takes great pride in its service and ability to pay the utmost attention to every detail. Spacious and comfortable rooms are all individually detailed with works from local artists and in addition we offer 10,000 square feet of newly designed function space.

Located in Boston's historic Back Bay, the cultural hub of the city, The Colonnade is adjacent to the magnificent Copley Place shopping plaza, directly across from the new Prudential Shopping and Tower and the Hynes Convention Center and only steps away from the delights of Newbury Street, Symphony Hall, Fenway Park and Boston's fabulous museum and theatre district. Whether travelling for business or pleasure, the Colonnade looks forward to welcoming you.

120 Huntington Avenue,
Boston, MA 02116
•
Tel 617 424 7000
Fax 617 424 1717
Freephone in US
800 962 3290
•
Managing Director:
David J. Colella
•
285 rooms
8 one-bedroom suites
4 two-bedroom suites

Doubles $195 - $275 EP
Suites $450 - $1050
•
Tax 9.7%
s.c. 15% on food services
•
Roof-top swimming pool and cafe, fitness center, conference facilities, children's programmes available
•
VS • MC • Amex

MASSACHUSETTS

DAN'L WEBSTER INN
SANDWICH

The Four Star Dan'l Webster Inn with beautifully landscaped grounds and swimming pool blends historic elegance with modern convenience. A Gathering Room invites one to sit a spell, relax and visit with other guests or the friendly staff. Three elegant dining rooms offer award-winning classic American cuisine and a wine list to tempt the most discerning palate. All rooms have air conditioning, phones and tv, many featuring four poster canopy beds. Fresh flowers, turndown service and suites with whirlpool tub and marble fireplace add to your enjoyment. The inn holds the prestigious DiRONA Award (Distinguished Restaurants of North America), while its wine list has been awarded the Wine Spectator "Best Of" Award for the last several years. Cape Cod Life Magazine also voted the Inn "Best Inn" and "Best Fine Dining" awards for the Upper Cape area.

Front desk staff are available 24 hours a day to help you plan your itinerary, whether to Plymouth or Provincetown, all area sights are a short drive away.

Recapture the romance, charm and heritage of this proud old inn.

149 Main Street,
Sandwich,
MA 02563
•
Tel 508 888 3622
Fax 508 888 5156
Freephone in US
800 444 3566
•
Innkeepers:
The Catania family
•
37 rooms
9 suites

Doubles $89 - $169 EP
Suites: $149 - $325
$89.50 - $190
per person MAP
•
Tax 9.7%
•
Outdoor swimming pool.
Nearby: tennis, golf,
bicycling, sailing, hiking,
sandy beaches and many
attractions
•
VS • MC•Amex • Diners

MASSACHUSETTS

DEERFIELD INN
DEERFIELD

The Deerfield is a full service country inn, set on what has been called the loveliest street in New England. Each room is individually and beautifully furnished and named after a person connected with the village's history. Modern comforts, however, include air conditioning and telephones. Our award winning restaurant uses only the freshest and finest local ingredients and some of our recipes are gathered from the old books in the village's archive library. Included in the room rate is a full country breakfast and afternoon tea.

Historic Deerfield Village was once an outpost of colonial America and maintains 14 museum houses which line the mile-long Street and encapsulate the cultural history, art and craftsmanship of the Pioneer Valley. When dusk starts to fall and horse-drawn carriages clop along the road you will find yourself transported back in time.

Nearby attractions are the world class art museum in Williamstown, historic villages of Shelburne Falls and Amherst, numerous craft shops and country walks.

The Street,
Deerfield,
MA 01342
•
Tel 413 774 5587
Fax 413 773 8712
Freephone in US
800 926 3865
•
Innkeepers:
Karl & Jane Sabo

23 rooms

Doubles $140 - $150
B&B
•
Tax 9.7%. s.c 10%
•
Nearby: boating trips,
white-water rafting
•
Children welcome
•
VS • MC
Amex • Diners

MASSACHUSETTS

HARBOR LIGHT INN
MARBLEHEAD

Winner of numerous national awards for excellence, the Harbor Light, now in its tenth year, offers first class accommodation and amenities in two elegantly furnished, side by side, period Federalist mansions in the heart of Marblehead - within walking distance of all the local attractions.

Formal fireplaced parlours, dining room and bed chambers, sparkling private baths, double jacuzzis, sundecks, patio, quiet garden and outdoor heated pool along with an extensive continental breakfast buffet, combine to ensure the finest in New England hospitality. Breakfast includes bagels, muffins, cakes, fruit breads, fruits in season, yogurts, fresh squeezed juice, tea and fresh brewed coffees. Located in the Historic Harbor District which includes many fine shops, art galleries and restaurants, the inn welcomes guests year round.

58 Washington Street
Marblehead
MA 01945
•
Tel 617 631 2186
Fax 617 631 2216
•
Owner:
Peter C. Conway
•
21 rooms
including
1 one bedroom suite
•
Doubles $95 - $245 B&B
Suite $150 - $175

Tax 5.7%
•
Outdoor pool,
conference facilities
•
Nearby: tennis, golf,
sailing
•
Children over 8
welcome.
•
Non-smoking
•
VS • MC • Amex

MASSACHUSETTS

JARED COFFIN HOUSE
NANTUCKET

The Jared Coffin House, a stately 1845 three-storey brick mansion built for a successful ship owner, is the centrepiece of the inn, a collection of six buildings in all. Comfortably elegant public areas and guest rooms combining period decor with modern amenities, offer you an ideal base for exploring Nantucket, the faraway island that takes you back in time to a gentler past.

Sense the history, as you walk along cobblestoned streets by grey shingled cottages and restored nineteenth century mansions. Dine on creative local cuisine, fresh seafood from the docks and traditional New England fare at Jared's our signature restaurant or relax in our Tap Room, a favourite gathering place for Nantucketers and visitors alike.

Springtime is glorious, as daffodils blanket the town in yellow. Summer is Nantucket's "season" with sailboats, beaches and wild roses on white picket fences. Autumn is coloured by russet heathlands, cranberry bogs and vivid blue skies while Winter is a time of quiet escape. We look forward to welcoming you to Nantucket and the Jared Coffin House.

29 Broad Street
Nantucket, MA 02554

•

Tel 508 228 2400
Fax 508 228 8549
Freephone in US
800 248 2405

•

Innkeepers:
Phil & Peg Read
General Manager:
Jonathan Stone

•

60 rooms

Doubles $150 - $200
B&B

•

Tax 9.7%

•

Conference facilities
Nearby: golf, sailing,
water skiing

•

Children welcome.

•

VS • MC
Amex • Diners
Discover

MASSACHUSETTS

LENOX HOTEL
BOSTON

Nearly 100 years after its founding, The Lenox enjoys a privileged position in the society of Boston hotels. Old-world Boston charm and elegance are paired with the latest conveniences in this 214-room landmark.

Located in historic Back Bay, steps away from the finish line of the Boston Marathon, The Lenox is convenient to boutique and department stores, art galleries, and the sidewalk cafés of Newbury Street. Just blocks away is the music of Symphony Hall and the collections and exhibitions at the Museum of Fine Arts.

The newly renovated, award-winning guest rooms are appointed with Italian marble bathrooms and terry bathrobes. Included are such modern amenities as a fax machine, personal voice mail, and a modem port. Simpler needs may be filled by a crackling fire in one of the hotel's select rooms with fireplaces, or a complimentary newspaper waiting at the door each morning. The hallmark service of the family-owned Lenox Hotel ensures a carefree holiday in Boston with the professional staff taking pride in providing every guest with warm, personal attention.

710 Boylston Street
Boston
MA 02116
•
Tel 617 536 5300
Fax 617 267 1237
Freephone in US
800 225 7676
•
General Manager:
Leszlie A. Purstell
•
214 rooms including
3 one bedroom suites
Doubles $210 - $275 EP
Suites $475 EP

Tax 9.7%
•
Conference facilities,
exercise room
•
Parking available
$26 per day
•
Children welcome
•
Non-smoking
•
VS • MC • Amex
Diners • Discover
JCB • EnRoute

68

MASSACHUSETTS

OCEAN EDGE RESORT & GOLF CLUB
BREWSTER

Ocean Edge was built in 1890 as a private mansion. Today, guests have the choice of staying in the handsomely renovated hotel or in spacious, fully equipped, beautifully furnished, private bayside or golf course villas with a choice of casual or gourmet dining featuring fresh regional ingredients.

The resort's 18-hole championship course, named by Golf Illustrated as one of the top ten conference golf destinations in the country, is the New England site of the prestigious Golf Digest Golf Schools. Ocean Edge is also a popular tennis destination featuring clay and plexi-pave courts. PGA and USPTA pros are available for coaching.

A private beach and six swimming pools are available throughout the property. Guests also enjoy jogging and cycle paths leading to the beautiful Cape Cod National Seashore. Nature lovers will appreciate the Audubon Wildlife refuge nearby or taking a whale-watching trip. A few minutes drive brings you to excellent museums, art galleries and theatres.

2907 Main Street,
Brewster, MA 02631

•

Tel 508 896 9000
Fax 508 896 9123
Freephone in US
800 343 6074

•

General Manager:
Kevin M. Howard

•

88 rooms including
2 one bedroom suites
One, two and three bedroom apartments and villas.
(Daily maid service)

Doubles $199 - $350 EP
Appts and villas
$190 - $775
Off-season rates available

•

Tax 9.7%
s.c. 18%

•

Private beach, tennis, golf, fitness center, hiking, spa.
Childrens' programmes available during the Summer

•

VS • MC • Amex
Diners • Discover

MASSACHUSETTS

PUBLICK HOUSE HISTORIC INN
STURBRIDGE

The Publick House, established by Colonel Ebenezer Crafts over 220 years ago, is today, a 60 acre resort offering a choice of accommodations ranging from the Publick House Inn itself, featuring colonial style furnishings to the 96-room Country Motor Lodge ideal for families, or the Chamberlain House, for authentic historic lodging.

In the dining room, with wide planks held fast by cast nails, winter breakfast buffets are served at the enormous original open hearth. Other dining choices include Ebenezer's Tavern, a menu of lighter fare and Charlie Brown's Steakhouse or visit the Publick House Bake Shoppe to sample their famous sticky buns. When the weather and the seasons are right, sheep leave their pens to graze on the meadows, extending to the bordering woods.

An ideal stopping point between New York and Boston and for a visit to Old Sturbridge Village, the Publick House maintains a programme of preservation and renovation, which assures both colonial atmosphere and contemporary conveniences.

Rt 131, PO Box 187,
Sturbridge,
MA 01566-0187
•
Tel 508 347 3313
Fax 508 347 5073
Freephone in US
800-Publick
•
Innkeeper:
Lenora Bowen
•
126 rooms
including 9 period suites
& 21 period bedrooms

Doubles $55 - $135 EP
•
Tax 9.7%
•
Outdoor swimming,
tennis, golf, fitness
center, conference
facilities.
•
Children welcome.
•
VS • MC
Amex • Diners

Experience 1830s Rural New England

Join costumed villagers as they go about their daily chores in their homes, farms, shops and meeting houses in New England's largest outdoor history museum. Enjoy the gardens! Participate in 19th century activities.

Savour traditional New England fare in the Bullard Tavern, and visit the Museum Gift Shop full of treasures, including some made by our own artisans.

A SAVING OF $1 is offered to holders of the Welcome Card or on presentation of a copy of **Selected Hotels & Inns, East Coast North America.**

Old Sturbridge Village

Old Sturbridge Village
1 Old Sturbridge Village Road, Sturbridge, MA 01566
Tel 508 347 3362   Fax 508 347 9012

We are just a one hour drive west of Boston on the Massachusetts Turnpike. Take exit 9, then Rt 20 West.

MASSACHUSETTS

RED LION INN
STOCKBRIDGE

The Red Lion Inn, a member of Historic Hotels of America, offers comfortable lodging and excellent food in a landmark setting, where nineteenth century atmosphere is combined with twentieth century efficiency. Warmth and charm welcome guests as they step into the main parlour. The inn has a fine collection of antique furniture and china. There is nowhere better than the long flower-filled verandah, with its rocking chairs, for sitting and watching the world go by.

Most guest rooms have television and all have air conditioning and phones. Dine in the elegant dining room or in the more intimate atmosphere of the Widow Bingham Tavern with its dark panelling. There is evening entertainment in the Lion's Den and in warm weather the courtyard is a delightful place for a meal.

The Red Lion is ideally situated for all Berkshire attractions; visit the Norman Rockwell museum, the Berkshire Playhouse or enjoy a concert on the lawn at Tanglewood. The Inn is a member of the Independent Innkeepers Association.

Main Street,
Stockbridge,
MA 01262
•
Tel 413 298 5545
Fax 413 298 5130
•
General Manager:
C. Brooks Bradbury
•
111 rooms
8 one bedroom,
2 two bedroom suites

Doubles $65 - $155 EP
Suites $165 - $235
•
Tax 9.7%
•
Outdoor swimming pool, exercise room, conference facility for up to 75 people
•
VS • MC
Amex • Discover

MASSACHUSETTS

SALEM INN
SALEM

Located in the heart of one of America's oldest seaport cities and only 17 miles from Boston, the lovely Federal-style Salem Inn was built in 1834 by sea captain Nathaniel West. It is within walking distance of the harbour and Salem's many museums, restaurants and historic sights.

The inn's accommodations include 31 spacious, comfortable, and individually decorated guest rooms featuring antiques, period detail and homey touches. Guest suites, complete with equipped kitchens are ideal for families. All rooms have a queen or dual-king bed, air conditioning, phone, tv and private bath. The inn's restaurant, Courtyard Café, offers two intimate dining rooms and, in warm weather, our secluded brick patio is the perfect place for enjoying a refreshing beverage or a delightful meal. A delicious, hearty continental breakfast is included in the room rates. The inn holds the AAA Three Diamond award.

7 Summer Street,
Salem, MA 01970

•

Tel 508 741 0680
Fax 508 744 8924
Freephone in US
800 446 2995

•

Innkeepers:
Diane & Richard Pabich

•

27 rooms
5 one bedroom suites
with kitchens

Doubles $99 - $175
B&B
Suites $119 - $175

•

Tax 9.7%

•

Facilities for
small conferences
(up to 20 people)

•

VS • MC • Amex
Diners • Discover

MASSACHUSETTS

THORNCROFT INN
MARTHA'S VINEYARD

Thorncroft Inn comprises three buildings on three and a half acres of treed grounds, on a peninsula on the lovely island of Martha's Vineyard. It is a secluded, first class country inn, with the Island's only ★★★★ Mobil Rating and only ♦♦♦♦ Award from the AAA. The inn is a couples oriented, honeymoon, anniversary and special occasion destination.

Rooms have private bath, antique furnishings, air conditioning, phone and colour cable tv. Buildings and grounds are completely non-smoking. Rates include full country breakfast in our dining room or, if you prefer, breakfast in bed; afternoon tea and pastries, evening turndown service, free parking and the Boston Globe delivered daily. Most rooms have working, wood-burning fireplaces and canopied beds. Some have furnished balconies or porches, private exterior entrances, two person whirlpool tubs or private 300 gallon hot tubs. There is a self-contained cottage with garage for the guest who prefers absolute privacy.

PO Box 1022, Main Street,
Vineyard Haven,
MA 02568
•
Tel 508 693 3333
Fax 508 693 5419
Freephone in US
800 332 1286
•
Proprietors/Innkeepers:
Lynn & Karl Buder
•
14 rooms
including a one bedroom
cottage (no kitchen)

Doubles $200 - $450
B&B
$150 - $350 (off season)
•
Tax 9.7%
•
Nearby: Atlantic ocean!
Indoor pool, tennis, golf,
riding, sailing, water skiing.
•
Does not meet the
needs of children
•
Non-smoking
•
VS • MC • Amex
Diners • Discover

MASSACHUSETTS

WHALEWALK INN
CAPE COD

The owners of the Whalewalk, Dick and Carolyn Smith, promise their guests a spoiled vacation in the unspoiled environment of outer Cape Cod, considered by many to be one of the country's most beautiful places.

The Whalewalk, an 1830's whaling master's home has been authentically restored and creatively redecorated with English, French and Danish antiques. It is set on 3 acres of lawns, gardens and trees on a back road, only minutes by car or bike to beaches or Orleans Village. The guest rooms provide a range of individual air conditioned accommodations, and there are 4 large suites or a delightful saltbox self-contained studio cottage, all with wet bars and fireplaces.

The hallmark of this award-winning inn is the warmth and friendship that prevails. Each day begins with a full breakfast served in the sunroom or on the patio, in the evening you can join other guests for a "happy hour" with complimentary hors-d'oeuvres. The inn is about two hours from Boston.

220 Bridge Road,
Eastham,
MA 02642
•
Tel 508 255 0617
Fax 508 240 0017
•
Innkeepers:
Carolyn & Richard Smith
•
7 rooms
5 one bedroom suites
(a two-bedroom suite can
be made available.)

Doubles $110 - $165
B&B
Suites $165 - $180
•
Tax 9.7%
•
Nearby: beaches,
cycling trails.
Small conference facility
•
Children over 12
welcome
•
VS • MC

MASSACHUSETTS

YANKEE CLIPPER INN
ROCKPORT

Family owned and operated for 50 years and offering gracious hospitality, this resort inn consists of four beautifully converted buildings; two of which are directly on the ocean. Landscaped gardens lead right down to the water and many rooms offer spectacular ocean views. Enjoy a full-service ocean-front restaurant, serving breakfast and gourmet dinner; heated saltwater pool, whirlpool and sauna and movie theatre. Additionally there is a fully equipped, completely private house for weekly rent, set on a hilltop with distant views to the open sea.

Located in a residential section of this delightful, quintessentially New England, seacoast village with its many galleries and shops, the Yankee Clipper is only one hour drive, but a world away from Boston. Our helpful concierge service is always more than delighted to assist with bookings for all local points of interest such as the Gloucester Stage Company, Rockport Art Association, a tour of the North Shore Lighthouses or an unforgettable whale-watch expedition from Cape Ann.

96 Granite Street,
Rockport,
MA 01966
•
Tel 508 546 3407
Fax 508 546 9790
Freephone in US
800 545 3699
•
Innkeepers:
Bob & Barbara Ellis
•
22 rooms
3 one-bedroom,
2 two-bedroom suites
3 bedroom house

Doubles $149 - $239 B&B
Suites $239
3 bedroom house
$2400 per week
(off season $1800
per week)
•
Tax 9.7%
•
Heated saltwater
outdoor pool.
Nearby: tennis, golf,
horseriding, hiking, spa
•
VS • MC
Amex • Discover

Visit New England
CIRCA 1627

Experience life in 17th-century Plymouth. Wander through timber frame homes, grainfields, and garden plots. Talk with Pilgrims and Wampanoag Indians as they go about their daily chores. Visit the 1627 Pilgrim Village, Hobbamock's *(Wampanoag Indian)* Homesite, Crafts Center, and on the harbor, *Mayflower II*.

PLIMOTH PLANTATION
PLYMOUTH, MASSACHUSETTS

(508) 746-1622

One hour from Boston. Near Cape Cod. Open April through November.
Write for information at P.O. Box 1620, Plymouth, MA 02362

Produced in cooperation with Plymouth County Development Council.

MASSACHUSETTS

BRADFORD INN
CHATHAM

The AAA Three Diamond Bradford Inn, on two secluded acres in the picturesque seaside village of Chatham, is a short step away from shops, theatre, restaurants, beach, golf and tennis facilities. Guestrooms, furnished for comfort and enjoyment are in seven different buildings. Breakfast is memorable – complimentary, prepared to order and served overlooking the swimming pool and flower-filled gardens. Start your day a special way – our full menu offers long-time New England favourites, along with some specialities of our own. Our fireplaced lounge area is a wonderful place to create or renew friendships, and a meal in our award-winning restaurant, Champlains, open for dinner, mid-May until mid-October, should not be missed. Each season here has its own special ambience...do come... share... and then savour the memories until you return.

| 26 Cross Street, Chatham, MA 02633 Tel 508 945 1030 Fax 508 945 9652 | Freephone in US 800 562 4667 Resident Owners: William & Audrey Gray | 29 rooms and suites, some with kitchens. 1 two-bedroom fully equipped house | Doubles/suites $139 – $199 B&B (lower rates off-season) Suites $179 - $249 | Tax 9.7% Outdoor pool. Nearby: tennis, golf, sailing, water skiing, beaches | Does not meet the needs of children under 7 VS • MC • Amex |

CAMBRIDGE HOUSE
CAMBRIDGE

Our 1892 colonial revival inn is unique for its attention to perfect period detail and unparalleled personalized service. Guests are treated to gourmet breakfasts of soufflé omelets surrounded by vibrant berry sauces, home-made sausage and oversized waffles. Fresh fruits and baked goods are available throughout the day, and on winter evenings guests gather for wine, cheese and hot hors-d'oeuvres served by a crackling fire in the inn's welcoming antique-filled parlour.

Ideally situated for sightseeing, close to Harvard Square and 5 minutes walk to the subway which takes you into the heart of downtown Boston. Your hosts, long-time Cambridge residents have an inexhaustible knowledge of the area and all it has to offer and extend to you the warmest of invitations.

| 2218 Massachusetts Avenue, Cambridge, MA 02140-1836 | Tel 617 491 0100 Fax 617 868 2848 Freephone in US 800 962 079 | Owner: Ellen Riley 16 rooms, 10 with bath en-suite, 4 with shared bath | Doubles $99 - $250 B&B Tax 9.7% | Non-smoking Children over 6 welcome | Complimentary off-street parking VS • MC • Amex |

78

MASSACHUSETTS

CAPTAIN NICKERSON INN
SOUTH DENNIS

Delightful 1828 sea captain's home with white wicker rockers on the comfortable front porch. Guest rooms are decorated with period four poster or white iron queen beds and oriental or hand woven rugs. The welcoming, fireplaced living room has a cable tv, vcr and stained glass windows and popular board games are available for guests, as are a selection of video movies.
Bicycles can be hired for a small fee and the inn is itself located on a bike path with the Cape Cod 20 mile bike Rail Trail ½ a mile away. Other area attractions include championship public golf courses, world class beaches, paddle boats, horseback riding, museums, Cape Playhouse, fishing, craft shops and a local church which houses the oldest working pipe organ in the U.S. Children of all ages are very welcome. Full breakfast is satisfying with homemade muffins and a hot entrée.

333 Main Street
South Dennis,
Cape Cod
MA 02660

Tel/Fax 508 398 5966
Freephone in US
800 282 1619

Owner/Innkeeper:
Patricia York

5 rooms, 3 with private bath.

Doubles $60 - $90
B&B
Tax 9.7%
Bicycles available

Nearby: tennis, golf, riding, sailing, 2 miles from beach.
Children welcome.

Non-smoking.
Smoking allowed on porch.
VS • MC • Discover

CORNER HOUSE INN
NANTUCKET

To travel to Nantucket Island and to Corner House is to step back in time to the romantic early 19th Century whaling era. At this attractive and historic village inn, brought gently into the 20th Century, enjoy civilized comforts including private baths, down comforters, pillows piled on handsome firm beds and some rooms with tv and refrigerator. Other joys include attractive sitting rooms, cosy fires on chilly days, a screened porch overlooking a charming garden terrace, homebaked continental breakfast and afternoon tea.
The superb location is a short walk to ferries, shops, restaurants, theatres, museums, beaches and tennis. A car is not necessary!
Resident owners John and Sandy Knox-Johnston are happy to share their favourite restaurants, quiet beaches, bicycle routes, birding walks or whatever your soul is seeking.

49 Centre Street,
Box 1828,
Nantucket,
MA 02554

Tel 508 228 1530
Innkeepers:
John & Sandy
Knox-Johnston

15 rooms
1 one bedroom suite
1 small apartment,
sleeps three people

Doubles $105 - $185
B&B
Suites $175 - $210
(lower rates
off season)

Tax 9.7%
60 miles of beaches surround
Nearby: tennis, golf, sailing, fitness center

Children over 8 welcome
VS • MC
Discover

MASSACHUSETTS

DIAMOND DISTRICT INN
LYNN

This 1912 Georgian style mansion on half an acre in Boston's North Shore is just steps from three miles of sandy beaches. Spacious mahogany trimmed living room and formal dining room overlook the veranda and gardens have partial ocean view.

Delicious home cooked full breakfast with fresh fruits is served in the elegant dining room and in winter, by a glowing fire. Vegetarian and low fat options available. Guest rooms offer antiques and custom queen or twin beds, good lighting, comfortable chairs, air conditioning, tv and phone.

Within walking distance to local restaurants and shopping and just 4 miles to Salem or Marblehead. The bus stop for the 30 minute ride into the centre of Boston is one block away. Sandra & Jerry are always delighted to furnish tourist information.

| 142 Ocean Street, Lynn, MA 01902-2007 | Tel 617 599 4470 Fax 617 595 2200 Freephone in US 800 666 3306 | Owner/Innkeepers: Sandra & Jerry Caron 9 rooms, 5 rooms with private bath. | Doubles $70 - $140 B&B Tax 9.7% Near sandy beach. | Parking available free of charge. Children over 6 welcome. | Non-smoking VS • MC Amex • Diners |

HAWTHORNE INN
CONCORD

Just 45 minutes from Boston and located in the historic area of Concord, the Hawthorne is steeped in history and literary associations standing as it does on land that once belonged to Ralph Waldo Emerson, the Alcotts and Nathaniel Hawthorne. Our rooms are appointed with antique furnishings, beautifully designed hand-made quilts, and wood floors graced with oriental and rag rugs all highlighted by wonderful colours that rest the soul and warm the heart.

Each morning at a common table our guests enjoy a continental breakfast – raspberries from our patch, grapes from our vines and soon, if the bees keep working, our own honey for your enjoyment.

Our town is alive with history, beauty and peacefulness. We at the Hawthorne Inn hope we have captured a small part of what is Concord.

| 462 Lexington Road, Concord, MA 01742 | Tel 508 369 5310 Fax 508 287 4949 | Innkeepers: Gregory Burch & Marilyn Mudry 7 rooms | Doubles $125 - $185 B&B Tax 9.7% | Nearby: swimming in Walden Pond, tennis, golf, boating, cross country skiing | Non-smoking Children welcome VS • MC • Amex |

MASSACHUSETTS

INN AT STOCKBRIDGE
STOCKBRIDGE

Just a mile from Main Street Stockbridge, a country lane leads into the circular drive of the twelve acre, owner-occupied, Inn at Stockbridge, an elegant Georgian colonial mansion.

Rooms are individually decorated with wonderful views over meadows and hills. Spacious public areas include living room with grand piano, library and tv room with board-games and puzzles. Relax on the wicker furnished porch, soak up the sun around the pool, or take a stroll in the woods.

An abundant breakfast is served round a sixteen place mahogany table, beautifully set with silver and china. Tanglewood, Summer theatre and the Norman Rockwell Museum are all nearby. The Inn holds the Three Star Mobil award.

| Rt 7 (north), Stockbridge, MA 01262 | Tel 413 298 3337 Fax 413 298 3406 Innkeepers: Alice & Len Schiller | 8 rooms Doubles $115 – $235 B&B Tax 9.7% s.c. 5% | Outdoor swimming pool. Nearby: tennis, golf | Non-smoking Children over 12 welcome | VS • MC Amex |

ISAIAH HALL
DENNIS

The warmth of true country ambience and hospitality in the heart of Cape Cod. On a quiet historic street, this lovely 1857 farmhouse offers relaxation in beautiful gardens or comfortable antique furnished parlour scattered with oriental rugs. Guest rooms are decorated with care and charm, and a delicious breakfast is served around the farmhouse table.

Take a leisurely walk to the beach or the village with its restaurants, shops, theatre and fine arts museum. Enjoy bike trails, tennis, golf and whale watching, take a day trip to Provincetown, Plymouth or the Islands.

Awarded AAA Three Diamonds and selected by various media as one of the best places to stay on the Cape, we invite you to join us for a while.

| 152 Whig Street, P.O. Box 1007, Dennis, MA 02638-1917 | Tel 508 385 9928 Fax 508 385 5879 Freephone in US 800 736 0310 | Owner/Innkeeper: Marie Brophy 11 rooms all except 1 with private bath | Doubles $85 – $122 B&B Tax 9.7% | Nearby: golf, tennis, horseriding, beaches, sailing, water skiing | Best meets the needs of children over 7 VS • MC • Amex |

MASSACHUSETTS

ISAIAH JONES HOMESTEAD
SANDWICH

This beautifully restored, 1849 Italianate Victorian home in historic Sandwich Village is steps away from most points of interest, and a short drive to many other historic attractions. Guests enjoy beautifully furnished rooms, taking them back to a gentler more romantic time, pampered with luxurious baths, some with oversize whirlpool tubs, robes, candles and other amenities.

Three guest rooms and the gathering room have fireplaces for a cosy retreat in cooler weather.

After a delicious full breakfast, served by candlelight, stroll through the charming village, enjoying its white steepled church, 1630 grist mill, Hoxie House and Sandwich Glass Museum. Beaches, Plimoth Plantation, Heritage Plantation, Provincetown and ferries to the Islands are nearby, as are fine restaurants, golf courses, antiquing and biking. Sandwich is just 65 miles from Boston.

| 165 Main St, Sandwich, MA 02563 | Tel 508 888 9115 Freephone in US 800 526 1625 | Innkeepers: Shirley & Bud Lamson 5 rooms | Doubles $75 - $155 B&B Tax 9.7% | Nearby: tennis, golf, conference facilities, biking Children over 12 welcome. | Non-smoking VS • MC Amex • Discover |

Heritage Plantation of Sandwich

A diversified museum of Americana and gardens on 76 acres. The Shaker Round Barn houses more than 35 antique and classic autos. The Military Museum has antique firearms, the Art Museum's working carousel hails from 1912. Museum, garden shops and cafe on site. Open May - October.

Grove & Pine Streets, Sandwich, Cape Cod, MA 02563
Tel. 508 888 3300 Fax 508 833 2917 E-mail museumcc@aol.com
Located just three miles from Cape Cod's Sagamore Bridge.

MASSACHUSETTS

JOHN CARVER INN
PLYMOUTH

In the heart of Plymouth, just 45 minutes from Boston/Logan Airport, sits the lovely John Carver Inn. From stately entrance to spacious overnight rooms, the staff of this quaint family-owned and operated Inn immediately makes you feel welcome. Guest rooms are thoughtfully and tastefully decorated with warm colonial furnishings. Delicious New England cuisine is served daily in the Hearth 'n' Kettle Restaurant with moderately priced meals sure to please all appetites, or sit in our pub for a drink after a day of sightseeing. We are steps from beaches, whale-watching and a host of historical and recreational attractions such as the historic Plimoth Plantation. Our front desk staff will be delighted to help you plan your excursions, share their favourite spots and even sell you discounted tickets right at the John Carver Inn.

| 25 Summer Street, Plymouth, MA 02360 | Tel 508 746 7100 Fax 508 746 8299 Freephone in US 800 274 1620 | Innkeepers: The Catania Family 79 rooms incl. 2 suites Doubles from $75 EP | MAP rates also available Tax 9.7% Outdoor pool | Nearby: tennis, golf, sailing, hiking, cycling, Plimoth Plantation and The Mayflower | Ideal with or without children VS • MC Amex • Diners |

LIGHTHOUSE INN
WEST DENNIS

The Stone family warmly welcomes you to an oceanfront, country inn complex, located on nine secluded acres on the shore of Nantucket Sound, ideal for relaxation whilst still being central to all points of interest on beautiful Cape Cod.
Enjoy the soothing sounds of the ocean, our private beach, the warm salt water of the Sound, and the sight of your child enjoying new-found friends in the childrens' programme. We offer a wide selection of accommodations, in cottages with fireplaces, Cape-style houses with guest rooms, individual suites, and rooms, in the Main House. In our dining room savour the five-course menu featuring a variety of fresh fish caught in Cape Cod waters. Each morning our full, American breakfast gets your day started on the right foot! For your next vacation, experience the rejuvenating spirit of old Cape Cod ... Lighthouse Inn!

| 1 Lighthouse Inn Road, West Dennis, MA 02670 Tel 508 398 2244 Fax 508 398 5658 | General Manager: Patricia Stone 61 rooms including 5 one bedroom suites, | 5 two bedroom suites & cottages Doubles & suites $124 - $336 B&B $214 - $648 MAP | Cottages $850 weekly Tax 10.2% s.c. included. | Outdoor pool, 700 feet of private ocean, tennis Nearby: golf, riding, sailing, water skiing | Children welcome. Childrens' summer programme. VS • MC |

MASSACHUSETTS

LONGFELLOW'S WAYSIDE INN
SUDBURY

Immortalized in 1863 by Longfellow in his *Tales of the Wayside Inn*, this National Historic Site is the oldest operating inn in America. Situated on more than 100 landscaped acres just west of Boston, the site includes the original inn with ten guest rooms, seven separate dining areas, museum rooms, a working grist mill (open Apr-Nov), a beautiful steepled chapel, and the Redstone Schoolhouse of Mary Had a Little Lamb fame.

Taste America's first cocktail, the cow-wow, while seated beside the roaring fireplace in the old bar, then feast on sumptuous yankee fare in our fireplaced dining rooms - complete with fresh corn muffins courtesy of the Grist Mill.

The Redstone Schoolhouse, rebuilt on the site by one time owner Henry Ford, is visited by thousands of school children every year, and hundreds of weddings take place at the Martha-May chapel.

Wayside Inn Road, Sudbury, MA 01776	Tel 508 446 1776 Fax 508 446 2312 Freephone in US 800 339 1776	Innkeeper: Robert Purrington 10 rooms Doubles $90 - $120 B&B	Tax 5.7% Nearby: golf, fishing, cross-country skiing	Parking available free of charge. Children welcome.	Non-smoking VS • MC • Amex Diners • Discover

THE MARLBOROUGH
WOODS HOLE

Romantic Cape Cod cottage complete with picket fence, trellis and garden, set on a hill among beautiful old maple trees. Rooms, all with private bath, are individually decorated with quilts, co-ordinated scented linens and collectibles.

Our large comfortable parlour is ideal for conversation, reading or television. Full gourmet breakfast with wonderfully brewed tea and our house blend of coffee. Informal afternoon tea with our own fresh home baked muffins is a great way to relax after a busy day on the Cape.

AAA 3 Diamond and 3 Star Mobil rated. Excellent restaurants nearby, plus ferries to Martha's Vineyard. Woods Hole Oceanographic Institute and the National Marine Biology Laboratories, quaint shops, beaches, golf course and bike paths are only minutes away. The Inn owner, Al, will do his best to point out hidden points of interest.

320 Woods Hole Road, PO Box 238, Woods Hole, MA 02543-0138	Tel 508 548 6218 Fax 508 457 7519 Freephone from the UK 0800 96 22 79	Owner: Al Hammond Innkeeper: Richard Hunt 5 rooms	Doubles $85 - $125 B&B (off season $65-$95) Tax 9.7%	Non-smoking Outdoor pool, paddle tennis Nearby: golf, bike path	Does not meet the needs of children under 2 VS • MC • Amex

MASSACHUSETTS

MARY PRENTISS INN
BOSTON

One hundred and fifty years ago the Mary Prentiss Inn was a country estate. Today it is surrounded by universities, museums, theatres, shops and restaurants. Conveniently located just off Massachusetts Avenue and a few blocks from Harvard University, the centre of Boston is easily accessed by subway, with the station a few minutes from the Inn.

Relax in comfortable spacious rooms, each individually decorated, many with working fireplaces and all appointed with carefully chosen vintage furnishings and your choice of down or hypoallergenic pillows. Enjoy your continental buffet breakfast, an array of juices, baked breads, home made jams and muffins with steaming pots of freshly brewed coffee and fine teas, in the parlour or on the outdoor deck.

6 Prentiss Street, Cambridge, MA 02140	Tel 617 661 2929 Fax 617 661 5989 Manager: Jennifer Rei Lewis	18 rooms, 16 of the rooms have wet bars, sinks, microwaves and refrigerators	Doubles $89 – $199 Suites $139 - $199 Tax 9.7% Non-smoking	Limited free parking available on site, spaces should be reserved ahead of time	Children welcome VS • MC

MOSTLY HALL
FALMOUTH

Built in 1849, a sea captain's wedding gift, the plantation-style house with wrap-around porch, lofty ceilings, tall shuttered windows and dramatic central hallway (hence the name!) is set in a landscaped park in Falmouth's historic district. The enclosed widow's walk, fitted out as a guest den with tv and travel library, and the garden gazebo are special places to relax.

Spacious air-conditioned guest rooms feature private baths, four poster queen size canopy beds, floral wallpapers, reading areas and antiques. Rates include full breakfast, afternoon refreshments and use of bicycles. A very special complimentary honeymoon package is available for a minimum stay of three nights. Close to restaurants, shops, beaches and ferries, and only 90 minutes from Boston, the inn is an ideal base from which to explore the Cape.

27 Main Street, Falmouth, MA 02540	Tel 508 548 3786 Freephone in US 800 682 0545	Owner/Innkeepers: Caroline & Jim Lloyd 6 rooms	Doubles $95 - $130 B&B Tax 9.7%	Non-smoking Nearby: tennis, golf, beaches, sailing	Does not meet the needs of children VS • MC Amex • Discover

MASSACHUSETTS

ONSET POINTE INN
ONSET

The Onset Pointe Inn is the unspoiled Cape you've always imagined. Quiet walks, romantic evenings, the lap of the surf, boats moored at the door, a wicker rocking chair, a bay-view from your own private balcony.

Our beautiful bed and breakfast inn offers accommodations directly on the beach. Days start with a delicious breakfast, available in the waterfront dining room or on the verandah.

Then the hours are yours to do as you please – shop, sightsee, play golf or tennis at nearby facilities, or just lounge on our own sandy beach.

At day's end the sun sets into the bay with a spectacular array of colours – this is truly Cape Cod life at its best!

| 9 Eagle Way, Onset, MA 02558-1450 | Tel 508 295 8342 Fax 508 295 5241 Freephone in US 800 35 ONSET | Innkeepers: Debi & Joe Lopes | 14 rooms, 7 in the Mansion and 7 in the Carriage House and Guest Cottages. 3 have kitchens | Doubles $75 – $150 B&B Tax 9.7% Non-smoking | Children welcome in guest cottages VS • MC • Amex |

PLEASANT BAY VILLAGE RESORT
CHATHAM

We have made it our goal over the years to offer the most distinctive and beautiful resort in Chatham. Accommodations are tastefully decorated with contemporary furnishings. Efficiencies and suites with one or two bedrooms offer fully equipped kitchens ideal for family or friends. Exotic gardens nestle among six acres of private woodlands on this lovely part of the Cape. In the centre of our grounds a cascading waterfall crowns an ornamental pond. Nothing is spared in the preparation of gourmet breakfasts right down to the pure maple syrup and freshly squeezed juices. In July and August, lunch is served poolside from the grill. From the Cape, take a whale-watch tour, a day trip to Martha's Vineyard or Nantucket or charter a sport fishing boat.

| PO Box 772, Chatham, MA 02633 Tel 508 945 1133 Fax 508 945 9701 | Freephone in US 800 547 1011 Proprietor: Howard L. Gamsey | 58 rooms/efficiencies Suites: 2 one-bedroom, 8 two-bedroom. Many offer self-catering facilities. | Doubles $135 - $215 EP Suites $315 - $375 Tax 9.7% s.c. 5% | Outdoor heated pool Nearby: tennis, golf, sailing | Children welcome VS • MC • Amex |

MASSACHUSETTS

QUEEN ANNE INN
CHATHAM

Over 150 years old and welcoming guests since 1874, while all rooms have today's amenities; private bathrooms, phones, and tv, many of the antiques have never left the inn. Rooms overlooking the garden have large private balconies and a beautiful view. Working fireplaces and private whirlpools add to the comfort of other rooms. A large, heated, outdoor pool, an indoor spa and three beautiful private clay tennis courts are at our guests' exclusive disposal. Our popular restaurant serves dinner from May 1 through January 1. Tucked away from the hectic life, Chatham sits between the Atlantic and the still waters of Nantucket Sound. Quiet lanes lead through clusters of shingled cottages. Others lead you to the bustling activity of the fish piers. We love Chatham and are sure you will too.

70 Queen Anne Road, Chatham, Cape Cod, MA 02633 Tel 508 945 0394 Fax 508 945 4884	Freephone in US 800 545 4667 Innkeeper: Guenther Weinkopf	31 rooms Doubles $167 - $295 B&B Tax 9.7%	Outdoor pool, indoor whirlpool, spa, tennis, conference facilities for 30.	Mountain bikes & boat excursions can be arranged by the inn. Nearby: golf, riding, sailing, water skiing.	Children welcome. VS • MC • Amex Diners • Discover

ROCKY SHORES INN & COTTAGES
ROCKPORT

A turn of the century hilltop mansion with panoramic Atlantic views, each bedroom has its own particular flavour, some reflecting a summery mood – white wicker and light colours, others with a period feel. Fresh flowers and sweets add to the sense of welcome, while complimentary buffet-style continental breakfast is served in the dining room.

The fully equipped clapboard-style cottages with their delightful rustic decor and garden or ocean views are ideal for families with children, seeking self-catering facilities.

Enjoy gazing at the natural beauty of the scenery from the huge outdoor porch which runs the entire length of the house or strolling around the three acres of landscaped lawns. Sandy beaches are only a ten minute walk away.

65 Eden Road, Rockport, MA 01966	Tel 508 546 2823 Freephone in US 800 348 0343	Owners: Renate & Gunter Kostka	11 rooms 11 cottages	Doubles $93 – $120 B&B Cottages $93– $130 Tax 9.7%	Cottages ideal for children of any age VS • MC • Amex

87

MASSACHUSETTS

SHARON INN
SHARON

City convenience, country charm – Phyllis and Ed Raider, are the third generation in more than 50 years to provide hospitality to travellers in their AAA Three Diamond rated motor inn with its beautifully tended lawns and inviting swimming pool. Special touches include complimentary tea and coffee in the rooms; availability of microwaves, refrigerators and vcrs, add to the welcome extended by the owners and their friendly, attentive staff.
From May through October two people can stay for two nights and enjoy a full day escorted tour of Boston (only 20 miles away) without having to drive in the city, an ideal way of sightseeing without hassle.
With easy access to Southern New England's most famous attractions, enjoy our "Close to the comforts of home" hospitality on your next trip.

775 Providence Highway, (Exit 9 off I-95), Sharon, MA 02067	Tel 617 784 3100 Fax 617 784 4862 Freephone in US 800 879 5432	Owners/Operators: Phyllis & Ed Raider 51 rooms	Doubles $69 – $89 EP Tax 9.7%	Outdoor swimming pool	Children welcome VS • MC • Amex

---

VILLAGE GREEN INN
FALMOUTH

The Federal style Village Green Inn, tastefully decorated in soft colours, antiques and reproductions, creates a comfortable and restful atmosphere in which to relish your Cape Cod stay. Guest rooms are large, immaculately clean and have air conditioning, private baths, cable tv and some have working fireplaces. In the lovely formal parlour, enjoy complimentary sherry, area restaurant menus and often, stimulating conversation while the gentle Cape Cod breeze fills the air with the scent of salt water. Large porches with white wicker furniture and hanging geranium plants invite you to relax with lemonade and freshly baked cookies, while enjoying the view of the historic Village Green. Fine restaurants, beaches, tennis, bike path and ferry within walking distance. Come, be pampered, enjoy the hospitality of the Village Green Inn.

40 Main Street, Falmouth, Cape Cod MA 02540	Tel 508 548 5621 Fax 508 457 5051 Freephone in US 800 237 1119	Co-owners: Diane & Don Crosby 5 rooms including 1 one bedroom suite	(accommodates 3 people, $25 additional person) Doubles & suite $85 – $140 B&B	Tax 9.7 % Nearby: Beaches, tennis, golf, riding, sailing.	Children over 12 welcome. Non-smoking VS • MC • Amex

MASSACHUSETTS

VILLAGE INN
LENOX

Lenox, a quaint New England village, located in the beautiful Berkshire hills of Western Massachusetts and just three hours from New York City and Boston, is the setting for the Village Inn. Whilst the Inn's original Federal style has been altered very little, the interior has just undergone a thorough renovation without changing its warm character. Our restaurant serves a full breakfast menu and gourmet dinners featuring creative regional cuisine. Open all year, the Inn is near the famous Tanglewood Music Festival and other summer cultural attractions, as well as the Norman Rockwell Museum and the Clark Art Institute (renowned for French Impressionists). Indescribably beautiful Fall foliage excursions, winter down-hill and cross-country skiing, and special Spring bargains, complement the Inn's calendar.

| 16 Church Street, P.O. Box 1810, Lenox, MA 01240 | Tel 413 637 0020 Fax 413 637 9756 Freephone in US 800 253 0917 | Owners: Clifford Rudisill & Ray Wilson | 32 rooms 1 two-bedroom suite with kitchenette | Doubles/suite $85 – $160 EP Tax 9.7% | Children over 6 welcome VS • MC • Amex |

WEATHERVANE INN
SOUTH EGREMONT

The Weathervane Inn began life as a 1785 farmhouse and still has the original fireplace with its beehive bake oven, rarely seen today, but a necessity in bygone days for both cooking and heating. Since purchasing the ten acre property in 1980, Anne and Vincent Murphy have completely renovated the old buildings to create the elegantly comfortable ambience today's guests enjoy.

Comfortably furnished guest rooms with plenty of common areas add to your enjoyment, as does the 20 x 40 ft swimming pool in the grounds. Located just 20 minutes from Tanglewood, summer theatre and the Jacob's Pillow Dance Festival, the inn is in an ideal location for enjoying all that Western Massachusetts has to offer.

| Route 23 P.O. Box 388 South Egremont MA 01258 Tel 413 528 9580 Fax 413 528 1713 | Freephone in US 800 528 9580 Owner/Innkeeper: Vincent & Anne Murphy | 12 rooms including 1 one bedroom suite. | Doubles $95 - $135 B&B $185 - $220 MAP Suites $200 - $245 Tax 5.7% s.c. 4.3% | Outdoor pool Nearby: tennis, golf, riding, skiing Children over 7 welcome. | Non-smoking VS • MC Amex • Discover |

MASSACHUSETTS

WEDGEWOOD INN
YARMOUTH PORT

A handsome, 1812 Greek Revival on two acres of lawn on the Cape's north side, ideal for those who appreciate stately colonial architecture, old maple and chestnut trees, a non-commercialised atmosphere and a warm welcome.

Guest rooms offer private bath and air-conditioning, most have working fireplaces, wide board floors and canopy beds. Fresh fruit and afternoon tea tray are thoughtfully placed in each room. The sunny bay-windowed dining room provides a pleasant setting for a delightful continental breakfast. The inn holds the AAA Three Diamond rating.

Yarmouth Port offers antique shops, historic sights, fine dining and whale-watching cruises. The Inn is ideally located just ten minutes from Hyannis and the island ferries.

83 Main Street, Yarmouth Port, MA 02675	Tel 508 362 9178/5157 Fax 508 362 5851 Innkeepers: Milt & Gerrie Graham	6 rooms including 2 full suites and a junior suite offering private sitting areas and screened porches	Doubles $115 – $150 B&B Suites $115 – $160	Tax 9.7% Does not meet the needs of young children	VS • MC • Amex

---

WILDFLOWER INN
FALMOUTH

The Wildflower Inn, where rocking chairs line the porch and a riot of vibrant flowers bloom in the gardens, is located on beautiful Cape Cod, just 70 miles south of Boston. Built in 1910, the newly renovated inn is located in the heart of Falmouth's historic district.

Guests enter through the fireplaced gathering room, from which a staircase winds its way to the upstairs guest rooms, beautifully decorated and each with its own distinct personality. An attached cottage, with its own private entrance and porch provides a full kitchen, living room and spiral staircase leading to a romantic loft bedroom (honeymooners take note!). A homemade breakfast, served each morning in the gathering room, on the wraparound porch or delivered to your room is included in the rates.

167 Palmer Avenue Falmouth, Cape Cod, MA 02540	Tel/Fax 508 548 9524 Freephone in US 800 294 5359 Owner/Innkeeper: Donna Stone	5 rooms 1 cottage with loft bedroom & full kitchen	Doubles $80 - $135 B&B 1 bedroom cottage plus sofabed $125 - $150 (weekly rate $600)	Tax 9.7 % Nearby: 7 miles of beaches, golf, short walk to ferry for Martha's Vineyard	Children welcome in cottage Non-smoking VS • MC • Amex

Let us put you
IN THE STATE YOU WANT TO BE IN
IN THE STATE YOU WANT TO BE IN

Take advantage of US WELCOME'S *completely free* booking service and our knowledge of the individual properties and areas to help you get the most out of your travels. We can help you plan a trip to exactly suit your taste, budget and individual requirements, just one phone call and we do the rest.

U.S. WELCOME DIRECTORIES

01923 821469
(U.K. OFFICE)
Fax 01923 827157
100127.2706@compuserve.com
Toll free number in US & Canada
1-888-INN VISIT

New Hampshire

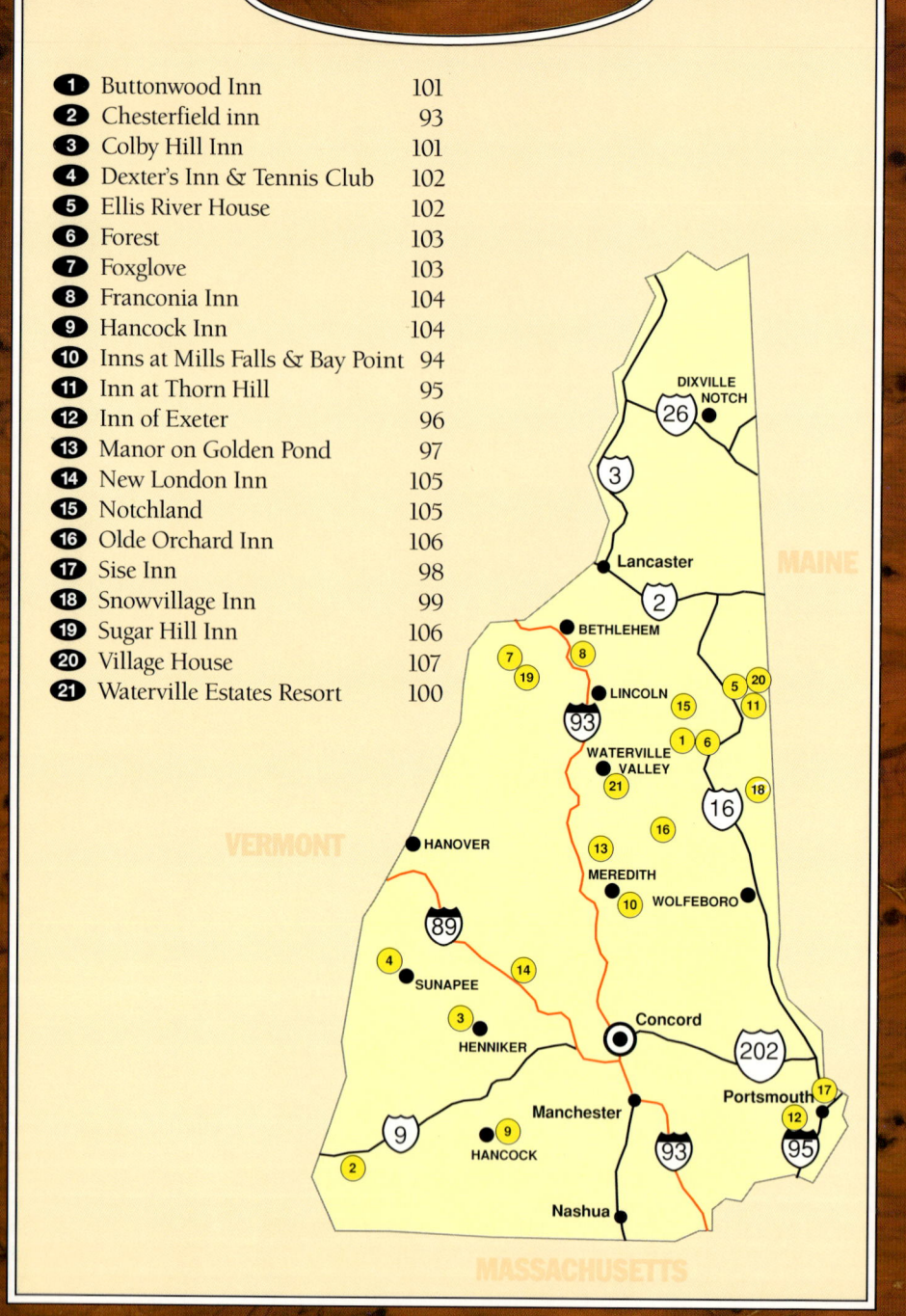

1. Buttonwood Inn — 101
2. Chesterfield inn — 93
3. Colby Hill Inn — 101
4. Dexter's Inn & Tennis Club — 102
5. Ellis River House — 102
6. Forest — 103
7. Foxglove — 103
8. Franconia Inn — 104
9. Hancock Inn — 104
10. Inns at Mills Falls & Bay Point — 94
11. Inn at Thorn Hill — 95
12. Inn of Exeter — 96
13. Manor on Golden Pond — 97
14. New London Inn — 105
15. Notchland — 105
16. Olde Orchard Inn — 106
17. Sise Inn — 98
18. Snowvillage Inn — 99
19. Sugar Hill Inn — 106
20. Village House — 107
21. Waterville Estates Resort — 100

NEW HAMPSHIRE

CHESTERFIELD INN
CHESTERFIELD

Originally a 1787 New Hampshire farm, now a luxurious Country Hotel and AAA Four Diamond award winning property with 13 guest rooms, stunning dining and entertaining facility and beautifully landscaped grounds offering sweeping views of the Vermont mountains.

Our guest rooms put comfort and privacy first. All are spacious, beautifully decorated, with plush bathrooms, self controlled heating and air conditioning, phone, tv and refrigerator. Many have fireplaces and/or garden terraces.

We love imaginative, delicious food with unique flavour combinations and create contemporary cuisine based on regional ingredients. Seafood is fresh from Boston, herbs from our garden and produce from local farmers. Bon appetit! The parlour, dining room and terrace provide a gracious setting for intimate dining as well as weddings and celebrations. The setting sun, panoramic views, fresh flowers and candlelight, provide the perfect backdrop for an incredible dining experience.

Rt 9, PO Box 155
Chesterfield
NH 03443

•

Tel 603 256 3211
Fax 603 256 6131
Freephone in US
800 365 5515

•

Innkeeper:
Phil & Judy Hueber

•

13 rooms
including 2 one bedroom suites.

Doubles $115 - $170
B&B

•

Tax 8%

•

Conference facilities

•

Children welcome

•

Non-smoking

•

VS • MC
Amex • Diners

NEW HAMPSHIRE

THE INNS AT MILLS FALLS AND BAY POINT
MEREDITH

One quaint New England village, two charming, multifaceted inns:

The Inn at Mills Falls envelopes guests in an atmosphere of warmth, comfort, and easy relaxation. By combining old-world charm with contemporary comforts such as spacious guest rooms, indoor pool and sauna and private deck - Mills Falls redefines the traditional country inn. A glass-enclosed heated bridge leading from the inn to eighteen delightful shops, galleries and restaurants allows you to shop, dine or explore.

Adjacent to Mills Falls, surrounded by over 2,000 feet of manicured lakefront park, The Inn at Bay Point sits directly on magnificent Lake Winnipesaukee offering the ultimate in accommodations and location. Guest rooms were designed with luxurious comfort in mind and many offer balconies, cozy fireplaces and personal whirlpool spas. All offer spectacular views of the lake and Gunstock Mountain beyond. Dine at your lakeside table, watch the colour of the distant mountains change, or, better yet, pamper yourself with a romantic dinner served on your private balcony.

Rt 3,
Meredith,
NH 03253
•
Tel 603 279 7006
Fax 603 279 6797
Freephone in US
800 622 6455
•
President & General Manager:
Rusty McLear
•
54 rooms at Mills Falls
24 rooms at Bay Point

Doubles $69 - $235 EP
•
Tax 8%
•
Indoor pool, golf, horseriding, sailing, water skiing, fitness center, hiking, spa
•
Children welcome
•
VS • MC
Amex • Diners

NEW HAMPSHIRE

INN AT THORN HILL
JACKSON

"A masterpiece among country inns", the Inn at Thorn Hill is a smokefree 1895 inn set on a knoll overlooking charming Jackson village, with spectacular views of the White Mountains. It is the perfect choice for honeymooners, romantics and those seeking adult sanctuary. The area offers numerous diversions throughout the year including swimming, golf and hiking in Summer; tobogganing, outdoor hot tub, cross-country and down-hill skiing, sleigh rides and ice skating in Winter.

Relax in the wicker furniture on the spacious porch, or in the fireplaced common rooms. The pub is intimate, the dining elegant with expertly prepared food and attentive service. There are 19 uniquely decorated, air-conditioned bed chambers in the Main Inn, Carriage House or Cottages where guests rest comfortably in their mountain quiet. Recommended by many Inn guides and Gourmet and Bon Appetit magazines, the Inn holds the Three Star Mobil and Three Diamond AAA awards. Special seasonal packages are available.

P O Box A,
Thorn Hill Road,
Jackson, NH 03846
•
Tel 603 383 4242
Fax 603 383 8062
Freephone in US
800 289 8990
•
Innkeepers:
Jim & Ibby Cooper
•
16 rooms
3 two bedroom suites

Doubles $150 - $250 MAP
Suites $230 - $275
•
Tax 8%. s.c. 15%
•
Outdoor swimming pool, cross country skiing from the door, outdoor hot tub
•
Conference facility
for up to 45 people
•
VS • MC • Amex .
Diners • Discover

NEW HAMPSHIRE

INN OF EXETER
EXETER

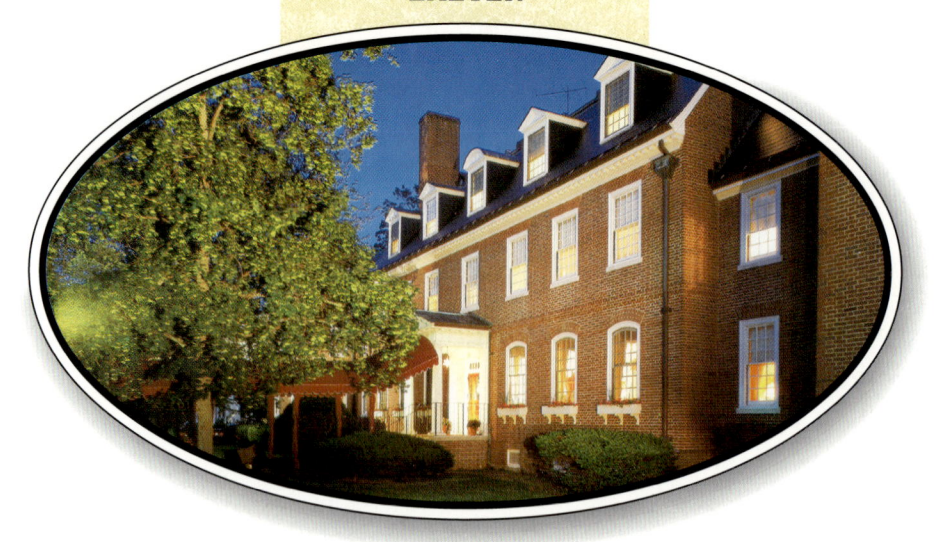

The hospitality at the Inn Of Exeter has been a tradition since the Inn was built in 1932.

A fine example of Georgian style architecture, the inn houses a variety of guest rooms and family suites with a blend of period antiques and all of the modern amenities a guest or business traveller could require.

Casually elegant dining at our Terrace Restaurant is another tradition. Full meal service is also provided in our comfortable and rustic lounge. For business or pleasure, the inn is a marvelous meeting place for lunch or dinner.

Conferences and social functions are memorable events and a beautiful courtyard, complete with old fashioned gazebo, is the perfect setting for wedding ceremonies and reunions.

Situated on the Campus of the renowned Phillips Exeter Academy, the inn is located within easy walking distance to many historical sites and shops.

90 Front Street
Exeter, NH 03833
•
Tel 603 772 5901
Fax 603 778 8757
Freephone in US
800 782 8444
•
Innkeeper: Carl G. Jensen
•
47 rooms
including 1 one bedroom suite
•
Doubles $83 - $115 EP
Suite $160 - $175 EP

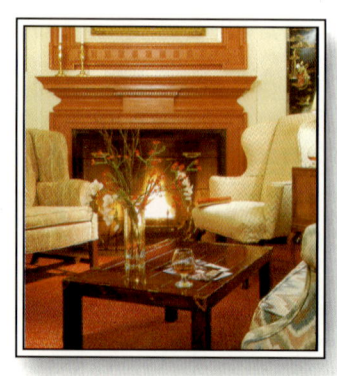

Tax 8%
•
Conference facilities
Nearby: golf, riding, sailing, cross-country skiing
•
Parking available free of charge.
•
Children welcome.
•
Non-smoking
•
VS • MC
Amex • Diners

NEW HAMPSHIRE

MANOR ON GOLDEN POND
HOLDERNESS

The Manor was originally built as a private estate and still provdes the warmth and charm of a country home, reflected in individually decorated bedrooms; most with wood burning fireplaces and views, and some whirlpools for two. Magnificently carved mouldings and rich wood panelling in the dining room provide a setting of classical elegance for nationally acclaimed cuisine. The Manor is an unforgettable romantic hideaway.

Situated in the village of Holderness, and set on the gentle slopes of Shepard Hill, rising above the western shore of pristine Squam Lake (site of the film On Golden Pond) the estate commands a panoramic 65-mile view of the Lake and surrounding mountains. Spacious 13-acre grounds provide a tranquil yet dramatic background for the mansion.

Your hosts, David and Bambi Arnold have dedicated themselves to providing guests with the ultimate in comfort, service and cuisine. They look forward to meeting you.

PO Box T, Rte. 3,
Holderness, NH 03245
•
Tel 603 968 3348
Fax 603 968 2116
Freephone in US
800 545 2141
•
Innkeepers/Owners:
Bambi & David Arnold
•
17 rooms, 4 two bedroom cottages with kitchens and screened in porches. Ideal for families.

Doubles $190 - $325 MAP
Cottages $950 - $1725
weekly 2 - 4 people EP
•
Tax 8% s.c. 15%
•
Tennis, swimming, boating
Nearby: golf, horseriding, skiing
•
Children over 12 welcome at the Manor House
•
Non-smoking
•
VS • MC • Amex

NEW HAMPSHIRE

SISE INN
PORTSMOUTH

Located in the heart of historic Portsmouth, New Hampshire, Sise Inn was originally the home of prosperous businessman and merchant John E. Sise and his family. The 1881 Queen Anne home enjoyed single ownership status until the mid-1930's.

The inn is located on the seacoast, just one hour north of Boston. Rooms and suites have been decorated in the Victorian style using antiques, period reproductions and museum prints. No two rooms are alike.

A complimentary light breakfast is available in the Breakfast Room daily.

The luxurious decor of the inn is reflected in the Sise Room, the Oak Room and the Boardroom, providing the right atmosphere for a serious business meeting or a gourmet dinner party.

Within walking distance from the inn are many fine restaurants, shops, museums and live entertainment. For the outdoor enthusiast, coastal beaches, forested state parks, cross-country skiing, harbour cruises and golf courses are within a ten minute drive.

40 Court St,
Portsmouth,
NH 03801
•
Tel 603 433 1200
Freephone in US
800 267 0525
•
General Manager:
Chris Passero
•
34 rooms
including 7 one bedroom
suites, 4 two bedroom
suites

Doubles $105 - $175 B&B
Suites $125 - $175
•
Tax 8%
•
Conference facilities
Nearby: outdoor pool,
tennis, golf, riding, sailing,
water skiing, skiing
•
Children welcome.
•
Non-smoking
•
VS • MC
Amex • Diners

NEW HAMPSHIRE

SNOWVILLAGE INN
SNOWVILLE

Located on a hillside with a sweeping view of the White Mountains, Snowvillage Inn is an ideal romantic getaway. No traffic, no noise. Just birds, crickets and the wind playing in the pines. Generous lawns, bordered with stone walls and brightened with award winning gardens offer chairs for mountain-gazing, reading and chatting while secluded hammocks provide excellent retreats for pure relaxation. In Spring and Summer, swimming and canoeing are available in nearby lakes and rivers.

All eighteen rooms at the inn are named after writers - the Robert Frost room with its twelve windows has a breathtaking view of Mount Washington - and are furnished with country antiques, fluffy comforters, quilts and comfortable chairs. Books and cosy places in which to read them, abound.

What makes this inn special? Guests rave about the view, the cuisine, the excellent service and the friendliness of the innkeepers, but most of all they treasure the sense of warmth and serenity experienced the moment they walk through the door.

PO Box 68
Snowville,
NH 03832
•
Tel 603 447 2818
Fax 603 447 5268
Freephone in US
800 447 4345
•
Innkeeper/owners:
Barbara & Kevin Flynn
•
18 rooms
•
Doubles $129 - $219 MAP

Tax 8% s.c. 15%
•
Cross-country skiing, hiking.
Nearby: beach with lake swimming, indoor pool, tennis, golf.
•
Children over 6 welcome.
•
Non-smoking
•
VS • MC • Amex
Diners • Discover

NEW HAMPSHIRE

WATERVILLE ESTATES RESORT
CAMPTON

Described as "the best kept secret in the White Mountains" Waterville Estates Resort, just two hours drive from Boston, offers a unique choice of lodging options ideal for family or friends travelling together, with the added freedom of self-catering. Choose from private, beautifully designed, fully furnished and equipped contemporary homes or comfortable condominiums ranging in size from one to four bedrooms many with additional sleeping areas.

Year-round enjoy our beautiful new sports centre with tennis, indoor and outdoor pools, fitness centre, white sandy beach, restaurant, mountain bike trails and trout fishing in the crystal clear Mad River. The ski area (lighted for evenings) with double chairlift, offers cross-country skiing with numerous other ski options at a choice of nearby resorts.

Waterville Estates Realty,
71 Waterville Estates,
Campton, NH 03223-9707
•
Tel 603 726 3716
Fax 603 726 4503
Freephone in US
800 222 5064
•
Owner: Tom Mullen
•
10 homes,
24 condominiums
•
One-bedroom units
from $96 - $120 EP

Four-bedroom units from $180. Special rates available for visits of over 3 nights.
•
Tax 8% s.c. 7%
•
Indoor, outdoor pools, tennis, fitness centre, conference facilities, children's summer and winter programmes. Nearby golf, sailing, water skiing
•
Children welcome
•
VS • MC

NEW HAMPSHIRE

BUTTONWOOD INN
NORTH CONWAY

Allow us to pamper you with personal service. As native New Englanders we help you with knowledgeable travel tips. Located on five wooded acres at the end of a no-through road on the side of a little mountain, we're only two miles from the village of North Conway. The nearby White Mountain National Forest's 780,000 acres offer unlimited outdoor activities year round.

Of our five acres, three are lawns and award-winning gardens, ideal for a summer stroll, finishing with a refreshing dip in the pool. Cross-country ski from our back door, Alpine skiing a mile away. We're happy to suggest hikes or walks and ensure you're fully equipped. Early risers enjoy hot coffee or tea from 7.00 am. Breakfast specials include To Die For French Toast, whilst for the faint-hearted, eggs and cold cereals are always available.

PO Box 1817, Mount Surprise Road
North Conway
NH 03860
Tel 603 356 2625
Fax 603 356 3140

Freephone in US
800 258 2625
Innkeepers:
Peter & Claudia Needham

9 rooms, 5 with private bath, including 1 two bedroom suite

Doubles $70 - $150 B&B
Suite $135 - $150
Tax 8%

Outdoor pool
Nearby: indoor pool, tennis, golf, riding, down-hill & cross-country skiing.

Children over 3 welcome.
Non-smoking
VS • MC • Amex

COLBY HILL INN
HENNIKER

Congenial inn-dogs Bertha and Delilah await with a handshake, and the cookie jar beckons at this rambling 1797 inn, a complex of farmhouse, carriage house, and barns. Enjoy the antique-filled guestrooms, some with working fireplaces, each with private bath and telephone and the comfortable common rooms which are a popular gathering place for visitors.

Five acres are lush with perennial gardens and feature a gazebo tucked between ancient apple trees for a quiet retreat. Memorable food begins and ends the day from the bountiful country breakfast to the acclaimed candlelit dinner served every night in the gardenside dining room

Classic New England scenery abounds in this delightful village on the river, just 90 minutes from Boston.

3 The Oaks,
PO Box 779
Henniker,
NH 03242
Tel 603 428 3181
Fax 603 428 9218

Freephone in US
800 531 0330
Innkeepers:
Ellie & John Day,
Laurel Day Mack

16 rooms
Can configure to have 2 three room suites
Doubles $85 - $175 B&B

Suites vary according to total of 3-room rate.
Tax 8% s.c. 10%

Outdoor pool, winter ice-skating, conference facilities
Nearby: tennis, golf, Canterbury Shaker Village.

Children over 7 welcome
Non-smoking
VS • MC
Amex • Diners

101

NEW HAMPSHIRE

DEXTER'S INN & TENNIS CLUB
SUNAPEE

Located on twenty acres in the lovely Sunapee Region of lakes and mountains, Dexter's embodies the essence of a true New England Country Inn. Warm, friendly, and unassuming hospitality is as much in evidence now as it has been for 45 years. Bountiful breakfasts and dinners are served daily and there are three all-weather world-class tennis courts with our resident professional available for tuition should you require.

Relax in the pool, stroll along country lanes, read on the terrace, or enjoy croquet, horseshoes or shuffleboard. We are ideally located for day trips to some of the most beautiful and interesting parts of New England. You will find Dexter's an idyllic setting evoking a charming reminder of a time and way of life that has never left this special inn.

PO Box 703 MM, Stagecoach Road, Sunapee, NH 03782	Tel/Fax 603 763 5571 Freephone in US 800 232 5571	Innkeepers: Michael W. Durfor, Holly Simpson-Durfor 17 rooms Holly Cottage sleeps 4	Doubles $135 - $190 MAP Cottage $380 B&B rates available on request	Tax 8% s.c. 15% Outdoor pool, tennis courts, conference facilities	Nearby: golf, sailing Children welcome VS • MC • Discover

ELLIS RIVER HOUSE
JACKSON

An enchanting, family run, country inn set on three acres overlooking the river and at the base of spectacular Mt Washington, the highest peak in the Northeast. Views from the inn are breathtaking. Amenities include: romantic fireplace guest rooms, spacious two room family suites, an indoor jacuzzi spa, outdoor swimming pool, delicious full country breakfast. Scenic balconies, outdoor patios and comfortable common rooms encourage conversation. In Winter there are 160 kms of world class groomed trails outside the back door, with four major downhill slopes minutes away. Summer activities include hiking, cycling, swimming and factory outlet shopping, while Fall offers spectacular foliage colours. Only three hours from Boston – join us for a taste of Old New England!

Rt 116, PO Box 656, Jackson, NH 03846 Tel 603 383 9339 Fax 603 383 4142	Freephone in US 800 233 8309 Innkeeper/Owner: Barbara Lubao	16 rooms, all with private bath. 1 cottage, 4 suites.	Doubles $79 – $229 B&B Cottage/suites $109 – $229	Tax 8% s.c. 10% Non-smoking Outdoor swimming pool, golf, horseriding	Children welcome VS • MC • Amex

NEW HAMPSHIRE

THE FOREST, A COUNTRY INN
NORTH CONWAY

On a winding country road, midway between North Conway and Jackson, The Forest, a classic three storey Victorian, began operating in 1890 and has welcomed vacationers ever since. The front yard is enclosed by a low picket fence, while across the gravelled driveway is a small stone guest cottage with fireplace - perfect for that special getaway. The inn carries a Three Diamond rating from the AAA.

With only eleven charming, fireplaced, guest rooms, you're assured of personal, friendly attention. Our beautifully served complimentary breakfast includes fresh fruits, juices and an array of homemade baked goods – spiced belgian waffles, apple pancakes, and more! Tea and refreshments are served each afternoon. Enjoy our large screened verandah, heated outdoor pool, tennis court and lovely gardens.

Rt 16A, (at the Intervale), North Conway, NH 03860 Tel 603 356 9772 Fax 603 356 5652	Freephone in US 800 448 3534 Owner/Innkeepers: Bill & Lisa Guppy	11 rooms, 9 with private bath. Garden Cottage	Doubles $80 – $130 B&B Cottage $100 – $160	Tax 8% Outdoor swimming pool, tennis	Non-smoking Children welcome VS • MC • Amex

FOXGLOVE
SUGAR HILL

Elegance atop Sugar Hill. Newly renovated, designer-decorated, turn-of-the-century country home. Cosy romantic bedrooms and suites, private baths. Crackling fires, park-like woodland setting, hideaway porches, terraces and quiet glades.

Trickling fountains, soft music, swaying hammocks fabulous sunsets. Foxglove offers guests a tranquil and impeccable setting from which to explore and enjoy the charm of this historic mountain village with its magnificent views - Franconia Notch, the White Mountains, The Upper Connecticut River and Mount Washington Valley. Foxglove is open year round and surrounded by a myriad of all-seasons sports and activities.

Rooms for two include a sumptuous breakfast with silver, china, crystal and other amenities. Casual comfort and attention to detail prevail.

Route 117 at Lovers Lane, Sugar Hill, NH 03585	Tel 603 823 8840 Fax 603 823 5755 Owner/Innkeeper: Janet G. Boyd	6 rooms including 1 one bedroom suite, 1 two bedroom suite	Doubles $85 – $145 B&B $135 - $195 MAP Tax 8%. s.c. 5% (15% on dinner)	Nearby: outdoor pool, tennis, golf, riding, sailing, water skiing, down-hill & cross-country skiing	Children over 12 welcome. Non-smoking VS • MC

NEW HAMPSHIRE

FRANCONIA INN
FRANCONIA

Not just a Winter Ski Lodge... as the snow melts in Spring, four beautiful red clay tennis courts and a large, sunny swimming pool appear. Skis, boots and poles disappear, replaced by horses, saddles and stirrups. Cross-country trails become scenic bridle paths. Where snowbanks once reigned, gardens flourish. The formidable snowcapped White Mountains shed their snow blanket to become a hiker's paradise.

On 107 acres in the Easton Valley, the inn affords the same magnificent view of Franconia Notch that inspired Robert Frost's poem "The Road Not Taken". Guest and common rooms invite relaxation and become part of your home when you stay with us.

Located 2½ hours north of Boston, we hold the AAA Three Diamond and Mobil Three Star ratings.

| 1300 Easton Valley Road, Franconia, NH 03580 | Tel 603 823 5542 Fax 603 823 8078 Freephone in US 800 473 5299 | Owners: Alex & Richard Morris 34 rooms | Doubles $140 – $170 MAP Tax 8% | Outdoor swimming pool, tennis, horseriding, cycling, hiking, skiing, sleigh-rides | Children welcome VS • MC • Amex |

HANCOCK INN
HANCOCK

Retreat to the authenticity and gentility of 18th century New England with all the amenities of the 20th century.

Each guest room has private bath, telephone, comfortable four-poster or canopy bed, handsewn quilts and air conditioning. Rich colonial colours and antiques decorate every corner of the inn and the tavern is now a cosy common room where guests gather fireside to play checkers on an antique board.

In the award-winning restaurant rediscover authentic American fare such as cranberry pot roast. Nearby, pick apples, browse in antique shops, hike or simply gaze upon majestic Mount Monadnock. Local protected woodlands provide habitat for bear, moose, deer, bobcat and coyote. Explore miles of uncrowded hiking and cross-country skiing trails as well as clean lakes and ponds for skating, boating and fishing.

| 33 Main Street, Hancock, NH 03449 | Tel 603 525 3318 Fax 603 525 9301 Freephone in US 800 525 1789 | Owner/Innkeepers: Joe & Linda Johnston | 11 rooms Doubles $98 - $158 B&B Tax 8% s.c. 10% | Conference facilities Nearby: tennis, golf, riding, sailing, water skiing, down-hill & cross-country skiing | Children over 12 welcome. Non-smoking VS • MC Amex • Diners |

NEW HAMPSHIRE

NEW LONDON INN
NEW LONDON

This classic 1792 country inn, on the Town Green, in one of the most picturesque villages in New England at the heart of the Dartmouth Lake Sunapee Region offers 29 rooms, many with sitting areas. The inn's restaurant features delicious upscale New England fare such as hardwood grilled and house-smoked appetisers and entrées.

Fireplaced, comfortably furnished, sitting rooms, dining room and library invite you to relax after a day spent browsing in unique shops. A short walk brings you to the New London Barn Playhouse - one of the oldest, best-loved summer theatres or visit Colby-Sawyer College, just across the green. Historic Claremont Opera House and Dartmouth College, both under half an hour away, offer year-round cultural activities.

| 140 Main Street
PO Box 8
New London
NH 03257
Tel 603 526 2791
Fax 603 526 2749 | Freephone in US
800 526 2791
Innkeepers:
Kimberley & Terance
O'Mahoney | 29 rooms
Doubles $85 - $150
B&B
Tax 8% | Conference facilities
Nearby: tennis, golf, riding, sailing, down-hill skiing, cross-country skiiing | Children over 2 welcome. | Non-smoking
VS • MC
Amex • Discover |

NOTCHLAND INN
HART'S LOCATION

Get away from it all, relax and rejuvenate at our comfortable 1860's granite mansion located on 400 acres in the midst of beautiful mountain vistas.

Settle into one of our seven deluxe rooms or four spacious suites, each individually appointed and all with wood-burning fireplaces and private bath. In the evening, Notchland's wonderful 5-course dinner is served in a romantic fireplaced dining room looking out to the gazebo by our pond.

We have 8,000 feet of Saco River frontage on our property and two of the area's best swimming holes. Coco our Bernese Mountain dog will greet you on arrival while Dolly, the Belgian Draft Horse pulls our sleigh in the Winter. Mork & Mindy are miniature horses with large personalities and as for our Llamas, DC & Sid - well come and meet them for yourselves.

| Rt 302,
Hart's Location,
NH 03812
Tel 603 374 6131
Fax 603 374 6168 | Freephone in US
800 866 6131
Owners/Innkeepers
Les Schoof & Ed Butler | 11 rooms
including 4 one bedroom suites
2 suites in renovated 1850 "schoolhouse" | Doubles $170 - $230
MAP
Suites $190 - $250
Tax 8% s.c. 15% | River swimming, cross-country skiing.
Nearby: outdoor & indoor pools, hiking, tennis, golf, riding, sailing, | Children over 12 welcome.
Non-smoking
VS • MC • Amex
Diners • Discover |

105

NEW HAMPSHIRE

OLDE ORCHARD INN
MOULTONBOROUGH

A restored farmhouse on twelve country acres with fruit orchards, a pond and a paddle boat for guest use. In the heart of New Hampshire's Lake region, only a mile from Winnipesaukee where a host of sailing, and water sport options are open to you.

Spring is a wonderful time to visit, as from mid-May to early June our eight acre orchard of several hundred fruit trees, apples, pears, cherries and plums, come into bloom. In late July the fruit begins to ripen, continuing into early November through the stunning Fall foliage displays. In Winter, ski from the front door with five major ski areas within an hours drive.

Children are always welcome at the inn and we offer our guests a large country breakfast with home-baked goods and all the fixin's!

RR Box 256 Moultonborough NH 03254 Tel 603 476 5004 Fax 603 476 5419	Freephone in US 800 598 5845 Owner/Innkeepers: Jim & Mary Senner	9 rooms including family suite 1 one bedroom cottage Doubles $70 - $125,	Family suite $135 B&B Cottage $80 for 2 people EP Tax 8%	Small meeting facilities Nearby: tennis, golf, riding, sailing, water-skiing,	down-hill skiing, cross-country skiing Children welcome. Non-smoking VS • MC

SUGAR HILL INN
FRANCONIA

A quintessential country inn. This authentic 18th century farmhouse has been impeccably restored and appointed. Each bedroom has comfortable canopy, beehive or four poster beds, private baths (many with deep soaking tubs), most offer spectacular mountain vistas and several feature romantic fireplaces.

Mornings start with a scrumptious country breakfast, afternoon refreshments of homemade sweets and tea are provided daily. The award-winning cuisine and warm hospitality are unmatched. Please join us in a most pristine setting, where unlimited outdoor activities, chamber concerts and summer theatre are a special treat. While away your afternoon sipping lemonade on a cosy porch rocker.

Rt 117, Franconia, NH 03580	Tel 603 823 5621 Fax 603 823 5639 Freephone in US 800 548 4748	Innkeepers : The Quinn Family Jim , Barbara,Kelly & Stephen 16 rooms	Doubles $155 – $245 MAP $105 - $145 B&B Tax 8% s.c. 15%	Nearby: golf, hiking, swimming, cycling, skiing, museum, antiquing, art & gift shops	Non-smoking Does not meet the needs of young children

NEW HAMPSHIRE

VILLAGE HOUSE
JACKSON

Just beyond the covered bridge lies the pretty village of Jackson and the Village House, with a tradition of hospitality going back 100 years – the charm and personality of a small B&B with many of the amenities of a larger resort. The Village House offers affordable lodging throughout the year. In Summer, enjoy our swimming pool, jacuzzi, tennis court and wrap-around porch, plus our convenient location to all area sights and attractions. In Winter, warm yourself by a roaring fire, or in our all-season outdoor jacuzzi. Cross country from our door or downhill within minutes. Year-round enjoy our delicious breakfasts. Welcome to the charm and peacefulness of the village of Jackson and one of the loveliest, most relaxing vacations of your life. The place is the Village House... the time is of your choosing... the delights are many...

PO Box 359, Rt 16A, Jackson, NH 03846
Tel 603 383 6666
Fax 603 383 6464

Freephone in US
800 972 8343
Owner/Innkeeper:
Robin Crocker

14 rooms, all with private bath
4 rooms offer kitchenettes

Doubles $65 - $130
With kitchenettes
$75 - $140
B&B

Tax 8%
Outdoor swimming pool. Nearby: tennis, golf, horseriding, hiking

Children welcome
VS • MC

The WELCOME NEWS

OUR new, quarterly, full-colour newsletter for independent travellers to East Coast North America.
Packed full of interesting news and views, items of information, tempting places to stay plus seasonal special offers and some delicious innkeepers' recipes for you to try.
Just give us a call and we will despatch a FREE copy to you straight away.

U.S. Welcome Ltd (U.K. Office)
Tel 01923 821469 Fax 01923 827157
100127.2706@compuserve.com

Toll free number in US & Canada 1-888-INN VISIT

Rhode Island

1. Bed & Breakfast on the Point — 111
2. Block Island Resorts — 109
3. Cliffside Inn — 110
4. Grandview — 111
5. Larchwood Inn — 112
6. Villa — 112

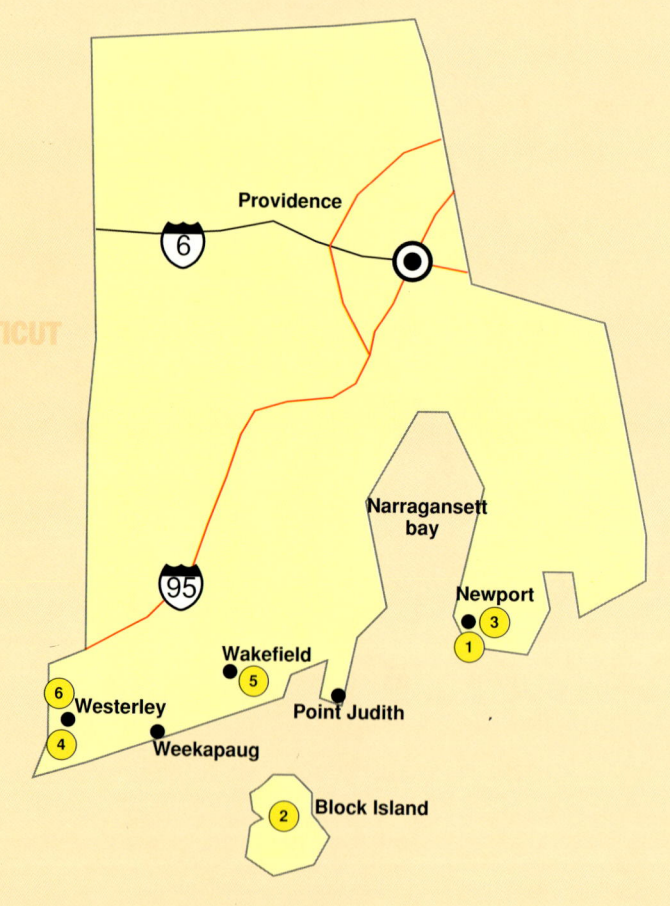

RHODE ISLAND

BLOCK ISLAND RESORTS
BLOCK ISLAND

Sail 13 miles out to sea to discover 19th Century New England at the Hotel Manisses, an elegantly restored Victorian Hotel featuring seventeen meticulously appointed rooms with private baths and phones, some rooms with jacuzzis.

Also owned and run by the Abrams family is the 1661 Inn & Guest House and the Nicholas Ball Cottage, all recently refurbished to provide further luxury accommodations with ocean views, jacuzzis and fireplaces. Hotel Manisses' dining room serves dinner nightly. Choose delicious selections from a widely varied menu. Flaming coffees, after dinner drinks & desserts are served in the upstairs parlour. Complimentary full breakfast buffet and wine and nibble hour are included in the rates.

Life on the Island is slow-paced and relaxing – beaches, harbours, gently rolling hills and flower strewn meadows as well as a quaint Victorian town. If you're looking to get away from it all, this is for you.

Spring Street,
Box 1,
Block Island,
RI 02807

•

Tel 401 466 2421/2836
Fax 401 466 2858

•

Innkeepers:
Joan & Justin Abrams,
Rita & Steve Draper

•

38 rooms
1 three bedroom cottage

Doubles $106 - $318
B&B

•

Tax 12%. s.c.
included in rate

•

Nearby: tennis,
horseriding, sailing,
hiking

•

Children welcome

•

VS • MC • Amex

RHODE ISLAND

CLIFFSIDE INN
NEWPORT

This delightful Second-Empire Victorian manor house was built in 1880 by Maryland Governor Thomas Swann and later owned by noted artist Beatrice Turner whose life and times were chronicled by LIFE magazine in 1950.

The inn's distinctive interior decor features more than 100 Beatrice Turner artworks. The fifteen elegant guest rooms are furnished with antiques, luxurious designer fabrics and linens. Twelve rooms have fireplaces, eleven have whirlpool tubs and one has a steambath.

Located in a quiet residential neighbourhood, the inn is steps from the beginning of the Cliffwalk, Newport's world famous Atlantic seaside walking trail; a five minute walk to Newport's main beach and ideally located for visiting the magnificent Newport mansions. Amenities include complimentary coffee service and full gourmet breakfast in the mornings, and afternoon Victorian tea. We look forward to welcoming you and hope that you will make Cliffside Inn your home-away-from-home.

2 Seaview Avenue,
Newport,
RI 02840

•

Tel 401 847 1811
Fax 401 848 5850
Freephone in US
800 845 1811

•

Innkeeper:
Stephan Nicolas

•

15 rooms including
7 one bedroom suites.

Doubles $175 - $325
B&B

•

Tax 12 %

•

Conference facilities
Nearby: indoor pool,
tennis, golf, sailing

•

Children over 14
welcome.

•

Non-smoking

•

VS • MC • Amex
Diners • Discover

RHODE ISLAND

BED & BREAKFAST ON THE POINT
NEWPORT

This century-old Victorian style home is 1½ blocks from Narragansett Bay, just fifteen minutes walk to the centre of Newport. Take a guided tour of Newport's historic sites; the harbour or the Mansions. Other attractions are the International Tennis Hall of Fame and the Museum of Newport History.

Your hosts, local history buffs, have an excellent collection of nineteenth century photos and art work displayed on walls. The bedrooms feature King size or twin beds and are furnished with some antique furniture and colourful fabrics. A substantial continental breakfast is served in the wicker filled common room. Most important of all, New England hospitality is featured.

| 102 Third Street Newport RI 02840 | Tel 401 846 8377 Innkeeper: George C. Perry | 4 rooms including 1 two bedroom suite. (3 rooms have private bath) | Doubles $95 - $155 B&B (May-Oct) Suite $150 - $190 (Off season rates lower) Tax 12% | Nearby: tennis, golf, sailing, water skiing, Parking available free of charge. | Children over 9 welcome. Non-smoking VS • MC |

GRANDVIEW BED & BREAKFAST
WESTERLY

Enjoy a splendid ocean view from the stone wrap-around porch of this turn of the century hilltop home. A large comfortable living room offers a haven to read, visit with friends – new and old, or just relax on the oversized couch in front of the beautiful stone fireplace. Hearty continental breakfast is served on the large cheery sunporch. Watch Hill and Westerly Beaches are nearby.

Enjoy local theatre, shopping, antiquing or dining in one of the area's many fine restaurants. Explore the delightful fishing village of Stonington, visit Mystic Seaport and Aquarium or drive to lively Newport with its shops, restaurants and the fabulous "Summer Cottages". Foxwoods and Mohegan Sun, two new casinos, are only a short drive away.

| 212 Shore Road, Westerly, RI 02891 | Tel 401 596 6384 Freephone in US 800 447 6384 | Owner: Pat Grande | 10 rooms, 4 of which have private bath Doubles $75 – $95 | Tax 12% Nearby: golf, tennis, beaches | Non-smoking Children welcome VS • MC • Amex |

RHODE ISLAND

LARCHWOOD INN
WAKEFIELD

The village of Wakefield is the perfect setting for a visit to a real, family-run country inn, which has kept pace with the twentieth century without sacrificing any of its rural beauty and traditions. The three storey Larchwood Inn, surrounded by wide expanses of landscaped grounds and located at the quiet end of the village, has also survived the necessities of modernisation, whilst carefully, preserving the charm of its 150 years of history.

Comfortable guest rooms and the choice of four different dining rooms and a cocktail lounge, enhance the warm hospitality of your welcome and offer you an ideal location for exploring all of Rhode Island. Take a ferry to lovely Block Island, tour the incredible Newport mansions, or simply enjoy the nearby sheltered beaches, boating, horseriding and cycling. Whatever your mood, the Larchwood Inn can suit it!

| 521 Main Street, Wakefield, RI 02879 | Tel 401 783 5454
Fax 401 783 1800
Freephone in US
800 275 5450 | Innkeepers:
Francis & Diann Browning
20 rooms,
11 with bath en suite | Doubles $60 - $110
EP
Tax 12% | Nearby: tennis, golf, horseriding, sailing | Children over 12 welcome
VS • MC
Amex • Diners |

THE VILLA
WESTERLY

Open year round, The Villa is situated at the crossroads of historic Westerly and Watch Hill, minutes from the pristine shoreline of Rhode Island and within easy reach of attractions such as the Newport Mansions and Old Mystic Village. On 1½ landscaped acres and surrounded by beautiful gardens and lawns, the inn offers both privacy and luxury in seven individual and delightfully decorated suites. Friendliness and personal care are provided by your host Jerry Maiorano.

Swim in the sparkling sapphire pool surrounded by lush green plants or relax in the outdoor Jacuzzi spa. Summers are warm and golden with cool ocean breezes and a breakfast buffet is served by the pool, in the dining area or brought to your room. In the winter enjoy the privacy and cosiness of your own fireplace or jacuzzi suite.

| 190 Shore Road, Westerly RI 02891 | Tel 401 596 1054
Fax 401 596 6268
Freephone in US
800 722 9240 | Owner:
Jerry Maiorano
7 suites, 5 with separate sitting areas. | Doubles $75 - $205
B&B
Tax 12% | Outdoor pool, hot tub
Nearby: tennis, golf, riding, sailing, water skiing | Does not meet the needs of children
VS • MC • Amex |

You Can Still Holiday in the Colonies...

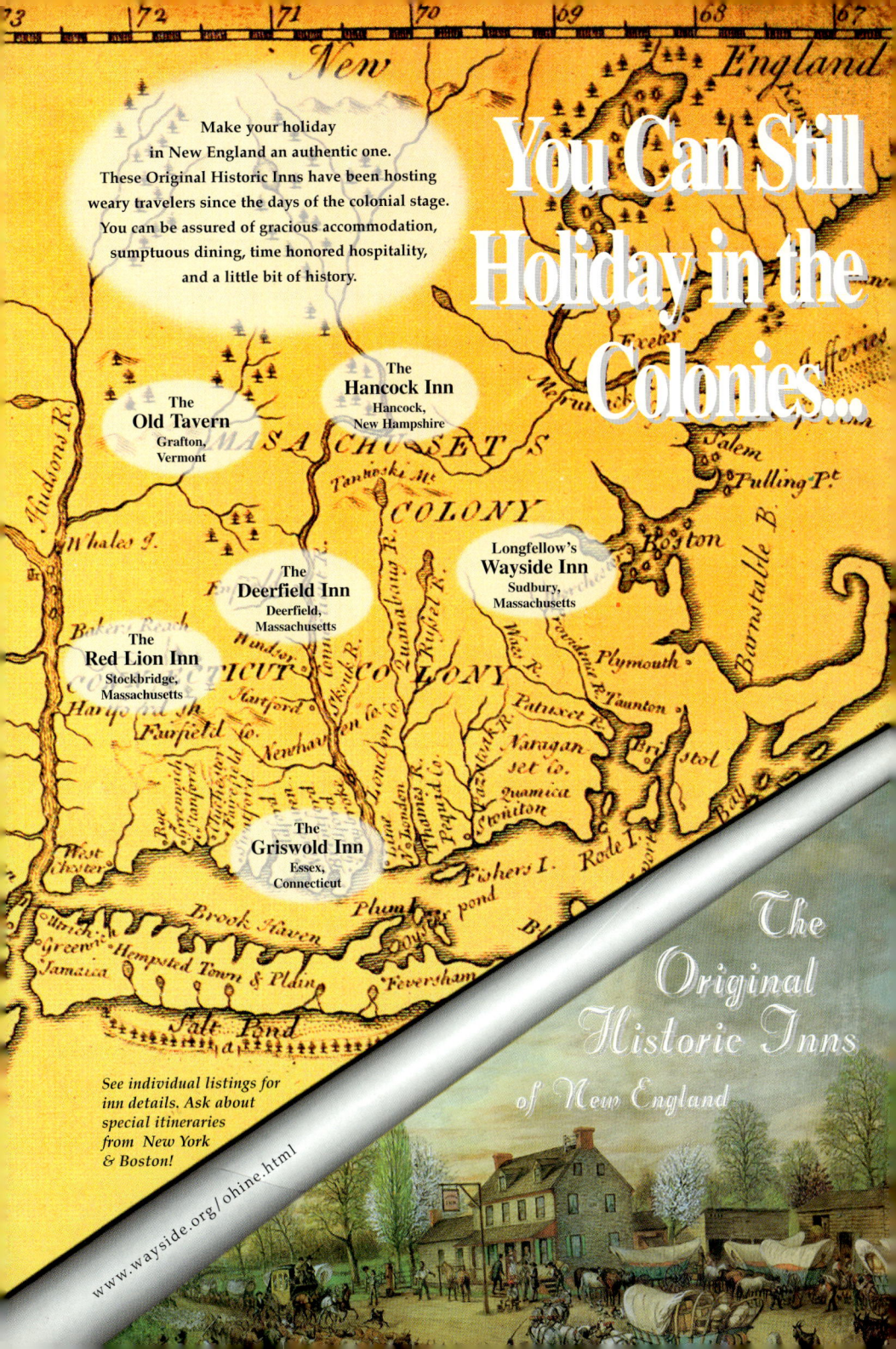

Make your holiday in New England an authentic one. These Original Historic Inns have been hosting weary travelers since the days of the colonial stage. You can be assured of gracious accommodation, sumptuous dining, time honored hospitality, and a little bit of history.

The Old Tavern
Grafton, Vermont

The Hancock Inn
Hancock, New Hampshire

The Deerfield Inn
Deerfield, Massachusetts

Longfellow's Wayside Inn
Sudbury, Massachusetts

The Red Lion Inn
Stockbridge, Massachusetts

The Griswold Inn
Essex, Connecticut

See individual listings for inn details. Ask about special itineraries from New York & Boston!

The Original Historic Inns of New England

www.wayside.org/ohine.html

Vermont

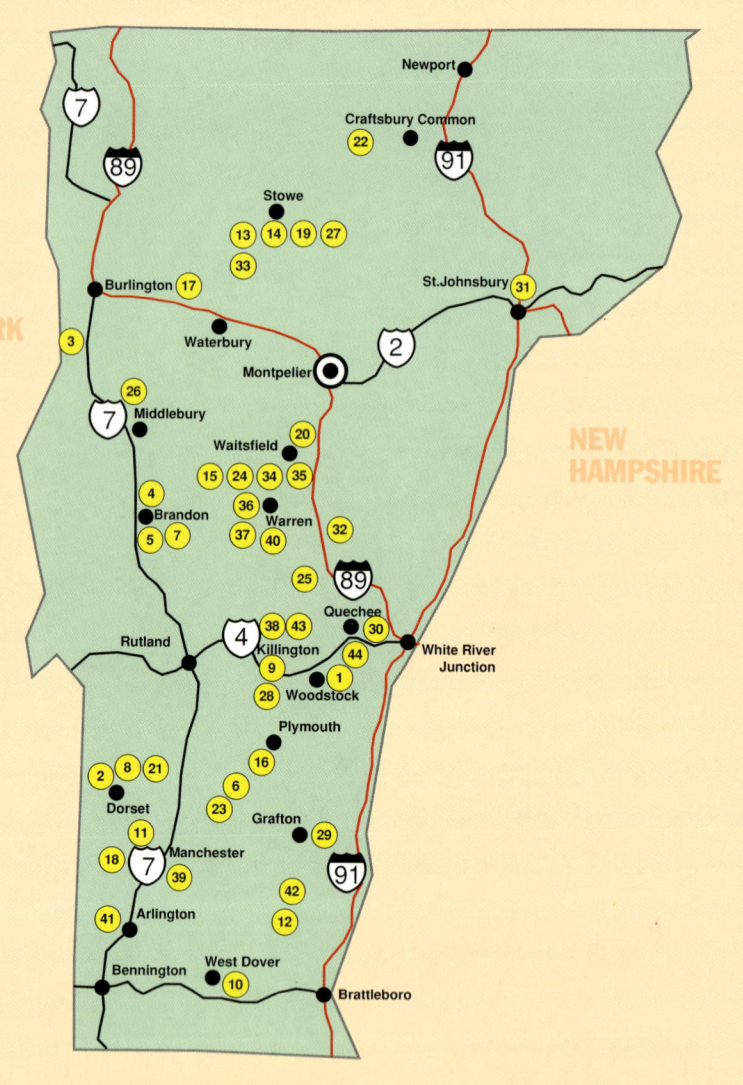

Vermont

① Ardmore Inn	134
② Barrows House	134
③ Basin Harbor Club	117
④ Blueberry Hill Inn	135
⑤ Brandon Inn	135
⑥ Castle	136
⑦ Churchill House Inn	136
⑧ Cornucopia of Dorset	118
⑨ Cortina Inn	119
⑩ Deerhill Inn	137
⑪ Equinox	120
⑫ Four Columns Inn	121
⑬ Gables	137
⑭ Golden Eagle Resort	122
⑮ Hamilton House	138
⑯ Hawk Inn & Resort	123
⑰ Inn at Essex	124
⑱ Inn at Ormsby Hill	125
⑲ Inn at the Brass Lantern	138
⑳ Inn at the Round Barn Farm	139
㉑ Inn at West View Farm	139
㉒ Inn on the Common	126
㉓ Landgrove Inn	140
㉔ Lareau Farm Country Inn	140
㉕ Maple Leaf Inn	141
㉖ Middlebury Inn	141
㉗ Mountain Road Resort	127
㉘ October Country Inn	142
㉙ Old Tavern at Grafton	128
㉚ Quechee	142
㉛ Rabbit Hill Inn	129
㉜ Shire Inn	143
㉝ Siebeness	143
㉞ Sugarbush	130
㉟ Sugartree	144
㊱ Sugar Lodge	144
㊲ Tucker Hill Lodge	145
㊳ Vermont Inn	145
㊴ Village Country Inn	146
㊵ West Hill House	146
㊶ West Mountain Inn	147
㊷ Windham Hill Inn	131
㊸ Woods	147
㊹ Woodstock Inn & Resort	132

A Week in Vermont Lasts a Lifetime in a Photo Album.

You'll have the opportunity virtually anywhere you turn in Vermont: from cozy villages to forested mountains... from simple clapboard houses to pristine church spires... from sparkling lakes of blue to endless fields of green.

Yes, Vermont says "New England" like nowhere else. But a picture is worth a thousand words. So, pack plenty of film when you come. And leave some pages open in that album. A lot of pages.

INTERNATIONAL **(802) 828-3237** FAX **(802) 828-3233**
or write: VERMONT TOURISM & MARKETING, DEPT. 729
134 STATE STREET, MONTPELIER, VT 05602 U.S.A.
http://www.travel-vermont.com

VERMONT
the nature of
New England

VERMONT

BASIN HARBOR CLUB
VERGENNES

Since 1886 the Beach family has welcomed travellers to Vermont's historic Champlain Valley. This seven hundred acre resort features sweeping lawns and gardens, rolling meadows and stands of ancient trees, with spectacular views of Lake Champlain. Families have vacationed here for generations. Recreational amenities include an 18 hole golf course, five tennis courts, sailing, water skiing, canoeing and swimming (lake and large pool), bicycling, nature walks and just plain loafing. Daily activities feature an active children's programme, lectures, movies, dancing and entertainment. Accommodations include seventy seven picturesque cottages with one to three bedrooms and baths, all within easy walking distance of the resort's facilities. Fine dining and the Wine Spectator's Award of Excellence round out a grand vacation.

Basin Harbor is just two hours drive from Montreal, four and a half hours from Boston and five hours from New York. Connecting flights via Burlington, VT. are available from major East Coast hubs in the U.S.

Vergennes,
VT 05491
•
Tel 802 475 2311
Fax 802 475 6545
Freephone in US
800 622 4000
•
Innkeepers, Owners:
The Beach Family
•
44 rooms
77 one, two and three
bedroom cottages

Doubles $230 - $280 AP
Cottages $260 - $300
B&B rates also available
except in July & August
•
Tax 7%. s.c. 15%
•
Outdoor swimming pool,
tennis, golf, horseriding,
sailing, water skiing,
hiking, exercise room
•
VS • MC

VERMONT

CORNUCOPIA OF DORSET
DORSET

Cornucopia, an 1880 colonial surrounded by colourful country gardens, offers the intimacy of a bed and breakfast and the service and amenities of the finest full service inn, including champagne check-in, full evening turn-down, wake-up trays of coffee or tea with fresh flowers and sumptuous, candlelit breakfasts.

Most rooms have fireplaces and all have sitting areas, with thoughtful extra touches to enhance your visit – oversized bath sheets, terry cloth bathrobes, Crabtree and Evelyn toiletries, fresh fruit, chocolates, luxurious down comforters or colourful Vermont made quilts, (depending on the season) and in-room telephones.

Visit this quintessential New England Village with its craft and antique shops, fine restaurants and live theatre, all a short stroll from the inn.

Come and be pampered at Cornucopia.
"We'd like to make our home, your home".

PO Box 307, Rt 30,
Dorset, VT 05251
•
Tel 802 867 5751
Fax 802 867 5753
Freephone in US
800 566 5751
•
Innkeepers:
Linda & Bill Ley
•
5 rooms
including 1 one-bedroom
cottage suite with self-
catering facility

Doubles $115 - $155 B&B
(special rates for stays of
7 nights or longer)
Cottage suite $205 - $225
•
Tax 7%
•
Nearby: swimming, tennis,
golf
•
Children over
12 welcome
•
Non-smoking
•
VS • MC • Amex

VERMONT

CORTINA INN
KILLINGTON

Killington's most luxurious inn... it's the little things that make a difference.

A staff that caters to your every wish, fresh flowers, afternoon tea, delicious breakfasts, room service, and award winning food bring guests back time and time again to our AAA Three Diamond, Mobil Three Star award winning inn.

We have blended the hospitality and cosy charm of a country inn with the amenities of a resort hotel. We offer continuous transport to skiing slopes, indoor pool, sauna, fitness center, games room, sleigh rides, snowmobiling and beautifully decorated fireplaced rooms and suites.

It is all of this which goes to make Cortina a truly four-season destination.

HC 34, Box 33,
US rt 4,
Killington, VT 05751
•
Tel 802 773 3333
Fax 802 775 6948
Freephone in US
800 451 6108
•
Innkeepers:
Bob & Breda Harnish
•
97 rooms and suites

Doubles $89 - $169 B&B
Suites $169 - $269
•
Tax 7%
•
Indoor pool,
8 tennis courts, golf,
fitness center,
games room
•
Children welcome
•
VS • MC • Amex

VERMONT

THE EQUINOX
MANCHESTER

A member of Historic Hotels of America, the Equinox has recently been beautifully and painstakingly restored to its original splendour and stands on 1,100 acres of land. The hotel offers deluxe accommodations in air-conditioned rooms or deluxe townhouses with cable tv, in-room movies and a choice of mountain, village or garden views. The new Charles Orvis Inn at the Equinox comprises one and two bedroom suites. Hotel services include laundry, dry-cleaning, shoe-shine, concierge, valet parking, room service and nightly turn down.

The hotel holds the AAA Four Diamond award and offers superb sporting facilities both on site and in the surrounding areas. The newly renovated Gleneagles Golf Course has been awarded Golf Magazine's Silver Medal.

There are three restaurants at the resort, The Colonnade Room, The Marsh Tavern and the Dormy Grill offering a range of dining choices from elegant to casual.

The Equinox is a drive of about 4 hours from New York and about 3½ hours from Boston.

PO Box 46
Manchester Village,
Manchester, VT 05254
•
Tel 802 362 4700
Fax 802 362 4861
Freephone in US
800 362 4747
•
General Manager & Vice President: S.L. Bowden
•
163 rooms
10 one-bedroom suites
27 additional rooms and suites in townhouse units, some with self-catering facilities
Doubles $169 - $299 EP
Suites $339 - $559
•
Tax 7%
•
Indoor and outdoor pools, tennis, golf, horseriding, fitness center, hiking, spa, conference facilities, British School of Falconry, Equinox Cross Country Ski Touring Centre
•
VS • MC • Amex • Diners

VERMONT

FOUR COLUMNS INN
NEWFANE

The magic begins to work when you first see the Four Columns Inn, set in the picture book village of Newfane, it continues as you enjoy quiet comforts, escaping for a time the hectic everyday world. Individually decorated guest rooms, each with private bath, await your arrival. Whether you choose a room with a fireplace, a view of the common, or a jacuzzi for two, the result will be the same, a feeling of serene contentment.

Spring, Summer, Fall or Winter, our 150 acres of woodland, gardens, ponds and trails offer you a chance to whet your appetite for some of the best food in New England. Greg Parks has been our Chef for 13 years, his culinary imagination and use of Vermont's abundance of local ingredients has earned us Four Diamonds from the AAA and the Distinguished Restaurants of North America Award in 1993.

Come to our inn any time of the year, and enjoy innkeeping as it was when life moved at a more comfortable pace.

West Street,
PO Box 278,
Newfane,
VT 05345
•
Tel 802 365 7713
•
Owners/Innkeepers:
Pam & Gorty Baldwin
•
12 rooms
4 one bedroom suites
•
Doubles $110 - $125 B&B
$210 - $225 MAP

Suites $140 - $195 B&B
$240 - $295 MAP
•
For the last week in September and first two weeks in October, MAP rates only
•
Tax 7%.
•
Outdoor swimming pool.
Nearby: golf, tennis, riding
•
VS • MC • Amex
Diners • Discover

VERMONT

GOLDEN EAGLE RESORT
STOWE

The Golden Eagle is one of New England's most affordable AAA Four Diamond resorts. Family owned and operated for 30 years, this 4-season resort is located ½ mile from picturesque Stowe Village, minutes from Mt. Mansfield State Park and Ski area, and a short drive from Burlington International Airport.

Nestled on 80 acres of landscaped lawns, flower gardens, mountain and pondside views, this is the perfect setting for a vacation escape. Accommodations range from spacious rooms to one and two bedroom apartments with fireplaces. Some rooms have whirlpools, all have private bath, telephones, tv, refrigerators, individual heat and air conditioning. A coffee shop and two dinner restaurants offer a variety of New England specialities.

Relax in the library by a wood-burning stove, surrounded by literature, magazines and classical music. Experience a tradition of warm hospitality and service.

The Mountain Road,
PO Box 1090, Stowe,
VT 05672

•

Tel 802 253 4811
Fax 802 253 2561
Freephone in UK
0800 969 240

•

General Manager/President:
Neil Van Dyke

•

42 rooms. 10 suites
(1 & 2 bedrooms)
2 & 3 bedroom chalets
and houses available

Doubles $89 - $159 EP
Suites/apartments
$159-$259

•

Tax 7%

•

Heated indoor & outdoor
pools, fitness center, tennis,
trout ponds, hiking, skiing,
ice-skating. Childrens'
activities & playground

•

VS • MC • Amex
Diners • Discover

VERMONT

HAWK INN & MOUNTAIN RESORT
PLYMOUTH

Step from the hearthside warmth of a luxurious Hawk mountain villa, surrounded by endless sunlit Green Mountain vistas in summer, silent snow-ribboned peaks in winter or the glorious fall colours of a New England autumn. Hawk's 1,200 acres invite you to experience the essence of Vermont's unspoiled natural beauty.

In the valley below, Hawk's fifty room, Four Diamond inn meanders along the banks of the Black River, flowing into the crystal clear waters of a chain of mountain lakes. Guests are pampered with cool mountain air in summer, down comforters and plush robes in winter. After a day of activities, enjoy fine dining at the River Tavern, on the terrace overlooking the river or by the warmth of the fieldstone fireplace.

In summer, hike and bike through the valley, paddle, row and sail from Hawk's mountain lake marina, fly fish for trout, enjoy the challenges of the riding stable, tennis courts, twenty meter pool or six nearby golf courses and a clay shooting preserve. Winter brings challenging downhill skiing, ice skating, fishing, cross-country skiing and snowshoeing and evening sleigh rides under the stars.

HCR 70, Box 67, Rt 310
Plymouth, VT 05056
•
Tel 802 672 3811
Fax 802 672 5067
Freephone in US
800 685 Hawk
•
Executive Vice President/General Manager:
James M. Nielsen
Innkeeper: Jurgen Dinger
•
50 inn rooms. 2, 3 & 4- bedroom villas

Doubles $142 - $293 B&B,
Villas $209 - $761 EP
•
Tax 7%
•
Outdoor & indoor pools, tennis, riding, sailing, biking, skiing
Nearby: golf
•
Children welcome.
•
Non-smoking
•
VS • MC • Amex
Diners • Carte Blanche
Discover

VERMONT

INN AT ESSEX
ESSEX

The Inn at Essex is an AAA Four Diamond small country hotel on the outskirts of Burlington, the town on Lake Champlain. It is a colonial style building set on 18 acres and is ideally located between the beautiful Green Mountains of Vermont and the scenic Adirondacks of New York State.

The Inn offers 97 elegantly furnished and spacious rooms with all amenities for business or pleasure, 30 rooms have woodburning fireplaces for the colder months. Dining is an experience not to be missed at the Inn, savour the glorious food of our two restaurants, prepared by 18 chefs and 100 students of the New England Culinary Institute. Choose Butler's fine dining room with continental cuisine or the more casual Birch Tree Cafe with new American fare.

A host of museums and shops are within 30 minutes of the Inn and not to be missed is a tour round Ben & Jerry's Ice Cream Factory or the Vermont Teddy Bear Company.

70 Essex Way,
Essex,
VT 05452
•
Tel 802 878 1100
Fax 802 878 0063
Freephone in US
800 727 4295
•
General Manager:
James Lamberti
•
94 rooms
2 one bedroom,
1 two-bedroom suite

Doubles $99 - $185 EP
Suites $185 - $385
•
Tax 7%
•
Indoor pool, fitness center, outdoor heated pool conference facilities
Nearby: tennis, golf, horseriding, sailing, water skiing, Vermont's premier factory-outlet shopping
•
VS • MC • Amex • Diners

VERMONT

INN AT ORMSBY HILL
MANCHESTER CENTER

When you visit Ormsby Hill, you will be surrounded by a spectacular setting with breathtaking views of the Battenkill Valley and the Green Mountains, a patio and porch inviting you to relax and renew, classical music in the background, a place so serene that once you pass through our antique wrought-iron gates and enter our front door, you will never want to leave.

Ormsby Hill is a restored manor house, circa 1764, listed on the Register of Historic Places. Enjoy our nationally-acclaimed dining, served in the magnificent Conservatory/Dining Room, featuring a full gourmet breakfast, with dinner offered on Friday and Saturday evenings.

Our romantic bed chambers have canopies, fireplaces, air-conditioning and luxurious bathrooms with Jacuzzis for two. Ormsby Hill is renowned for comfort, heartfelt hospitality and profound attention to detail.

Historic Route 7A
Manchester Center
VT 05255
•
Tel 802 362 1163
Fax 802 362 5176
Freephone in US
800 670 2841
•
Innkeepers:
Ted & Chris Sprague
•
10 rooms
Doubles $110 - $210 B&B
Dinner served on Friday & Saturday only

Tax 7%
•
Conference facilities for 20
Nearby: outdoor & indoor pools, tennis, golf, riding, cross-country & downhill skiing, fly fishing, hiking, cycling
•
Does not meet the needs of children
•
Non-smoking
•
VS MC Amex

VERMONT

INN ON THE COMMON
CRAFTSBURY COMMON

Perched on 15 hilltop acres with unrivalled views of the surrounding Green Mountains, the Inn is a renowned sanctuary of comfort, fabulous food, caring service and true Vermont hospitality. Enjoy one of the sixteen impeccably decorated bedrooms and suites, many with fireplaces, innovative cuisine from a talented young chef and an award winning wine cellar. For 15 consecutive years, the Inn has received the distinguished AAA Four Diamond Award.

Surrounded by landscaped gardens the Inn is perfectly situated in the unspoiled Northeast Kingdom. The town, Craftsbury Common, is one of Vermont's uncommon gems - historically designated, every building painted white whilst the surrounding countryside is quintessential New England. The Inn is proud to be a member of the Independent Innkeepers Association.

Main Street,
Craftsbury Common,
VT 05827
•
Tel 802 586 9619
Fax 802 586 2249
Freephone in US
800 521 2233
•
Innkeepers/Owners:
Michael & Penny Schmitt
•
14 rooms
2 two bedroom suites

Doubles from
$220 - $270 MAP
Suites from $240 - $270
•
Tax 7% s.c. 15%
•
Outdoor pool, tennis,
golf, biking,
canoeing, hiking,
skiing

VS • MC

VERMONT

MOUNTAIN ROAD RESORT
STOWE

Stowe's newest AAA Four Diamond Award Winner! Superlative country accommodations ranging from deluxe guest rooms to luxury condo-suites, many with fireplaces and romantic jacuzzis. We offer the atmosphere of a country inn, the amenities of a distinctive resort and the savoir faire of innkeepers who have travelled the world. Afternoon refreshments are included by the pool or by the fire in the Living Room. A deluxe continental breakfast and spirits are available in the Library or from room service. Enjoy our deluxe outdoor and indoor heated pools, whirlpool spas, sauna and mini-gym. Spacious lawns, flowering gardens and tall pines frame Stowe's intimate resort in Spring, Summer and Fall, while blankets of snow sparkle in Winter.

Exclusive Dine Around® and Vermont Romance plans available. Among our British guests, we've welcomed the Campbells from Herts, who said "A1. A most enjoyable stay." From Dorset, the Vastenhouts commented "Excellent. Beautiful location, lovely resort." You'll love the friendly atmosphere and feel as the Eatwells from Surrey, who said "Best accommodations we have had in two weeks of travel."

PO Box 8 (rt 108)
Stowe, VT 05672
•
Tel 802 253 4566
Fax 802 253 7397
Freephone in US
800 367 6873
Freephone in UK
0800 89 4581
•
Innkeepers:
Bill Mintzer & Jeff Knox
•
32 rooms and suites

Doubles $95 - $205
B&B
Suites $215 - $395
•
Tax 7%
•
Outdoor and indoor pools, tennis, fitness center, spa, French petanque.
Nearby: golf
•
Children welcome
•
VS • MC • Amex
Diners • Discover

VERMONT

OLD TAVERN AT GRAFTON
GRAFTON

Since 1801, the Old Tavern at Grafton has been the choice of the discriminating traveller. The centrepiece of beautifully restored historic Grafton village, the Old Tavern offers 66 individually appointed accommodations and seven guest cottages, all within walking distance of the main Tavern and fine dining room. Meals are offered three times daily, with breakfast included in the room rate. Cuisine embraces the traditional and seasonal qualities of Vermont fare.

Bountiful leisure activities include bicycling, tennis, golf, fishing, nature trails, spring-fed swimming pond, nordic and alpine skiing and the historic beauty of Grafton village.

Grafton is easily reached by car off exit 5 of Interstate 91. Major airlines service Hartford's Bradley International Airport. Direct flights are available to Rutland or Keene, both one hour away.

Recognized as the fifth oldest continuously operating Inn in America, the Old Tavern is a member of Historic Hotels of America.

Grafton,
VT 05146

•

Tel 802 843 2231
Fax 802 843 2245
Freephone in US
800 843 1801

•

President-Windham
Foundation: Stephan Morse

•

65 rooms
1 one bedroom suite
7 guest cottages, 5 with fully equipped kitchens, living rooms etc.

Doubles
$95 - $170 B&B
Cottages
$480 - $570

•

Tax 7%

•

Outdoor swimming pond, tennis, hiking, snow-making at cross country ski centre

•

VS • MC

VERMONT

RABBIT HILL INN
LOWER WATERFORD

A tiny, enchanting hamlet that is an Historic District, is the setting for this 1795 American classic country inn, in two Federal period buildings on 15 acres above the Connecticut River. Rated Four Diamond by the AAA and Four Star by Mobil, elegantly stylish and romantic, the Inn is renowned for exceptional personal service and caring attention to detail. It has been repeatedly designated one of America's Ten Best Inns by travel and guide writers.

The 20 bedrooms and suites, each with private bath, and many featuring canopied beds, fireplaces and two person jacuzzis, offer a sense of timelessness and pampered relaxation.

From oil lamps on porches to unusual turn-down service, discover whimsical surprises. Start your day with a delicious full country breakfast and, in the evening, relax and enjoy acclaimed gourmet dining in two stunning dining rooms, soothed by a chamber musician. We invite you to join us in our partnership with the past. Rabbit Hill is our home, and the hospitality is from our hearts.

Lower Waterford,
VT 05848
•
Tel 802 748 5168
Fax 802 748 8342
Freephone in US
800 76 BUNNY
•
Innkeepers:
John & Maureen Magee
•
16 rooms 4 suites
•
Doubles $179 - $269 MAP
Suites $229 - $269

Tax 7%. s.c. 15%
•
Book and film library, swimming pond, hiking, fishing, sledding, cross-country skiing, ice skating and snow shoeing. Nearby: cycling, mountain climbing, golf, down-hill skiing, museum, antiquing
•
Children over 12 welcome
•
VS • MC

VERMONT

SUGARBUSH INN & RESORT
WARREN

Sugarbush offers the undisturbed beauty of quiet villages, steepled churches, clapboard buildings, covered bridges, sparkling rivers and a valley filled with rolling meadows and farms. Readers of Snow Country magazine rank Sugarbush among the top ten ski resorts in North America for quality and variety of accommodation. Lodging options include deluxe condominiums and homes to a full-service 46 room country inn.

Sugarbush winter activities are cross-country skiing with 300 km of groomed trails, ice skating, tobogganing, snowshoeing, horse-drawn sleigh rides, Icelandic pony rides, snowmobiling or the indoor sports centre. Summer means mountain biking and guided hikes; an 18-hole Robert Trent Jones golf course or tennis at two of the top 50 tennis resorts in the US. In addition there's canoeing, kayaking, swimming in the Mad River or soaring in a glider.

Sugarbush/Mad River Valley boasts over 40 shops and boutiques, ranging from country quaint to extremely elegant and a range of superb dining options.

RR1 Box 350
Warren, VT 05674
•
Tel 802 583 3333
Fax 802 583 3209
Freephone in US
800-53-SUGAR
•
250 rooms
including one bedroom -
four bedroom fully
equipped houses &
apartments.
•
Doubles $104 - $230 B&B
w/ski tickets in winter

Houses & Apartments
$104 - $880
•
Tax 7%
•
Outdoor & indoor pools,
tennis, golf, conference
facilities, down-hill, &
cross-country skiing
•
Children welcome. Varied
programmes available. Cost
on application.
•
Non-smoking
VS • MC • Amex

VERMONT

WINDHAM HILL INN
WEST TOWNSHEND

Most Windham Hill guests journey here looking for a retreat - a quiet and natural setting in which to relax and unwind. Discover a peaceful country house with spotless rooms, an elegant-yet-approachable cuisine, "comfortable" dress code, books, puzzles and music in many forms. Experience pampering by a caring staff and innkeepers eager to share the pleasures of their Green Mountain home and the warmth of their Vermont hospitality.

In Spring, Summer and Fall, hike the inn's trails, 10 km of pine and maple forest with waterfall and swimming hole. In winter, ski 20 km of groomed cross-country trails (lessons and rental equipment available), sample down-hill skiing 25 minutes away at Mount Snow, take a toboggan ride, skate our pond or snowshoe from the back door.

We are conveniently located in central southern Vermont, a comfortable drive from country fairs, art and craft shows, picturesque villages and numerous events and attractions.

RR1 Box 44,
West Townhend,
VT 05359
•
Tel 802 874 4080
Fax 802 874 4702
Freephone in US
800 944 4080
•
Innkeepers:
Grigsby & Pat Markham
•
18 rooms
•
Doubles $210 - $285 MAP

Tax 7%. s.c. 15%
•
Outdoor pool, tennis,
cross-country skiing
Nearby: golf, riding, down-hill skiing
•
Children over 12 welcome.
•
Non-smoking
•
VS • MC • Amex
Diners • Discover

VERMONT

WOODSTOCK INN & RESORT
WOODSTOCK

The ultimate New England country inn with resort facilities, located in the heart of quintessential Woodstock, offers 144 comfortably luxurious rooms and suites, many with fireplaces. The elegant dining room serves continental and New England cuisine, while a more casual alternative is the Eagle Café for country kitchen dining.

Play the 18 hole Robert Trent Jones golf course, or enjoy the fully equipped Health & Fitness Center. Close by are the Woodstock Ski Touring Center with 60km of cross country trails plus the "Suicide Six" downhill ski area.

Stroll one of America's prettiest sidewalks, lined with unique shops, galleries and restaurants, laze by the outdoor pool amidst beautifully landscaped gardens, browse in the cosy library, enjoy complimentary tea and cookies in a delightful wicker furnished sitting room complete with grand piano, or relax in front of the huge stone hearth in the comfortable lobby. The Inn holds the AAA Four Diamond and Mobil Four Star awards, and is a member of the prestigious Small Luxury Hotels of the World.

14 The Green,
Woodstock,
VT 05091-1298
•
Tel 802 457 1100
Fax 802 457 6699
Freephone in US
800 448 7900
•
President &
General Manager:
Chet Williamson
•
146 rooms
7 one bedroom suites
3 townhouses

Doubles $149 - $265 EP
Suites $399 - $499
Tax 7%
•
Ooutoor and indoor pools and tennis courts, racquetball, squash, golf, horseriding, fitness center, hiking, skiing, sleigh rides.
•
VS • MC • Amex

Shelburne Museum
FORGE AHEAD

NOT SO MUCH A MUSEUM MORE A WAY OF LIFE ★★★

Founded in 1947 by Electra Havemeyer Webb, and set on 45 beautifully landscaped acres in north west Vermont, three centuries of the American way of life are reflected in an amazing collection of over 80,000 everyday and unusual objects.

A superb decoy collection; exquisite quilts, each with its own history; a 500 foot miniature circus parade; weather vanes; tools; carriages; a museum of hats; paintings and prints from folk art to impressionist; complete historic houses; blacksmith, printing and weaving shops all in full working order; a schoolhouse, a stagecoach inn, a lighthouse, a jail and a general store, not to mention the 220 foot steamboat Ticonderoga – we could continue, but why not come and see?

Open daily 10.00 - 5.00 May to October (daily guided tours of selected buildings available the rest of the year scheduled at 1.00pm) with daily demonstrations of printing, weaving and blacksmithing; an operating circus carousel and weekly talks. Free shuttle tram provides transport throughout the 37 buildings of the museum.

Shelburne Museum
FORGE AHEAD

PO Box 10, Shelburne, VT 05482
Tel 802 985 3346   Fax 802 985 2331
Located on US rt 7
Seven miles south of Burlington VT.

VERMONT

ARDMORE INN
WOODSTOCK

A small, classic New England Inn, the Ardmore offers spacious, gracious accommodations together with the charm and warmth of personal service, in what has been acclaimed as one of the ten most beautiful villages in the U.S.

A talented chef will surprise and delight you with delicious and imaginative breakfast creations. Each of the guest bedrooms is individually decorated and furnished in a variety of delightful styles.

Woodstock is a quaint, historic village, offering a variety of attractions including antiquing, theatre, galleries, and some of New England's finest restaurants. Delight in Vermont's fresh air; walking or biking on back roads and mountain trails, golf, tennis, fishing and polo. In winter enjoy sleigh rides or down-hill and cross-country skiing at the many nearby outstanding Vermont ski areas.

| 23 Pleasant Street, Woodstock, VT 05091-0466
Tel 802 457 3887
Fax 802 457 9006 | Freephone in US
800 497 9652
Innkeeper:
Giorgio Ortiz | 5 rooms
Doubles $85 - $165
B&B
Tax 7% | Nearby: outdoor & indoor pools, tennis, golf, riding, water skiing, down-hill & cross-country skiing | Does not meet the needs of children. | Non-smoking
VS • MC
Amex • Diners |

BARROWS HOUSE
DORSET

Set on 11 flower-filled acres in a small picturebook village the Barrows House offers a unique blend of charm and country hospitality, whether you stay in one of the charming outbuildings or the main inn.

Furnished with comfort foremost in mind, there are plenty of antiques but they are the sort that beg to be used. Enjoy a hot drink in front of the fire after skiing, or a cool drink on the patio in the warmth of a summer evening, we want you to feel equally at peace and at home.

Best of all, meals in the inn's lovely plant-filled airy dining extension are an informal, delicious and unforgettable experience. A member of the Independent Innkeepers Association, and holder of the 3 Diamond and 3 Star Awards, come and experience Barrows House for yourselves - you'll be welcome!

| Rt 30 Dorset, VT 0521
Tel 802 867 4455
Fax 802 867 0132 | Freephone in US
800 639 1620
Innkeepers:
Linda & Jim McGinnis | 19 rooms
8 one-bedroom,
1 two-bedroom suite
Doubles $145 - $205
MAP | Suites $200 - $240
Tax 7%. S.c. 15%
Outdoor pool, tennis, lawn games | Nearby: golf, horseriding, fishing, sailing, small conference facility | Children welcome
VS • MC • Amex |

134

VERMONT

BLUEBERRY HILL INN
GOSHEN

Share with us a special way of life. Within the restored 1813 farmhouse lies another world - intimate, isolated, tranquil. Bask in the morning sun of the greenhouse, sipping coffee among the flowers; stretch out under the apple trees on the lawn; pick all the sun-ripened blueberries you can eat; stroll up Hogback Mountain for a spectacular view of the world; swim in the spring-fed pond, hike and cross-country ski, miles of trails from the front door.

At the end of the day soak in a hot bath before joining other guests for a convivial social hour, followed by a sumptuous four course meal served dinner-party style in the candlelit dining room.

We offer no radios, no televisions, no bedside telephones - just Vermont!

Goshen VT 05733 Tel 802 247 6735 Fax 802 247 3983	Freephone in US 800 448 0707 Owner: Tony Clark & Shari Brown	24 rooms Doubles $164 - $210 MAP Tax 7% s.c 15%	Swimming pond, sauna, gardens, hiking, cross-country skiing.	Nearby: tennis, golf, horseriding Children welcome	Non-smoking VS • MC

BRANDON INN
BRANDON

Restored 1786 family run inn, listed on the National Historic Register and set on the village green in a charming Vermont town, within an hour of many tourist attractions.

Visit Fort Ticonderoga, tour the Maple and Marble Museums or Ben and Jerry's Ice Cream Factory. The Inn also houses the Vermont Ski Museum.

Large individually decorated guest rooms, beautifully appointed and spacious public rooms, cosy tavern and secluded back acres with an outdoor pool. Award-winning cuisine.

We are 15 miles north of Rutland, on rts 7 and 73, a 3½ hour drive from Boston or Montreal.

20 Park Street Brandon VT 05733	Tel 802 247 5766 Fax 802 247 5768 Freephone in US 800 639 5335	Innkeepers: Louis & Sarah Pattis 35 rooms & suites	Doubles $125 - $175 MAP. B&B rates also available Suites $155 - $195	Tax 7% s.c. 15% Nearby: tennis, golf, horseriding, sailing, water skiing, fitness center, skiing.	Children welcome VS • MC • Amex

VERMONT

THE CASTLE
PROCTORSVILLE

Follow a winding drive to a grand three storey, stone manor house, nestled amongst six beautifully landscaped acres and surrounded by rolling hills. Wonderful summer days great for hiking, biking, fishing, or plain relaxing; the spectacular glory of leaf season; or the winter season with terrific skiing and, at all times, craft and antique shopping, museums, art and a rich history.

The 1901 inn, built as a private home, and recently, lovingly restored by Dick & Erica Hart has ten wonderfully spacious guest rooms, magnificently crafted woodwork, moulded ceilings and a unique feeling of space, elegance and comfort. Rooms, in deep rich colours but full of sunshine and light, offer oriental rugs, sitting areas with couches, fireplaces and a wonderful sense of privacy.

| PO Box 547, Ludlow, VT 05153 Tel 802 226 7222 Fax 802 226 7853 | Freephone in US 800 697 7222 Owners Dick & Erica Hart | 10 one bedroom suites Doubles $95 - $195 B&B $153 - $255 MAP | Tax 7% s.c. 15% Outdoor pool, tennis, conference facilities | Nearby: golf, riding, water skiing, down-hill & cross-country skiing | Children over 12 welcome. Non-smoking VS • MC • Amex |

CHURCHILL HOUSE INN
BRANDON

This charming, century old country inn is located at the edge of the spectacular Green Mountain National Forest. Known for its excellent cuisine, rates include dinner and breakfast. Dinner around the candlelit antique oak table creates a wonderful party atmosphere. We do not hold a liquor license so bring along your favourite beverage.

The Inn offers eight individually decorated guest rooms with private baths and three common rooms where guests gather for hors d'oeuvres and congenial company. Within easy reach of Vermont attractions, we also organise self-guided inn to inn hiking, biking and skiing trips and small leader-guided hikes. In Winter you can cross-country ski from the door. Located 4 miles east of Brandon on rt 73.

| RR#3, Box 3165 Brandon, VT 05733 | Tel 802 247 3078 Fax 802 247 6821 | Innkeepers: The Jackson family 8 rooms | Doubles $150 - $180 MAP. Special packages available Tax 7% s.c. 15% | Outdoor pool and sauna, bicycle rentals, hiking, cross-country skiing, golf, fishing. | Children welcome VS • MC |

VERMONT

DEERHILL INN & RESTAURANT
WEST DOVER

The Deerhill is set amidst the stunning scenery of the Green Mountains. Linda and Michael Anelli (confirmed Anglophiles!), are fully attuned to the needs of their UK guests - tea in one of the creatively furnished sitting rooms, cocktails in the English-style "Snug" bar and lively discussions of flyfishing or gardening!

Enjoy candlelit dining, gourmet cuisine and thoughtful service in one of Vermont's most popular restaurants! Hearty breakfasts, beautifully appointed rooms, an ever-changing art gallery and attention to detail are all reasons to visit. The seasons and variety of activities make you want to stay; Winter offers Nordic and downhill skiing, Spring, golf and fishing, Summer, music and museums and the Fall the dazzling spectacle of Autumn

| Valley View Road, Box 136, West Dover, VT 05356-0136 Tel 802 464 3100 Fax 802 464 5474 | Freephone in US 800 99 DEER 9 | Owners/Innkeeper & chef: Linda & Michael Anelli 15 rooms including 2 suites | Doubles $90 - $150 B&B. MAP rates available Suites $200 - $260 Tax 7% s.c. 15% | Outdoor pool, tennis. Nearby: golf, horseriding, hiking, biking, skiing, swimming | Children over 8 welcome VS • MC • Amex |

GABLES INN
STOWE

Originally an 1800s farmhouse, and converted around 1934, our family run inn offers individually and comfortably furnished rooms in traditional New England style, several offering views of spectacular Mt Mansfield and the valley. These views can also be enjoyed from our dining room, front porch and lawns, where our deservedly famous breakfast (voted best in Stowe) and garden lunch is served.

In Summer enjoy complimentary bicycles, swim in our outdoor pool, or take part in the many special events hosted by Stowe. Autumn brings unbelievable colours with the evocative scent of woodsmoke rising from chimneys. Winter offers alpine and cross country skiing, snowshoeing, sleigh rides and gloriously crisp air. Come, join us to celebrate life at its best!

| 1457 Mountain Road, Stowe, VT 05672 | Tel 802 253 7730 Fax 802 253 8989 Freephone in US 800 GABLES 1 | Owner/Innkeepers: Sol & Lyn Baumrich 19 rooms | Doubles $150 – $200 MAP. $90 B&B Tax 7% s.c. 10% Summer 15% Winter | Outdoor swimming pool. Nearby: golf, tennis, horseriding, skiing | Children welcome Non-smoking VS • MC • Amex |

VERMONT

HAMILTON HOUSE
WARREN

With just four guest rooms, Hamilton House offers a privacy that is rare. An elegant English country house to be enjoyed as if it were your very own retreat "far from the madding crowd". Set in twenty five wooded, landscaped acres, the spacious house is easy to get to but quietly remote.

Each guest room has its own distinct style such as the Garden Room, complete with king-size bed, fresh flowers and garden colours. Breakfast may be taken informally in the conservatory or in the more formal dining room with afternoon tea served on the terrace in fine weather. Dine at one of the many excellent restaurants nearby, or at Hamilton House itself where an extensive array of international dishes, from simple suppers to formal dinners, may be offered during your stay.

| Warren, VT 05674-9712
Tel 802 583 1066
Fax 802 583 1776 | Freephone in US
800 760 1066
Owners/Innkeepers:
James & Joyce
Plumpton | 4 rooms
including 2 one
bedroom suites
Doubles $140 - $160
B&B | Suites $180 - $200
Tax 7%
gratuities
not accepted | Cross-country skiing
Nearby: outdoor &
indoor pools, tennis,
golf, horseriding,
skiing. | Does not meet the
needs of children.
Non-smoking
VS • MC
Amex • Discover |

INN AT THE BRASS LANTERN
STOWE

A traditional New England Bed and Breakfast Inn, located in the heart of Stowe, with views of Mt. Mansfield, Vermont's highest peak.

This is an award-winning restoration - a labour of love by the innkeeper. Guest rooms are decorated with period antiques and are individually heated and air-conditioned, some with fireplaces, others with whirlpool tubs. The Inn won a Restaurant of Distinction award in 95/96 from the Gourmet Dinners Society of North America.

The bustling village of Stowe offers endless activities; hiking, skiing, theatre, craft fairs and more and the innkeeper takes pride in helping guests find activities that will interest them most.

The Inn holds the AAA 3 Diamond rating and is about 3½ hours drive from Boston.

| 717 Maple Street,
Stowe,
VT 05672 | Tel 802 253 2229
Fax 802 253 7425
Freephone in US
800 729 2980 | Innkeeper:
Andy Aldrich | 9 rooms
Doubles $75 – $185
B&B | Tax 7%
Non-smoking | Does not meet the
needs of children
VS • MC • Amex |

VERMONT

INN AT THE ROUND BARN FARM
WAITSFIELD

The inn that lives in your imagination; rich in history, elegant, luxurious and charming, without the least bit of pretension. Dream-like guest rooms, roaring fireplaces, relaxing steamshowers, Jacuzzi tubs and canopied beds so comfortable you'll feel like you're sleeping in a big hug! The only thing worth getting out of bed for is a scrumptious breakfast of blueberry Belgian waffles and cinnamon coffee.

In Summer, stroll our 85 acres of lush gardens, meadows, ponds and woodlands, our sculpture gardens provide a wonderful walking path that takes you on a journey through Vermont's history, complete with swans. In Winter enjoy the best views in the valley on 30 km of cross-country ski trails.

Rated AAA Three Diamond, Mobil Three Star.

| RR1, Box 247, East Warren Road, Waitsfield, VT 05673 | Tel 802 496 2276 Fax 802 496 8832 | Owners/Manager: Jack & Doreen Simko, AnneMarie Defreest | 11 rooms Doubles $115 – $195 B&B ($15 added to rates 15/9 - 25/10) | Tax 7% Indoor swimming pool, hiking Non-smoking | Children over 10 welcome VS • MC • Amex |

INN AT WEST VIEW FARM
DORSET

The Inn at West View Farm enjoys a tradition of fine hospitality and has welcomed guests since the turn of the century. Our restored farmhouse, offers the amenities of a full service inn and excellent restaurant in a beautiful pastoral setting and has been chosen by Glamour Magazine as one of Vermont's great romantic country inns.

Our historic buildings have undergone loving restoration and await your arrival. Come and experience the tranquility of a Vermont vacation.

In summer, enjoy our wrap-around porch and the shade of the majestic maples which dot our lawns and meadow. In winter, cosy up to one of our two fireplaces, unwind in the Tavern or relax in our cheerful sunroom.

| Rte 30 Dorset VT 05251 Tel 802 867 5715 Fax 802 867 0468 | Innkeepers: Dorothy & Helmut Stein | 10 rooms including 1 two bedroom suite. | Doubles $85 - $140 B&B Tax 7%. s.c. 15% | Nearby: golf, riding, sailing, water skiing, down-hill skiing, cross-country skiing | Children over 12 welcome. Non-smoking VS • MC • Amex |

VERMONT

LANDGROVE INN
LANDGROVE

Three generations of the Snyder family are currently active in operating this cheerful red clapboard country inn in rural Vermont, where cows graze in undulating fields and horse-drawn carriages amble along miles of canopied roads. Comfortable guest rooms are furnished in an antique colonial style with stencilling on the walls, hard-rock maple armoires and rocking chairs.

A day at the inn begins with a hearty country breakfast and in the evening you may choose one of the fine restaurants in the area or enjoy a candlelit meal at the inn itself, finishing up with one of Kathy's delicious desserts. Whether you choose to partake of the many activities available at the inn, visit the surrounding areas or simply relax in the quiet beauty of the landscape, the Landgrove Inn provides you with the true Vermont experience!

R D 1 Box 215, Landgrove/Weston Road, Landgrove, VT 05148	Tel 802 824 6673 Fax 802 824 3055 Freephone in US 800 669 8466	Owners: Jay & Kathy Snyder 16 rooms Doubles $85 - $120 B&B	Tax 7% Outdoor pool, tennis, cross country skiing, conference facilities fishing, horse-drawn sleigh.	Nearby: indoor pool, golf, horseriding, down-hill skiing Children welcome.	Non-smoking VS • MC Amex • Discover

LAREAU FARM COUNTRY INN
WAITSFIELD

A restored 1832 Greek Revival farmhouse nestled in a picturesque meadow beside the Mad River, but within minutes of shopping and skiing. We offer views of the woods and river, together with hospitality that is "a cut above", filling our inn with guests seeking restful getaways, ski holidays, outdoor excursions and country romance in a peaceful rural setting.

Delicious aromas from the kitchen, the heart of the house, are a welcome wake-up. It is here that fancy country breakfasts and home baked goods are prepared and guests linger long over coffee with the innkeepers. Dinners can be arranged for groups or special evenings and on Fridays and Saturdays our Flatbread Kitchen produces the best pizza in New England from a wood-fired earthen oven.

P.O. Box 563, Route 100 Waitsfield VT 05673	Tel 802 496 4949 Freephone in US 800 833 0766	Owners: Dan & Susan Easley 13 rooms including 1 one bedroom suite	Doubles $70 - $125 B&B Tax 7%	Nearby: outdoor & indoor pools, tennis, golf, riding, down-hill skiing, cross-country skiing	Children welcome. Non-smoking VS • MC

VERMONT

MAPLE LEAF INN
BARNARD

The Maple Leaf is a faithful Victorian farmhouse reproduction, nestled snugly within sixteen acres of maple and birch trees a stone's throw from historic Woodstock. As you approach the inn, trees unfold to reveal gables, dormers, wrap-around porch, gingerbread trim windows, and soaring chimneys.

Stencilling, stitchery, and handmade quilts blend with antique and reproduction furnishings, contributing to the warm, welcoming atmosphere. Most guest rooms feature king-size bed, sitting area, wood-burning fireplace, tv, vcr, phone, and whirlpool tubs.

Enjoy the bright and airy parlour and savour late afternoon refreshments by the fire. Books and artefacts collected from world travels adorn the walls and shelves in the library where comfortable chairs invite guests to read or relax.

P.O. Box 273 Barnard VT 05031	Tel 802 234 5342 Freephone in US 800 51-MAPLE	Owner/Innkeeper: Gary & Janet Robison 7 rooms	Doubles $100 - $160 B&B Tax 7%	Cross-country skiing Nearby: tennis, golf, riding, sailing, down- hill skiing	Does not meet the needs of children Non-smoking VS • MC

MIDDLEBURY INN
MIDDLEBURY

The Middlebury Inn has presided over happenings since 1827, establishing a great tradition of hospitality, comfort and service. There are 76 recently redecorated rooms with each area of the inn having its own charm, combining past traditions with present day amenities.

Dining choices vary seasonally with plentiful New England fare in the Founders Room and Stewart Library. During warm weather, the wide sweeping porch is a natural for lunch or dinner. Our Tavern provides the best in liquid refreshment and the Country Peddler is a unique combination of café, gifts, New England crafts and antiques. There is never any lack of choices for "what to do today," or for that matter, tomorrow, and the day after.

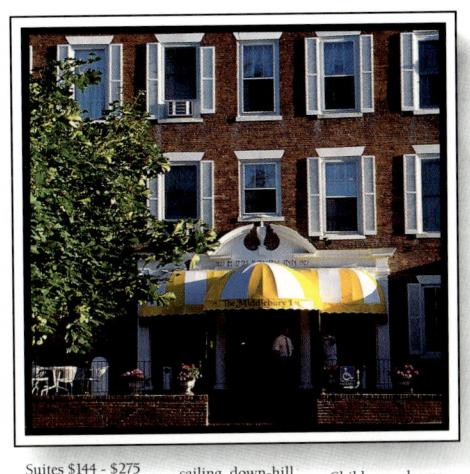

Court Square, PO Box 631 Middlebury VT 05753 Tel 802 388 4961 Fax 802 388 4563	Freephone in US 800 842 4666 Innkeeper: Frank Emanuel	76 rooms including 8 one bedroom suites Doubles $80 - $200 B&B including afternoon tea	Suites $144 - $275 Tax 7% Conference facilities Nearby: outdoor pool, tennis, golf, riding,	sailing, down-hill skiing, cross-country skiing Parking available free of charge.	Children welcome. Non-smoking VS • MC • Amex Diners • Discover

VERMONT

OCTOBER COUNTRY INN
BRIDGEWATER

Arrive at a cozy, casual, rustic 19th century farmhouse to pots of fresh coffee, tea or lemonade, just-baked cookies, and welcoming smiles. Relish Patrick's hearty breakfast feasts and family-style evening meals - sociable and fun - with international dishes to delight you. In warmer weather enjoy gardens, apple trees, lilacs and swimming pool, or settle by the fireplace or potbellied stove to read and doze.

Guests often join the innkeepers (devout and knowledgeable theatre buffs themselves) for a delicious pre-performance picnic on the riverbank behind one of New England's best summer theatres. Actors and directors often come too! Located near Woodstock, Hanover and Weston, October Country offers plenty to do...whilst still being off the beaten track. Kick off your shoes, put up your feet - you've found the perfect place to relax.

| PO Box 66 Upper Road Bridgewater Corners VT 05035 Tel 802 672 3412 | Freephone in US 800 648 8421 Innkeeper: Richard Sims | 10 rooms, 8 with private baths Doubles $124 - $157 MAP | Tax 7% s.c. 10% Outdoor pool, conference facilities | Nearby: indoor pool, tennis, golf, riding, sailing, water skiing, down-hill & cross-country skiing | Children welcome. Non-smoking VS • MC • Amex |

QUECHEE BED & BREAKFAST
QUECHEE

Welcome to a warm and gracious AAA 3 Diamond, Mobil 3 Star, colonial country inn set on a cliff overlooking the Ottauquechee River – a spectacular and memorable view at all times of year. Spacious guest rooms are thoughtfully furnished with comfort and privacy in mind. Enjoy a hearty country breakfast served at individual tables, or relax in the spacious living room, with striking brick and granite fireplace and stunning views. Annual, perennial and herb gardens together with locust and chestnut trees surround the inn.

A short walk through the covered bridge brings you to the waterfall and Quechee Village, famous for its glassblowing, antique shops and restaurants. This is an area rich in natural beauty, a wonderful blend of country and sophistication.

| Rt 4 and Waterman Hill, PO Box 80, Quechee, VT 05059 | Tel 802 295 1776 Innkeeper: Susan Kaduboski | 8 rooms Doubles $94 – $139 B&B | Tax 7% | Four season sports activities all available nearby Non-smoking | Does not meet the needs of children VS • MC |

VERMONT

SHIRE INN
CHELSEA

In a quintessential New England Village, white and serene, your recently redecorated room in this Federal-style inn awaits you. Tall windows, excellent beds, hand-ironed, soft, 100% cotton, sheets, cosy down comforters and quilts, and a crackling fire. Modern private baths with the softest, plushest towels we could find. Rocking chairs. Privacy. Comfort!

Karen, innkeeper and chef, believes dining should be an event to please all senses, candlelight, and soft background romantic music add to your pleasure. After a meal which may include Dijon-mustard chicken breast or veal scallopine stuffed with wild rice and apricots, followed by homemade cheesecake or chocolate torte with raspberry sauce, sip a cup of hot coffee as you sigh with contentment.

| Main Street P.O. Box 37 Chelsea VT 05038-0037 | Tel 802 685 3031 Fax 802 685 3871 Freephone in US and Canada 800 441 6908 | Owner/Innkeeper: Jay & Karen Keller 6 rooms | Doubles $140 - $185 MAP Tax 7% s.c. 15% | Cross-country skiing Nearby: golf, riding, down-hill skiing | Children over 7 welcome. Non-smoking VS • MC |

THE SIEBENESS
STOWE

A warm welcome is guaranteed at our charming country inn nestled in the foothills of Mt. Mansfield. Romantic guest rooms are uniquely decorated with beautiful country antiques and homemade quilts. Two bedrooms in our country cottage have jacuzzis, gas fireplaces, refrigerators, air-conditioning, tv and beautiful views.

Relax in our outdoor hot tub, or in our comfortable fireplace lounge. Wake up to the aroma of a freshly cooked country breakfast – our food has made us famous. Enjoy the mountain views from our pool and grounds, take a bike ride, a walk, or in the winter, skate or ski to the picturesque village of Stowe with its delightful array of shops and restaurants.

| 3681 Mountain Road, Stowe, VT 05672 Tel 802 253 8942 Fax 802 253 9232 | Freephone in US 800 426 9001 Owner/Innkeepers: Sue & Nils Andersen | 10 rooms. Doubles $70 - $150 B&B | Cottage rooms $130 - $170 Tax 7% s.c. 10% | Outdoor pool. Nearby: tennis, golf, skiing. Non-smoking. | Children welcome VS • MC • Amex |

VERMONT

THE SUGARTREE
WARREN

In summer, the chalet-style Sugartree's window boxes overflow with colourful flowers and you may find a hummingbird outside your window. In winter, views are of glistening trees and the snow covered trails of the Sugarbush ski area just ¼ mile away.

Quilts, comforters and antiques adorn guest rooms, some of which have canopy beds and throughout the inn, needlework, Frank's handcarved Santas, whimsical and interesting pictures, books and games. Join a singalong by our 100 year old pump organ or curl up by the fire with a good book. Thoughtful extra touches make your stay more comfortable ... phones, hair dryers, a guest pantry with refrigerator, maps, attraction brochures and in winter, a free ski shuttle to the mountain. Cricket spoken here! Frank is a member of the local team and organiser for the area's annual cricket festival.

| RR1 Box 138 Sugarbush Access Road Warren, VT 05674 Tel 802 583 3211 Fax 802 583 3203 | Freephone in US 800 666 8907 Innkeepers: Frank & Kathy Partsch | 9 rooms including 1 one bedroom suite. Doubles $80 - $124 B&B | Suites $100 - $135 Tax 7% Nearby: Outdoor pool, indoor pool, tennis, | golf, riding, conference facilities, down-hill & cross-country skiing | Children over 7 welcome. Non-smoking VS • MC • Discover |

SUGAR LODGE AT SUGARBUSH
WARREN

Located in central Vermont at Sugarbush Resort, we offer the privacy and amenities of a small hotel with the hospitality of a country inn.

Our rooms offer all home comforts with a choice of king, queen or two double beds, full private baths, colour cable television and telephone. In the evenings, relax by the fire in our living room with a cup of hot chocolate or spiced cider and home-made chocolate chip cookies!

Enjoy the snow covered Vermont countryside as the shuttle takes you to the slopes, or one of the many fine nearby restaurants or shops. In summer enjoy, all of the numerous outdoor and indoor sports facilities in the immediate area.

| Sugarbush Access Road Warren VT 05674 Tel 802 583 3100 Fax 802 585 1148 | Freephone in US 800 982 3465 Innkeeper David B. Jackson | 22 rooms Doubles $59 - $119 B&B Tax 7% s.c. 3% | Nearby: outdoor & indoor pool, tennis, golf, riding, sailing, conference facilities, down-hill & cross- | country skiing, hiking, canoeing, fishing Children welcome. | Childrens' programme Summer or Winter $55 daily. Non-smoking VS • MC • Amex |

144

VERMONT

TUCKER HILL LODGE & RESTAURANT
SUGARBUSH/MAD RIVER VALLEY

Set on 14 acres of wooded hillside, with swimming pool and lovely country gardens, this inn offers homey, rustic rooms with handmade quilts, bouquets of flowers, a mountain cabin feeling and a good restaurant. Dinner can be enjoyed in the panelled and beamed dining room or the delightful greenhouse style addition. Entrees are beautiful to see and heavenly to eat, homemade desserts are spectacular – try the maple creme brulee, or perhaps go for the strawberry praline torte.

To work off those calories, in Summer there are tennis courts, an outdoor pool and cycling trails while in Winter there is skiing from the back door.

RD 1, Box 147, Sugarbush Mad River Valley, VT 05673	Tel 802 496 3983 Fax 802 496 3203 Freephone in US 800 543 7841	Owner/Innkeepers: Susan & Giorgio Noaro	22 rooms, 16 of which have private baths. 2 one bedroom suites	Doubles $70 – $90 B&B Suites $110 – $115 Tax 7%	Outdoor pool, tennis, hiking Children welcome VS • MC • Amex

VERMONT INN
KILLINGTON

Please join us at our small country inn on five acres in the Green Mountains, we offer the charm of a family-run inn with excellent New England and Continental cuisine. We are proud to have been awarded the Killington Champagne Dine-Around Award for fine dining for three consecutive years.

Built as a farmhouse in 1840, original wood beams are exposed in the living room, where you can listen to music, watch television or simply relax in front of a crackling fire when there is a chill in the air. Our lounge offers an intimate setting with wood stove and beautiful mountain views. Guest rooms are unique and cosy, with country charm and the inn also offers a sauna, hot tub, tennis court and swimming pool.

Rt 4 Killington VT 05751 Tel 802 775 0708 Fax 802 773 2440	Freephone in US 800 541 7795 Innkeepers: Megan & Greg Smith	18 rooms Doubles $90 - $225 MAP Tax 7% s.c. 15%	Outdoor pool, tennis Nearby: indoor pool, golf, riding, down-hill skiing, cross-country skiing	Children over 6 welcome Non-smoking	VS • MC Amex • Diners

VERMONT

WEST HILL HOUSE B&B
WARREN

Our peaceful nine acre property is less than one mile from Sugarbush Ski slopes and adjacent to the (Robert Trent Jones) Sugarbush Golf Course and cross country ski centre. Lovely perennial gardens, meadows, a beaver pond and splendid views of the nearby mountains from our great front porch provide a setting for relaxation and getting away from the pressures of daily life.

There is much to do as you enjoy the ever changing beauty of the surroundings. The area offers fishing, canoeing, horseback, riding, soaring, hiking, biking, tennis, golf and superb cross-country and down-hill skiing. Fine restaurants, quaint villages with shops, covered bridges, antiquing, galleries, summer concerts and theatre are all nearby.

| West Hill Road RR1 Box 292 Warren VT 05674 Tel 802 496 7162 Fax 802 496 6443 | Freephone in US 800 898 1427 Proprietor: Dotty Kyle | 7 rooms including 1 one bedroom suite | Doubles $85 - $135 B&B Suite $105 - $135 Tax 7% | Nearby: outdoor & indoor pools, tennis, golf, riding, down-hill skiing, cross-country skiing | Children over 10 welcome. Non-smoking VS • MC • Amex |

VILLAGE COUNTRY INN
MANCHESTER

Rose chintz fabrics; lace; antiques; rocking chairs on a porch bedecked with baskets of flowers; formal gardens cascading with colour; a romantic gazebo and a terrace of fountains. Choose Le Fleur suite with its King-sized bed, separate sitting room, white wicker furniture and clawfoot tub on a platform; Rose Noir with sitting area, fireplace and a two-person bathtub; or one of the Garden rooms where you can open your door and walk directly into the beautiful gardens.
Your stay at the inn includes full country breakfast and a delicious four-course candlelit dinner with time to enjoy a cocktail in the inviting Tavern in the Green first.
In historic Manchester Village with its wonderful shops and galleries there is plenty to see and do, or perhaps your preference is to just pick a rocking chair and watch the world go by.

| PO Box 408 Route 7A Manchester Village VT 05154 Tel 802 362 1792 Fax 802 362 7188 | Freephone in US 800 370 0300 Owners: Anne & Jay Degen | 33 rooms including 9 one bedroom suites, 9 deluxe suites & rooms | Doubles $150 - $185 MAP Deluxe rooms & Suites $200 - $300 Tax 7% s.c. 15% | Outdoor pool Nearby: golf, riding, down-hill & cross-country skiing, | Children over 12 welcome. Non-smoking VS • MC Amex • Discovery |

VERMONT

WEST MOUNTAIN INN
ARLINGTON

This view is reserved for you. Nestled on 150 mountainside acres, cradled between the Taconic and Green Mountain ranges, this full-service inn has welcomed travellers for nearly two decades. From its perch overlooking the famous Battenkill River and historic village of Arlington, guests relax in comfortable surroundings, dine on creative country cuisine and partake of a myriad of outdoor adventure opportunities.

Antiques and country furnishings invite you to relax and rejuvenate in a setting where nature surrounds you, whether it's the fishpond, bird sanctuary, woodland wildflower trails, or llamas and goat in residence in the pasture.

Candelit dinners, hearty country breakfasts and warm and spacious common spaces - this indeed is a "special peace of Vermont" where you enter as a cherished guest and leave as one of the folks.

River Road Arlington VT 05250	Tel 802 375 6346 Fax 802 375 6553 Innkeeper: Paula Maynard	18 rooms including 3 one bedroom suites, 3 two bedroom suites	Doubles $145 - $199 MAP (reflects seasonally variable rates) Suites $209 - $239 Tax 7% s.c. 15%	Conference facilities, cross-country skiing Nearby: tennis, golf, riding, down-hill skiing	Children welcome. Non-smoking VS • MC • Amex Diners • Discover

---

THE WOODS
KILLINGTON

Immerse yourself in luxury at The Woods' unique condominium and cluster homes. Three miles from the base of Killington, offering unmatched comforts and unexpected amenities; full kitchens with microwave and dishwasher; oversized whirlpool tubs; colour cable tv, vcr and basic supplies for your convenience. Daily housekeeping service is provided.

A complimentary shuttle transports you to the finest skiing in the East. Ice skating, horse-drawn sleigh rides - all only minutes away. Indulge yourself in such apres ski offerings as Swedish massage, a swim in the 75 foot lap pool, or a workout in our fully equipped exercise studio. Tempt your palate at one of the best restaurants in the area - Panache, featuring unique award winning cuisine in a casual yet elegant atmosphere.

RR#1, Box 2325, Killington, VT 05751 Tel 802 422 3244 Fax 802 422 3320	Director Guest Services: Tammy Howard Euber	40 fully equipped one, two and three bedroom apartments & houses with jacuzzi and fireplaces.	Houses $266 - $425 EP Tax 7%	Indoor pool, tennis, conference facilities, down-hill & cross-country skiing (shuttle service to slopes)	Nearby: golf, riding, sailing, water skiing Children welcome. Non-smoking VS • MC • Amex

Welcome to the Capital Region USA. The states of Maryland and Virginia and the city of Washington, DC, invite you to discover a wealth of unique sightseeing options found around the nation's capital.

From the gleaming white marble national Capitol building to monumental Civil War battlefields, travellers here will see a variety of historic and cultural sites. Visit the famous Smithsonian Museums and galleries, enjoy narrated city tours aboard sightseeing trolleys, then sample fine local wines and

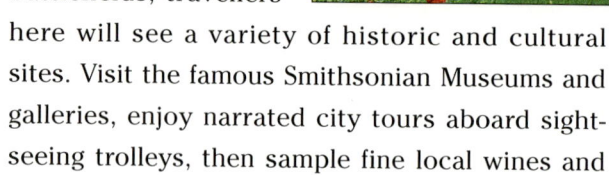

Capital

international cuisine in charming neighbourhood restaurants. Relax and play in the surf at sandy ocean beaches, or skim across the waters of the sparkling sailboat-dotted Chesapeake Bay. Step back in time as you explore charming colonial cities, elegant plantation estates, or native American villages. Then zoom into the 20th century for some world-class shopping and theme park thrills.

Outdoor enthusiasts will enjoy a hike through brilliant autumn foliage along the famous Appalachian Trail and Blue Ridge Mountains, or golfing at some 300 public courses found in the region. Whether you choose to soar above the trees in a hot air balloon or explore the deep recesses of the earth in million-year-old limestone caverns, new adventures await at every turn.

Many of the region's major tourist attractions are within minutes of each other and accessible by well-marked interstate highways or serene scenic byways. And if you choose to stopover in one of the major cities, such as Washington, Baltimore, or Richmond, it's not essential to have a car at all for city and area excursions.

Region USA

When you overnight at country inns throughout the region, your bed and breakfast experiences will include everything from a working farm holiday or romantic country interlude, to a pampered stay in an historic city. All specialise in spoiling their guests with the kind of good service that makes a vacation memorable.

Come for a holiday... discover the birthplace of a country ...and, along the way, meet the remarkable people and places of the Capital Region USA who are destined to become your new best friends.

For further information call: 0181 651 4743 (VA); 01295 720 789 (MD); 0181 392 9187 (DC)

Mid-Atlantic

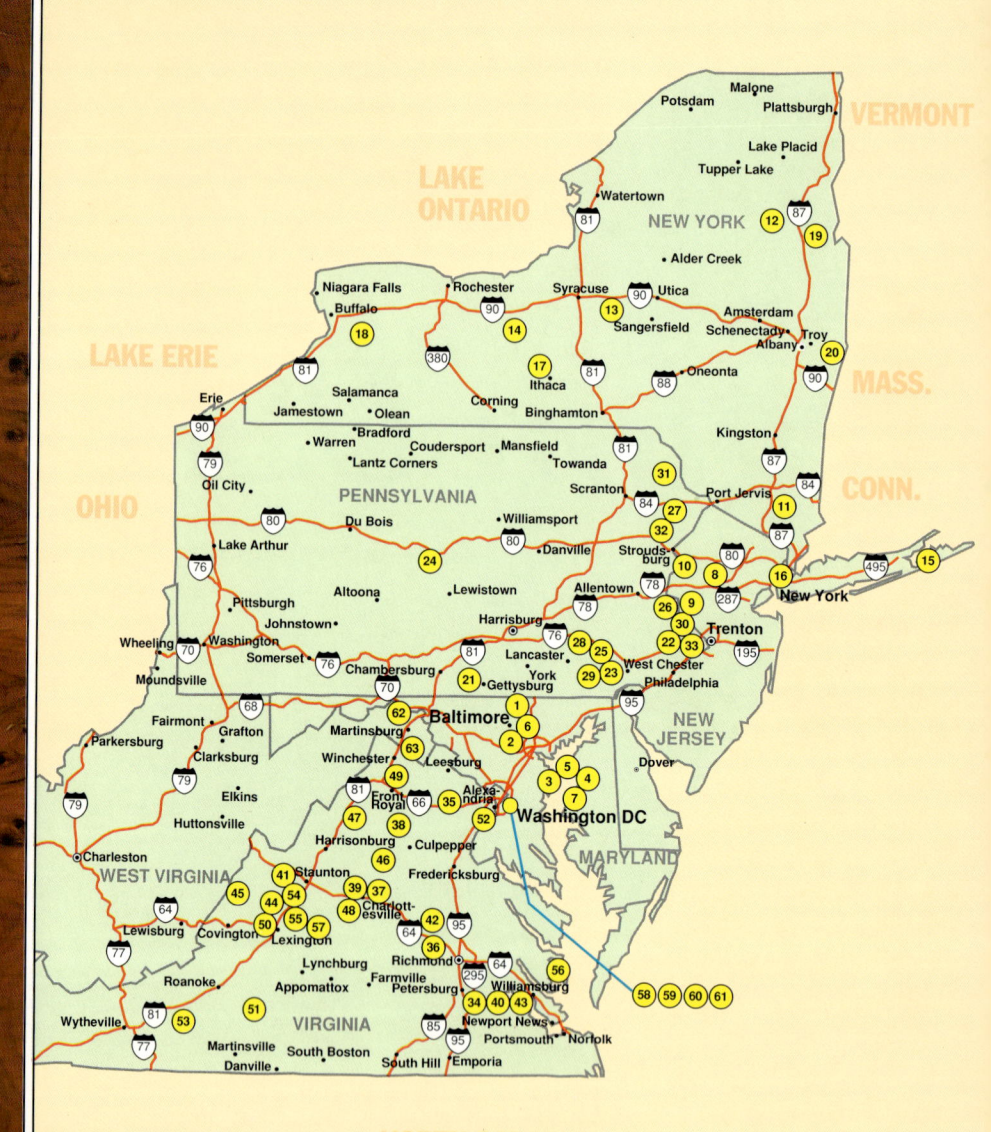

Mid-Atlantic

MARYLAND
- 1. Antrim 1844 — 152
- 2. Harbor Court Hotel — 153
- 3. Historic Inns of Annapolis — 155
- 4. Inn at Perry Cabin — 154
- 5. Kent Manor Inn — 155
- 6. Mr. Mole — 156
- 7. Wades Point Inn on the Bay — 156

NEW JERSEY
- 8. Bernards Inn — 157
- 9. Chimney Hill Farm — 158
- 10. Inn at Millrace Pond — 158

NEW YORK
- 11. Bird & Bottle Inn — 165
- 12. Copperfield Inn — 159
- 13. Craftsman Inn — 160
- 14. Geneva on the Lake — 161
- 15. Halsey House — 165
- 16. Manhattan East Suites — 162
- 17. Rose Inn — 166
- 18. Roycroft Inn — 163
- 19. Sagamore on Lake George — 164
- 20. Sedgwick Inn — 166

PENNSYLVANIA
- 21. Baladerry Inn — 167
- 22. Barleysheaf Farm — 167
- 23. Boxwood Inn — 168
- 24. Carnegie House — 168
- 25. Doneckers — 169
- 26. Evermay on the Delaware — 169
- 27. French Manor — 170
- 28. Historic Smithton Inn — 170
- 29. King's Cottage — 171
- 30. Pineapple Hill — 171
- 31. Settlers Inn — 172
- 32. Sterling Inn — 172
- 33. Wedgwood Inn — 173

VIRGINIA
- 34. Applewood Colonial — 182
- 35. Bailiwick Inn — 174
- 36. Berkeley Hotel — 175
- 37. Boar's Head Inn — 176
- 38. Chester House — 182
- 39. Clifton — 183
- 40. Colonial Capital — 183
- 41. Frederick House — 184
- 42. Henry Clay Inn — 184
- 43. Homestay — 185
- 44. Hummingbird Inn — 185
- 45. Inn at Gristmill Square — 186
- 46. Inn at Meander Plantation — 186
- 47. Inn at Narrow Passage — 187
- 48. Keswick Hall — 177
- 49. L'Auberge Provencale — 178
- 50. Llewellyn Lodge — 187
- 51. Manor at Taylor's Store — 188
- 52. Morrison House — 179
- 53. Oaks — 188
- 54. Staunton Hill Country Inn — 180
- 55. Steeles Tavern Manor — 189
- 56. Tides Inn — 181
- 57. Trillium House — 189

WASHINGTON DC
- 58. Embassy Inn — 191
- 59. George Washington Inn — 190
- 60. Normandy Inn — 191
- 61. Windsor Inn — 192

WEST VIRGINIA
- 62. Country Inn — 193
- 63. Hillbrook Inn — 194

MARYLAND

ANTRIM 1844
TANEYTOWN

Forty miles west of Baltimore, sixty miles north of Washington DC, on twenty three acres of gardens and orchards nestled in the rolling Catoctin Mountains, experience the grace, elegance and hospitality of 19th century America that is Antrim 1844.

Guest rooms at this beautifully restored country inn resort feature antiques, fireplaces, canopy feather beds and marble baths, or for a truly romantic stay choose one of the secluded suites. Located beside the formal gardens the "Ice House" has the atmosphere of a country cottage. "The Barn" has two rooms, each with its own private deck overlooking woods and a brook.

The Condé Nast Flagship Inn for Maryland, Antrim 1844 is acclaimed for superb cuisine and during the warmer months guests will find dinner served on the veranda overlooking the gardens. With the arrival of chillier weather, dinner is served in the "Smokehouse" with brick floor and walk-in fireplaces. The inn has proved to be an ideal environment for small business meetings and magnificent wedding receptions held in the Pavillion.

30 Trevanion Road,
Taneytown, MD 21787
•
Tel 410 756 6812
Fax 410 756 2744
Freephone in US
800 858 1844
•
Owners/Innkeepers:
Dorothy & Richard Mollett
General Manager:
Stewart Dearie
•
14 rooms including
5 one-bedroom suites

Doubles $150 - $175 B&B
Suites $200 - $300
5-course set-price dinner $50
•
Tax 5%
•
Outdoor pool, tennis, croquet, putting, conference facilities. Nearby: Indoor pool, golf, horseriding.
•
Children over 12 welcome
•
Restricted smoking
•
VS • MC • Amex

MARYLAND

HARBOR COURT HOTEL
BALTIMORE

Located on Baltimore's revitalised Inner Harbor the Four Diamond, Four Star Harbor Court Hotel offers an elegant retreat with a sweeping view of the heart of the city.

Relax in the sumptuous library containing volumes from all over the world, or enjoy the Explorers Lounge with handpainted African scenes and exotic objets d'art. Savour a delicious dinner in Hamptons with its acclaimed American Cuisine and unique view of the harbour, or enjoy a more informal meal in Brightons. All of the Harbor Court's guest rooms, staterooms and suites offer elegant furnishings and decor designed for maximum comfort.

One of the special pleasures awaiting guests is the Fitness Center located on the beautifully landscaped rooftop complete with a croquet court. Just steps away from the hotel visit attractions such as the National Aquarium, The Maryland Science Center or simply enjoy the numerous shops and vital nightlife.

550 Light Street
Baltimore, MD 21202
•
Tel 410 234 0550
Fax 410 659 5925
Freephone in US
800 824 0076
•
Managing Director:
Werner Kunz
•
203 rooms including
10 one bedroom,
10 two bedroom suites
•
Doubles from $175 EP

Tax 12%
•
Parking available
at $15 per day
•
Indoor pool, tennis courts,
conference facilities,
full service fitness center.
•
Nearby: Outdoor pool,
golf, horseriding
•
Children welcome
•
VS • MC • Amex

153

MARYLAND

AT PERRY CABIN
ST. MICHAELS

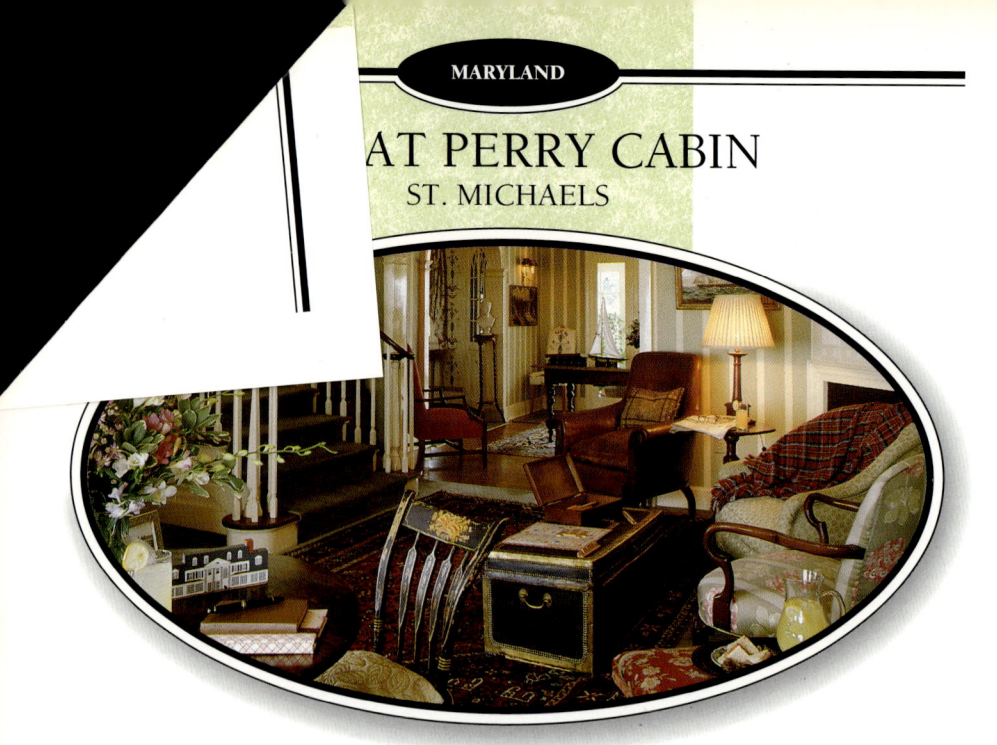

Built in 1820, The Inn at Perry Cabin was restored, expanded and re-opened in 1990 by Sir Bernard Ashley. The Inn is under two hours from Washington DC on a twenty-five acre waterfront site. With forty-one rooms and suites, it is a perfect "Country House Hotel", in harmony with its natural surroundings on Maryland's Eastern Shore.

The charm and elegance of the Laura Ashley interiors are beautifully complemented with fine antiques and objets d'art throughout the Inn. The mood is one of peace and character. Luxury is achieved through attention to detail, complete comfort and courteous, unobtrusive service.

The Inn's award-winning Chef, Mark Salter, bases his specialities on the riches of the locality, fresh fish and produce mixed with fine international fare. Guests also enjoy the Inn's indoor pool and health facility with exercise room, sauna and steam room.

308 Watkins Lane
St. Michael's, MD 21663
•
Tel 410 745 2200
Fax 410 745 3348
Freephone in US
800 722 2949
•
General Manager:
Stephen Creese
•
41 rooms including
3 one-bedroom suites
•
Tax 8%

Doubles and suites
$195 - $575 EP
•
Sailing, indoor pool,
conference facilities, exercise
room, sauna and steam.
•
Nearby: horseriding,
water skiing.
•
Children over 10 welcome
•
No smoking in dining room
•
VS • MC • Amex • Diners

MARYLAND

HISTORIC INNS OF ANNAPOLIS
ANNAPOLIS

A town as historic as Annapolis calls for accommodations as historic as ours. Four charming inns take you back in time; handsomely restored and tastefully furnished in original and reproduction antiques whilst at the same time offering all modern conveniences. Soak up more historic atmosphere in our elegant yet cosy Treaty of Paris Restaurant, our Drummer's Lot Pub or our King of France Tavern.

Whether you stay for a couple of nights or a week, Annapolis with its cobblestone streets, quaint shops, historic attractions and colourful waterfront has a great deal to offer – tour the U.S. Naval Academy or charter your own yacht. We're just 45 minutes from Washington DC, 40 minutes from Baltimore and a short drive from Baltimore Washington International Airport.

58 State Circle,
Annapolis,
MD 21401

Tel 410 263 2641
Fax 410 268 3813
Freephone in US
800 847 8882

General Manager:
Russ Finch
137 rooms

Doubles $110 - $165
B&B
Tax 12%
Parking available $10

Conference facilities
Nearby: swimming,
tennis, golf,
horseriding, sailing.

Children welcome
Non-smoking
VS • MC
Amex • Diners

KENT MANOR INN & RESTAURANT
STEVENSVILLE

Situated on 226 waterfront acres, Kent Manor Inn (circa 1820) has 24 individually decorated, waterview guest rooms. Most have porches or balconies and several boast working fireplaces. Kent Manor Inn's fine dining restaurant is open to the public every day for lunch, dinner and a sumptuous Sunday brunch. Executive Chef Dennis Shakan came to the inn last year from a five-star, five diamond resort in Colorado and we are proud of his outstanding New American seasonal menus and artful presentations.

On our working farm, guests enjoy the swimming pool, hiking paths, bicycles, paddleboats at our new eight-slip pier, volleyball, horse-shoes and croquet. Nearby is world-class golf, outlet shopping, the historic towns of Annapolis, Easton and St. Michael's, antiquing, boating fishing, hunting and the scenic beauty of Maryland's Eastern Shore.

500 Kent Manor
Drive,
Stevensville,
Kent Island,
MD 21666

Tel 410 643 5757
Fax 410 643 8315
Freephone in US
800 820 4511
Managing Director:
Alan J. Michaels

24 rooms
including 1 one
bedroom suite
Doubles $120 - $190
B&B

Suite $205 - $225
Tax 8%
Outdoor pool, sailing,
conference facilities,

boat lock, bicycles,
free paddle boats
Nearby: tennis, riding,
water skiing

Children welcome.
Non-smoking
VS • MC • Amex
Diners • Discover

MARYLAND

MR. MOLE
BALTIMORE

Mr. Mole, Maryland's only Four Star B&B, is a large 1870 Baltimore house located in the quiet tree lined neighbourhood of historic Bolton Hill and close to the Inner Harbor with its numerous shops and restaurants. Within easy reach are Orioles Park, Antique Row, John Hopkins University, Meyerhoff Symphony Hall and other attractions.

Collin has decorated the house with great style and elegance, complete with 18th and 19th century antiques. The first floor living room, breakfast room and parlour feature 14-foot ceilings, bay windows and marble fireplaces. Of the five individually decorated suites, The London Suite and The Print Room include a private sitting room and two bedrooms.

Garage parking with an automatic garage door opener is included as is a large, Dutch-style continental breakfast.

1601 Bolton Street,
Baltimore, MD 21217
Tel 410 728 1179
Fax 410 728 3379

Innkeeper:
Collin Clarke

5 rooms including
3 one-bedroom suites
2 two-bedroom suites

Suites $97 - $155
B&B
Tax 12%

Free parking
Children over 10 welcome

Non-smoking
VS • MC
Amex • Diners

WADES POINT INN ON THE BAY
ST. MICHAELS

This country bed & breakfast inn overlooking Chesapeake Bay, is ideal for those seeking country serenity and the splendour of the bay. All rooms enjoy a waterview. The Inn's 120 acres of fields and woodland (with one-mile nature trail), a dock for fishing and crabbing, and the ever-changing view of boats, birds and water lapping the shoreline, provide a peaceful setting for relaxation and recreation.

Interesting shops and fine dining, the famed Chesapeake Bay Maritime Museum and abundant recreational opportunities are just a few miles away. Couples, families, executive retreats or seminars are welcome.

PO Box 7,
St. Michaels, MD 21663
Tel: 410 745 2500
Fax: 410 745 3443

General Partners:
John E. Feiler &
Elizabeth M. Feiler

26 rooms
including 2 two bedroom suites

Doubles $110 - $180
B&B
(rooms with shared bath $84 - $95)

Tax 8%
Nearby: tennis, golf, sailing

Children over 1 welcome
No smoking
VS • MC

NEW JERSEY

BERNARDS INN
BERNARDSVILLE

The Bernards Inn is a tranquil retreat where history surrounds you, graceful architecture shelters you, privacy comforts you and gracious hospitality envelopes you. Situated in the quaint country town of Bernardsville, in New Jersey's picturesque Somerset Hills, the inn has been the delight of weary New Yorkers and others for nearly ninety years.

It continues its tradition of gracious hospitality, welcoming guests with all the service, style, intimacy and elegance of a small European luxury hotel while preserving the discreet charm of an historic American country inn.

Awaken to the luxury of world-class accommodations, impeccable service and residential comfort. Enjoy lavish terry bathrobes, orchids in bloom and services by appointment such as in-room personal training and massage therapy.

Chef Edward Stone's menu of progressive American cuisine masterfully reflects nature's seasonal charms and culinary innovations are wonderfully enhanced by an award-winning wine list.

27 Mine Brook Road
Bernardsville
NJ 07924

•

Tel 908 766 0002
Fax 908 766 4604
Freephone in US
888 766 0002

•

General Manager/Owner:
Alice Rochat

20 rooms
including 4 one bedroom suites
Doubles $150 - $200 EP

•

Tax 6%

•

Conference facilities

•

Nearby: indoor pool, golf, riding

•

VS • MC
Amex • Diners

NEW JERSEY

CHIMNEY HILL FARM
LAMBERTVILLE

High on a ridge, overlooking the charming city of Lambertville, sits Chimney Hill Farm, situated on eight acres of naturally landscaped grounds filled with gardens and wildlife - an "architectural treasure" and an ideal base for exploring the Delaware Valley.

Enjoy a choice of five designer decorated guest rooms, some with fireplaces. Spend a quiet Winter weekend sipping mulled cider in front of a blazing fire or a Summer stay, kayaking on the Delaware River. Take a historic mule barge ride, visit a local winery, shop at Lambertville, New Hope or Lahaska, or perhaps take in a show at the Bucks County Theatre.

We look forward to meeting you.

| 207 Goat Hill Road Lambertville NJ 08530 | Tel 609 397 1516 Fax 609 397 9353 Owner: Terry Anderson | 5 rooms Doubles $85 - $160 B&B | Tax 6% Small business meetings | Nearby: outdoor pool, tennis, golf, down hill skiing, riding, cross country skiing | Children over 12 welcome. Non-smoking VS • MC • Amex |

INN AT MILLRACE POND
HOPE

The Inn at Millrace Pond is a gracious country inn situated on 23 acres in historic Hope. The main building with its fine restaurant and tavern was an active gristmill until 1952.

Rooms are decorated with the simple elegance of a fine Colonial American home. Besides the main building with nine rooms, there are six in the original Miller's house and two more in the original stone Wheelwright's Cottage. The parlour has a fireplace and library. In warm weather Cordie and Charles offer rides in a 1921 Cadillac touring car. There is a tennis court, and golfers have a good selection of courses nearby.

Situated on the wooded western side of New Jersey, Hope is no more than 90 minutes (75 miles West) from New York City, a mile south off Interstate 80.

| P.O. Box 359, Hope, NJ 07844 | Tel 908 459 4884 Fax 908 459 5276 Freephone in US 800 7 INNHOPE | Innkeepers: Charlie & Cordie Puttkammer | 17 rooms Doubles $85 - $165 B&B Tax 6% | Tennis Nearby: golf, horseriding. All children welcome | Non-smoking VS • MC Amex • Diners |

NEW YORK STATE

COPPPERFIELD INN
NORTH CREEK

In the heart of the spectacular Adirondacks rests the Copperfield Inn. In Winter, Gore Mountain Ski Area features a 2100 foot vertical drop, 9 lifts and 41 trails plus the state's only gondola.

When the snow melts it runs off into the Hudson, the water rises and races downriver to create Class IV white water rafting - spine chilling excitement for those who love the water. Summer tames the Hudson; float down the river in an inner tube or enjoy boating, fishing and swimming in numerous beautiful lakes. Hike, bike, rock climb and enjoy bird and wild-life watching in the mountains. When temperatures slowly descend, magical shades of autumn are created, as nature colours the majestic mountains in hues of red, orange and yellow. Soon the first snow begins to fall, the skiers return and the cycle of the seasons in the Adirondack Park begins anew.

Relax in comfort and style at the exquisite AAA Four Diamond Award winning Copperfield Inn.

P.O. Box 28,
North Creek,
NY 12853
•
Tel 518 251 2500
Fax 518 251 4143
Freephone in US
800 424 9910
•
General Manager:
Laura Hollenbeck
•
25 rooms
including 3 one bedroom
suites.

Doubles $120 - $190 B&B.
MAP available
Suites $150 - $200
•
Tax 7% s.c. $1.00 per person
•
Outdoor pool, tennis, conference facilities, health club, shuttle to Gore Mountain
Nearby: golf, riding, water skiing, skiing
•
Children welcome.
VS • MC • Amex Diners • Discover

NEW YORK STATE

CRAFTSMAN INN
FAYETTEVILLE

Comfortable and gracious, this elegant new country inn has been designed with all the modern amenities required by today's business and leisure travellers. Each room is individually decorated for your ultimate comfort, featuring tv, radio and large work areas. Complimentary light breakfast is served in the beautifully decorated breakfast room and, with the fire burning brightly, the lobby is an inviting place to relax and meet friends or colleagues. For your dining pleasure, our new restaurant will offer the same tasteful decor in which to enjoy a variety of delicious meals.

The Craftsman Inn puts you in the heart of New York State's business centres and area attractions. Only 17 minutes from Carrier Circle, Syracuse University and downtown, the inn is located near shopping areas, numerous restaurants and golf courses.

The staff at the Craftsman Inn is dedicated to making your stay comfortable, enjoyable and memorable.

7300 E. Gowesee St
Fayetteville
NY 13066
•
Tel 315 637 8000
Fax 315 637 2440
Freephone in US
800 797 4469
•
General Manager:
David Garrett
•
70 rooms
including 3 one bedroom
suites, 2 two bedroom
suites

Doubles $69 - $84 B&B
Suites $82 - $125
•
Tax 12%
•
Conference facilities.
Nearby: outdoor &
indoor pools, tennis, golf,
riding, sailing.
•
Children welcome.
•
Non-smoking
•
VS • MC • Amex
Diners • Discover

NEW YORK STATE

GENEVA ON THE LAKE
GENEVA

Set on ten acres in the heart of the beautiful wine-growing Finger Lakes region, is the elegant AAA Four Diamond, Italian Renaissance style Geneva-On-The-Lake. Formal gardens, outdoor sculpture, woodland walks to the lakeshore, natural landscaped paths, secluded nooks and a boathouse and dock with sailboats and canoe, are all designed with romance and relaxation in mind.

Enchanting architecture, marble fireplaces, antiques, 18th century panelled walls and heraldic tapestries in the public rooms set the tone for this small resort. Guest suites offer living rooms and fully equipped kitchens while thoughtful touches such as fresh coffee, flowers, fruit basket and wine add to the warmth of your welcome. Enjoy candlelight gourmet dining on Friday, Saturday and Sunday evenings with complimentary continental breakfast served daily.

Savour the elegance of this historical resort – the getaway for all seasons.

1001 Lochland Road,
Rt 14 South,
Geneva, NY 14456
•
Tel 315 789 7190
Fax 315 789 0322
Freephone in US
800 GENEVA
•
General Manager:
William J. Schickel
•
14 one bedroom, 10 two bedroom suites

Suites $162 - $481 B&B
•
Tax 7%
•
Outdoor pool, sailing, croquet, badminton, cycling
•
Nearby: tennis, golf, horseriding, wineries
•
Children welcome
•
VS • MC
Amex • Diners

NEW YORK STATE

MANHATTAN EAST SUITE HOTELS
NEW YORK CITY

A unique blend of convenient locations, spacious suites and outstanding service - staying at one of the Manhattan East Suite Hotels is like having your own apartment in New York. Kitchens so well equipped you can fix anything from simple snacks to full meals. A range of dining experiences from four star restaurants to the convenience of room service. The hotels are ideal for family travelling, impromptu meetings, entertaining or simply a great place to sit back and relax. At our family-owned, family run properties you're not a customer but our personal guest and we go out of our way to make your stay as special as possible.

Choices include the Surrey Hotel on the Upper East Side close to museums, art galleries and scenic Central Park, Plaza Fifty set in the dynamic centre of midtown Manhattan near Rockefeller Center, Park Avenue and Fifth Avenue or Lyden House, small, intimate and located in Sutton Place.

Nine locations in Manhattan's best neighbourhoods, from West 31st Street to Midtown and the Upper East Side.

Tel 212 465 3690
Fax 212 465 3663
Freephone 0800 89 6931

•

1,954 rooms & suites
Suites ranging from studio and junior to one and two bedrooms

•

Doubles $189 - $270 EP
Suites $224 - $545. Weekly & monthly rates available, also seasonal promotional packages.

•

Tax 13.25 % s.c. $2 per room per night.

Conference facilities, most hotels have fitness centers, some with saunas

•

Parking available
$20.75 - $35.00 per day according to location.
Tax 19%

•

Children welcome

•

Non-smoking suites available in all hotels

•

VS • MC • Amex
Diners

NEW YORK STATE

ROYCROFT INN
EAST AURORA

In 1895 the Roycroft Arts and Crafts Community, a self-contained group, based on the Medieval Guild system and supporting hundreds of craftspeople, was founded in East Aurora. In 1905, the Roycroft Inn opened to accommodate visitors to what had become a cultural Mecca. After the death of the movement's Founder, the writer-philosopher Elbert Hubbard, the Roycroft was operated by his son and then passed through several hands until being granted National Landmark Status in 1987. In June 1995 the Roycroft re-opened its doors to guests.

An exquisite collection of furniture and fixtures adorn the meticulously refurbished inn and the names of notable personalities remain carved into doors. Blending the historical significance of the Roycroft movement with completely modern amenities, the Inn provides the utmost in style, comfort and luxury. From unique guest suites to dining and function rooms, exceptional quality, service and hospitality abound. The Inn is located a convenient 30 minutes from downtown Buffalo.

40 South Grove Street,
East Aurora,
NY 14052
•
Tel 716 652 5552
Fax 716 655 5345
•
Innkeeper:
Martha Beardsley Augat
•
22 suites
•
Doubles $120 - $210 B&B
•
Tax 11%

Conference facilities
Nearby: outdoor pool, tennis, golf, down-hill skiing, cross-country skiing
•
Parking available free of charge
•
Children welcome
•
Non-smoking
•
VS • MC • Amex
Diners • Discover

NEW YORK STATE

SAGAMORE ON LAKE GEORGE
BOLTON LANDING

The Sagamore Resort offers an unrivalled setting on a private island on scenic Lake George. The hotel's main house is a restored Victorian landmark surrounded by landscaped gardens, walking and jogging trails, and a white sand beach. Dining ranges from casual to gourmet in a choice of four restaurants. Guests savour the charm of an historic hotel with all the modern amenities of a Mobil Four Star and AAA Four Diamond resort.

Year-round the Sagamore's indoor facilities include a spa, health club, tennis and racquetball. Outdoor activities include extensive water sports, golf or a leisurely cruise on the hotel's own deluxe yacht. In the winter enjoy cross-country skiing and ice skating. Value and holiday packages, and supervised childrens' programmes are available.

A 4 hour drive from New York City and Boston, and an easy driving distance from many cities in the mid-Atlantic, Quebec and Ontario regions the Sagamore is also accessible by train or plane to Albany, from where the resort provides transportation.

110 Sagamore Road,
Bolton Landing,
NY 12814

•

Tel 518 644 9400
Fax 518 644 3033
Freephone in US
800 358 3585

•

Managing Director:
Robert McIntosh

•

174 rooms
176 suites

Doubles $159 - $310 EP
Suites $255 - $390

•

Tax 7%
s.c. $4 per person per day

•

Indoor pool, lake swimming, tennis, golf, horseriding, sailing, fitness center, spa
Complete conference centre for groups up to 800

VS • MC • Amex

NEW YORK STATE

BIRD & BOTTLE INN
GARRISON

From 1761 when it began life as Warren's Tavern, the inn has had a colourful and romantic history. Restored with great care to its original 18th century appearance the re-named Bird & Bottle is dedicated to preserving the Central Hudson Valley's traditions of fine dining and hospitality and has attained an international reputation for its food, with the guest book full of compliments from satisfied patrons.

Recently the second floor rooms and a cozy cottage were beautifully refurbished, so now, after a 40-year lapse, overnight accommodations are once again available. Each of the guest rooms has a fireplace, as has the cottage and all are meticulously furnished with period furniture and either a four-poster or canopied bed.

Route 9, Old Albany, Post Road, Garrison, NY 10524	Tel 914 424 3000 Fax 914 424 3283 Freephone in US 800 782 6837	Innkeeper: Ira Boyar 4 rooms including 1 one bedroom suite 1 cottage	Doubles $210 - $240 MAP Suite or cottage $240 Tax 7.25%	Small meeting facilities Nearby: outdoor pool, tennis, golf, riding, sailing, cross-country skiing	Children over 12 welcome. Non-smoking VS • MC Amex • Diners

HALSEY HOUSE
LONG ISLAND

Located halfway between Southampton and Bridgehampton, Halsey House in Water Mill offers a relaxed and reflective pace, great white sand beaches, vast skies and a porch on which to gaze over acres of wildflowers rioting across the road, geese grazing cornfields in the distance, or Mecox Bay, shimmering a half mile to the south.

The Halseys have been in these parts for centuries - Thomas Halsey settled in Southampton in 1640- and in 1994 Jane Halsey and her mother Gwen, lovingly restored the two-storey brown shingle farmhouse her grandparents built in 1910.

You'll enjoy the festive Waverly wallpapers, lustrous fir floors and fresh flowers in the bedrooms, the pretty common sitting room with comfortable overstuffed couches, the big country kitchen and Jane's blueberry pancakes.

258 Halsey Lane, Water Mill, Long Island, NY 11976 Tel 516 726 6527	Innkeeper: Jane E. Halsey 3 rooms including 1 one bedroom suite,	2 two bedroom suites (2 rooms share 1 bath, 1 room has private bath)	Doubles $100 - $190 B&B Tax 9 %	5 minutes to beaches. Nearby: tennis, golf, riding, sailing, water skiing	Children over 12 welcome. Non-smoking VS • MC

NEW YORK STATE

ROSE INN
ITHACA

Rose Inn's magnificent setting with twenty landscaped acres of lawns and gardens is at the heart of New York's glorious wine-growing area, the Finger Lakes, half way between New York City and Niagara Falls, minutes from Cornell Univerity. This AAA Four Diamond and Mobil Four Star Award winning inn is a masterpiece of the woodcrafters art, with a unique and stunning circular mahogany staircase rising gracefully through the two storeys of the house to a cupola on the roof. Fifteen guest rooms with period furniture and imaginative and luxurious use of fabrics, reflect a mood of elegance from days gone by. The formal parlour is a delightful gathering place for guests to enjoy a fine library and good company whilst dinner, served Tuesdays to Saturdays, is a very special experience for which advance reservations are recommended.

Route 34 North, P.O. Box 6576, Ithaca, NY 14851-6576	Tel 607 533 7905 Fax 607 533 7908 Innkeepers: Charles & Sherry Rosemann	15 rooms including 5 one bedroom suites. Doubles $125 - $175 B&B	Tax 11%. s.c. 15% Conference facilities	Nearby: Outdoor & indoor pool, tennis, golf, riding, sailing, down-hill skiing, cross-country skiing	Children over 10 welcome. Non-smoking VS • MC

SEDGWICK INN
BERLIN

In the beautiful Taconic Valley on the New York side of the Berkshires, this 1791 historic colonial, described as the "Quintessential country inn" is a place of casual elegance and old world charm with well-stocked library and inviting fireplaced parlour.

There are five antique-filled bedrooms in the main house and six, with colonial style furnishings in the annexe. An old carriage barn houses unusual gift and craft items.

The Inn is renowned for its fine food and breakfast is included in the rates. The Inn is a member of the Independent Innkeepers Association and ideally located for all attractions in the Berkshires and Southern Vermont.

Rt 22, Box 250, Berlin, NY 12022	Tel 518 658 2334 Fax 518 658 3998 Freephone in US 800 845 4886	Owner/Innkeeper: Edith Evans 10 rooms including 1 one bedroom suite	Doubles $75 – $125 B&B Tax 11%	Nearby: tennis, golf, hiking, swimming, skiing	Annexe rooms best suited to families with children VS • MC

PENNSYLVANIA

BALADERRY INN AT GETTYSBURG
GETTYSBURG

Baladerry Inn is located at the edge of the Gettysburg Battlefield near Little Round Top. This circa 1812 brick Federal-style home served as a hospital during the War between the states. A large two-storied great room dominated by a massive brick fireplace is both a dining and gathering area. A brick terrace, off the great room, provides an outdoor area for socialising. Four guest rooms in the Carriage House, newly renovated in 1994, feature fireplaces or private patios plus a common area with fireplace, sunroom, and brick patio. Private and spacious, the Inn is an excellent choice for history buffs, leisure travellers, small business meetings and reunions. A full country breakfast is served each morning.

40 Hospital Road, Gettysburg, PA 17325 Tel 717 337 1342	Owner/Innkeeper: Tom and Caryl O'Gara 8 rooms	Doubles $85 - $99 B&B Tax 6%	Tennis, conference facilities Nearby: outdoor & indoor pools, golf, horseriding	Children over 14 welcome. Non-smoking	VS • MC Amex • Diners

BARLEY SHEAF FARM
HOLICONG

In an exquisite country setting, choose between the gracious accommodation at the Farm or escape to a truly pastoral retreat in our two distincitve barn suites, with long-distance, tranquil views of horse farms and meadows. All guest rooms are air-conditioned. Three fireplaced common rooms offer a peaceful ambience for relaxation, leisurely reading or socialising.

That all-important first meal of the day may include fresh seasonal fruit with yoghurt and granola, stuffed baked apples, fresh farm eggs, scrambled and served with salmon, or a sweet pepper and onion frittata, ham or sausage, complemented with a variety of fragrant, home-baked Swiss breads, home-made jams and genuine farm honey. Served in the Farm's rustic brick-floored dining room and sun porch overlooking the lawns, pool and pond.

5281 York Rd (Rte 202), PO Box 10, Holicong, PA 18928-0010	Tel 215 794 5104 Fax 215 794 5332 Owners: Peter & Veronika Suess	12 rooms including 2 one bedroom suites, 2 two bedroom suites	Doubles $105 - $175 B&B Suites $155 - $255 Tax 8%	Outdoor pool, conference facilities, cross-country skiing Nearby: indoor pool, tennis, golf, riding, sailing, skiing	Children over 8 welcome. Non-smoking VS • MC • Amex

PENNSYLVANIA

BOXWOOD INN
LANCASTER COUNTY

The AAA Three Diamond inn is set in four acres adjacent to well-kept Amish and Mennonite farms. Guests receive an extraordinary introduction into the simplistic lifestyle of the "Pennsylvania Dutch".

The 1768 stone farmhouse was fully renovated with guests in mind – classic simplicity with country elegance. Enjoy a full breakfast in our formal dining room followed by an activity-filled day exploring covered bridges and visiting farmers' markets, passing horse-drawn buggies en route.

Return to a relaxing cup of tea served in the Garden Room overlooking the patio and stream.

Plan your evening meal at a fine local restaurant. Your elegantly appointed room with private bath and cosy handmade Amish quilts awaits you.

PO Box 203, 12 Tobacco Road, Akron, PA 17501	Tel 717 859 3346 Fax 717 859 4502 Freephone in US 800 238 3466	Owners/Innkeepers: June & Dick Klemm	5 rooms Carriage house good for families	Doubles $85 - $145 B&B Tax 6%	Children welcome Non-smoking VS • MC

CARNEGIE HOUSE
STATE COLLEGE

A luxurious 22 room country inn nestled in woods near Penn State University, Carnegie House offers all the comforts of a European Country House Hotel. The oak panelled library, with its glowing fire; the comfortable dining room offering evening table d'hôte and a la carte menus, full Scottish breakfast on Sundays, leisurely luncheons and daily complimentary buffet breakfasts. Sunny sitting rooms and guest bedrooms with individually controlled heat and air conditioning, tv and telephones with computer outlets.

This Four Diamond AAA award winner is the first United States Outpost of The Carnegie Club of Skibo Castle in Scotland. Yours hosts are German born Peter and Helga Schmid who have created a relaxed, welcoming atmosphere for guests to enjoy.

100 Cricklewood Drive, State College, PA 16801	Tel 814 234 2314 Fax 814 231 1299 Freephone in US 800 229 5033	Hosts/Owner: Peter & Helga Schmid 20 rooms including 2 one bedroom suites.	Doubles $125 - $175 B&B Suites $195 - $275 Tax 6%	Conference facilities, Courtesy Van for airport service. Nearby: tennis, golf, skiing.	Children over 12 welcome. Non-smoking VS • MC • Amex

PENNSYLVANIA

INNS AT DONECKERS
EPHRATA

Experience Doneckers' warm hospitality in the picturesque setting of historic Lancaster County. Described as "an oasis of sophistication in Pennsylvania Dutch Country", the Doneckers Community includes four distinctive, handsomely preserved inns of 40 rooms and suites dating from 1777 to the Victorian era.

Appointed in fine antiques and hand-stencilled walls, the inns surround the award-winning restaurant, the Farmers Market and the Artworks, a complex of 30 artisans' studios and galleries featuring fine art, quilts and crafts.

Minutes from Amish farmlands and famous antique markets, Doneckers is conveniently located midway between Philadelphia and Gettysburg, ideally situated for a couple of nights stopover or a central point from which to explore the whole area.

318-324 N. State Street, Ephrata, PA 17522 Innkeeper: Jan Grobengieser	Tel 717 738 9502 Fax 717 738 9554 Freephone in US 800 377 2219	40 rooms 13 one bedroom suites 2 cottage suites, 1 with kitchenette	Doubles $59 - $185 B&B Suites and cottages $149 - $185	Tax 6% Nearby: swimming, tennis, golf	Children welcome VS • MC • Amex

---

EVERMAY ON THE DELAWARE
ERWINNA

Located on 25 woodland acres, Evermay offers country elegance in a rural setting, with formal gardens overlooking the historic Delaware River to the east and bordering Delaware Canal to the west. Deer come to drink at dusk, lambs frolic on green fields and colourful peacocks strut and display their plumage.

All guest rooms are air conditioned with private baths, individually controlled heat, telephones, laptop computer capability, and Victorian antiques and collectibles. Continental plus breakfast is served in the garden room and afternoon tea in the parlour. There is a wonderfully conducive atmosphere for small conference meetings. The Evermay and its staff offer a relaxing environment that can inspire creativity, along with the opportunity to sit back and unwind.

Headquarters River Rds, PO Box 60 Erwinna PA 18920	Tel 610 294 9100 Fax 610 294 8249 Owner/Innkeeper: William & Danielle Moffly	16 rooms including 1 two bedroom suite Doubles $85 - $220 B&B	Prix Fixe dinner Fri, Sat and Sun only Tax 8% Conference facilities	Nearby: outdoor pool, golf, riding, sailing, down-hill skiing, cross-country skiing	Children over 12 welcome. Non-smoking VS • MC

PENNSYLVANIA

FRENCH MANOR
SOUTH STERLING

An elegant storybook stone chateau, secluded and private and surveyor of the 45 acres it rests upon – miles of leafy treetops and a brilliant sunlit sky. Spacious, uncompromising accommodations, together with fine cuisine and service, make the French Manor perfect for a long or short-term stay. From our spacious stone veranda, enjoy the beautiful crests and ridges of the northern Pocono Mountains. Within our own grounds are miles of trails for hiking, biking and cross-country skiing. Alternatively, spend time in our cosy lounge where you can read, watch tv or relax with good company and your favourite liqueur. The French Manor's guest rooms are designed and decorated to emphasise luxury, whilst maintaining the intimate atmosphere of a country inn. Dinner is a celebration of authentic French cuisine. We invite you to join us.

| Box 39, Huckleberry Road, South Sterling, PA 18460 | Tel 717 676 3344 Fax 717 676 9786 Freephone in US 800 523 8200 | Owner/Innkeepers: Ron & Mary Kay Logan 9 rooms including 2 one-bedroom suites, 1 two-bedroom | Doubles $120 - $180 B&B Suites $175 - $225 Tax 6% s.c.10% | Hiking, fishing, guests are welcome to use facilities at the Sterling Inn (1½ miles). Nearby: sailing, water-skiing. | No facilities for children Non-smoking VS • MC • Amex |

HISTORIC SMITHTON INN
EPHRATA

Smithton with its large, square, sunny rooms is picturesque and historic. Each room has its own working fireplace and sitting area with comfortable chairs, reading lamps and writing desk; chamber music is provided as are good books and private refrigerators. Most beds have canopies, soft goose down pillows and bright, hand-made Pennsylvania Dutch quilts. Feather beds are available on request.

Long leisurely evenings can be enjoyed in the library and adjacent great room with a crackling fire in the cooler months. A delicious full country breakfast is served daily.

For extra privacy our suite offers a snack room, parlour with working fireplace, bedroom with queen canopy bed and bathroom with whirlpool tub and separate shower. At Smithton you will encounter matchless hospitality, provided by people who really care.

| 900 West Main Street, Ephrata, PA 17522 | Tel 717 733 6094 Innkeeper: Dorothy Graybill | 8 rooms including 1 one bedroom suite. | Doubles $ 75 - $150 B&B Suite $140 - $170 Tax 6% | Nearby: outdoor & indoor pools, tennis, golf | Children welcome Non-smoking VS • MC • Amex |

PENNSYLVANIA

KING'S COTTAGE
LANCASTER

The King's Cottage, recently listed in the American Historic Inns "Top Ten List", is snuggled in the midst of historic Lancaster County, the heart of the Amish country. It combines beautiful antiques with designer decorating, modern luxury with old fashioned hospitality. From polished oak floors to original crystal chandeliers, the inn envelopes guests in a warm elegant atmosphere.

Begin your day with a full breakfast including specialities such as Peaches 'n' Cream French toast and Lancaster County sausage. Your innkeepers will arrange tours, reserve you places at an Amish dinner and provide maps and information for exploring the beautiful Pennsylvania Dutch countryside.

After a days outing, relax in the library with hot cider or fresh lemonade. Located within easy reach of Washington DC, New York City, Philadelphia and Baltimore with airport and train terminals nearby.

1049 E. King Street, Lancaster, PA 17602
Owner/Innkeepers: Karen & Jim Owens

Tel 717 397 1017
Fax 717 397 3447
Freephone in US 800 747 8717

9 rooms
Carriage House, honeymoon cottage

Doubles $69 - $145 B&B
Cottage $139 - $180

Tax 6%
Nearby: swimming, tennis, golf, horseriding

Children over 12 welcome
Non-smoking
VS • MC

PINEAPPLE HILL
NEW HOPE

This beautifully restored, 16 room, 1790 colonial farmhouse, set on five acres, offers a charming blend of comfort and convenience. Eighteen inch walls and original woodwork exemplify a craftsmanship long forgotten.

In the grounds, the ruins of a stone barn enclose a beautifully hand tiled pool. Spacious guest rooms, three of which are accompanied by a separate living room with cable tv, offer comfortable furnishings and are thoughtfully stocked with books and magazines. Full gourmet breakfasts served in the common room each morning are always a treat.

In the 1700's it was customary to place a pineapple on your front porch as a way of letting friends and neighbours know that you were welcoming guests. We continue this tradition by offering the same hospitality to our guests - we hope you'll always feel welcome at Pineapple Hill.

1324 River Road, New Hope, PA 18938,
Tel 215 862 1790

Owners: Charles & Kathryn Triolo

8 rooms including 3 one bedroom suites.
Doubles $95 - $165 B&B
Suites $145 - $165

Tax 8%
Outdoor pool, conference facilities

Nearby: tennis, riding, sailing, water skiing, cross-country skiing
Children welcome.

Non-smoking
VS • MC
Amex

PENNSYLVANIA

SETTLERS INN
HAWLEY

Stone patios, flowers and herb gardens greet visitors to this restored Tudor Manor, whilst chestnut wood beams, enormous native bluestone fireplace and large comfortable chairs offer a continuing tradition of fine innkeeping and hospitality.
Eighteen rooms and suites are cheerfully decorated with white wicker furniture, antiques, flowered wallpaper and quilted bedcovers and have air-conditioning and phones. Some rooms have tv, all are non-smoking. Included in the rate is a hearty country breakfast with fresh home-baked goods. The dining room is widely known for its creative regional cuisine featuring locally grown produce, with seasonally changing menu to take advantage of the freshest fruits, vegetables and herbs. Delicious Amish farm cheeses, local maple syrup and Pennsylvania wines and beers are always available.

4 Main Avenue, Hawley, PA 18428 Tel 717 226 2993 Fax 717 226 1874	Freephone in US 800 833 8527 Innkeepers: Jeanne & Grant Genzlinger	18 rooms including 3 two bedroom suites. Doubles $85 - $120 B&B	Suites $110 - $150 Tax 6% Conference facilities, gardens & gift shop	Nearby: indoor pool, tennis, golf, riding, sailing, water skiing, down-hill skiing, cross-country skiing	Children welcome. VS • MC Amex • Discover	

STERLING INN
SOUTH STERLING

High in the beautiful Pocono mountains of north-east Pennsylvania, the Sterling Inn re-captures the charm and relaxed graciousness of times gone by, with personal attention from the Logan Family and their staff.

Enjoy boating, fishing, scenic hiking trails, nature programmes, swimming in our lake or indoor pool, tennis, volleyball, 9 hole putting course, shuffleboard, skiing, skating, tobogganing, horse drawn sleigh rides and weekend entertainment.

Choose from a variety of accommodations, charming rooms in the Main Inn, Lodge and Guest House, as well as individual cottages and suites. Enjoy hearty country breakfasts and candlelight dining in our Hearthstone Dining Room. Special diets always accommodated with advance notice.

Rt 191, South Sterling, PA 18460	Tel 717 676 3311 Fax 717 676 9786 Freephone in US 800 523 8200	Innkeepers: The Logan Family 36 rooms including 12 one-bedroom suites	Doubles $126 - $160 MAP Suites $153 - $220 Tax 6% s.c. 15%	Outdoor/indoor pool, tennis, cross-county skiing, sledding, ice-skating, hiking, fishing, boating.	Nearby: golf, horseriding Children very welcome Non-smoking VS • MC • Amex

PENNSYLVANIA

WEDGWOOD INN OF NEW HOPE
BUCKS COUNTY

Located between New York City and Philadelphia, the Wedgwood is made up of three buildings offering guest rooms distinctive in style and decor. Each house has its own parlour with fireplace, good books, board games, menus from local restaurants and friendly conversation.

Steps from the centre of New Hope, an artists colony and antiques centre, the inn combines period charm of lofty windows, hardwood floors, brass ceiling fans and handmade quilts with modern essentials such as private baths and air-conditioning.

Begin the day with a delicious breakfast including home-baked muffins, and hot croissants. Spend the evening relaxing in the gazebo or in front of a roaring fire. At bedtime find a mint on your pillow and a tiny glass of Carl's secret recipe almond liqueur.

111 West Bridge Street (Rt. 179), New Hope, Bucks County, PA 18938-1401	Tel 215 862 2520 Fax 215 862 2570 Owner/Innkeepers: Nadine & Carl Glassman	12 rooms including 4 one-bedroom suites, 2 two-bedroom.	Doubles $80 - $149 B&B Suites $150 - $200 Tax 8% s.c. 10%	Croquet, badminton. Nearby: swimming, tennis, golf, horseriding, sailing, waterskiing.	Children over 5 welcome Non-smoking VS • MC • Amex

---

FEEDBACK FEEDBACK FEEDBACK FEEDBACK
Your comments are valued!

Please write or call to tell us your opinion of the inns and hotels in which you stayed.

Were your expectations met? Was the welcome warm?

Did you feel you received good value for the money you spent?

Consumer feedback is a vital part of maintaining the standard of **U.S. Welcome Directories** and your input is of great value.

As a small token of thanks, it will be our pleasure to send you a **complimentary copy** of our next book which will reach the bookshops in January 1998.

Please send letters, *no stamp required to:*
U.S. Welcome Directories Ltd.,
FREEPOST (HA4595)
Northwood,
England
HA6 3BR
Telephone : 01923-821469 (U.K.)   888-INN-VISIT (U.S.)

VIRGINIA

BAILIWICK INN
FAIRFAX

As you walk through the door of this unique award winning inn and restaurant you'll step into the history and romance of days gone by, back to the early 1800's when this majestic house and the neighbouring Fairfax Courthouse were the centre of Northern Virginia's community life.

Enjoy the warm hospitality and fine details of our superbly restored and lovingly decorated Federal style inn – fourteen meticulously appointed guest rooms, with antiques and featherbeds, some with fireplaces or Jacuzzis. Revel in the exquisite cuisine of our gourmet chef. From polished balustrade and fresh cut flowers in the foyer, to cheery fires burning in book-lined parlours we invite you to discover Northern Virginia's hidden treasure.

Located midway between Dulles International Airport and Washington DC, the Bailiwick is an ideal base for the first or last few nights of your trip, with DC's museums, galleries and monuments only a short metro or auto trip away. Quaint shops and restaurants of Old Town Fairfax are steps from our door. Welcome to our past!

4023 Chain Bridge Road,
Fairfax,
VA 22030

•

Tel 703 691 2266
Fax 703 934 2112
Freephone in US
800 366 7666

•

Proprietors:
Bob & Annette Bradley

•

General Manager:
Stewart Schroeder

13 rooms including
1 one-bedroom suite

•

Doubles $130 - $195
B&B
Suite $295

•

Tax 8.5%

•

Parking available, no charge

•

Non-smoking

•

VS • MC • Amex

VIRGINIA

BERKELEY HOTEL
RICHMOND

The Berkeley Hotel is a small, elegant European-style hotel offering four diamond service and accommodations. The warm decor complemented by original maps hung throughout the hotel, the excellent restaurant and the lavish traditional furnishings of the guest rooms take one back to when innkeeping was an art.

Amenities for overnight guests include in-room Krup coffee-makers as well as complimentary valet parking and use of an exclusive health club. Located in historic Shockoe Slip, the city's oldest business district, and carefully designed to fit in with the surrounding cobblestoned streets and charming shops, The Berkeley is a short walk from many Richmond attractions and entertainment as well as a convenient headquarters for those wishing to explore the entire state of Virginia.

Guests looking for the personalised attention and hospitality of an elegant hotel will be delighted to find The Berkeley waiting to greet them in the Capital of the Confederacy.

1200 East Cary Street,
Richmond, VA 23219
•
Tel 804 780 1300
Fax 804 343 1885
•
General Manager:
Neal Rogers
•
55 rooms including
1 one bedroom suite
•
Doubles $118 - $395 EP

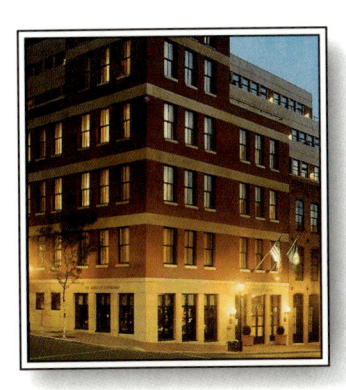

Tax 9.5%
•
Free parking available
•
Conference facilities
•
Nearby: indoor pool,
tennis, golf.
•
Children welcome
•
VS • MC
Amex • Diners

VIRGINIA

BOAR'S HEAD INN, A COUNTRY RESORT
CHARLOTTESVILLE

The Boar's Head Inn with the ambience of a Virginia gentleman's country estate, sprawls on 53 acres of genteel Virginia countryside. In this pristine setting, surrounded by manicured horse farms and in the burgeoning Monticello wine district, the Four Diamond Boar's Head continues to charm and relax guests as it has done for over three decades.

World class tennis, full service sports club and adjacent 18 hole championship Birdwood Golf Course offer unrivalled sports facilities while The Old Mill Room restaurant is one of only a handful in Virginia to hold the AAA coveted Four Diamond award. The wine list has won the Wine Spectator's Award of Excellence four years running.

Against the spectacular backdrop of the Blue Ridge Mountains, a stone's throw from Thomas Jefferson's Monticello and more than a century and a half later, at the Boar's Head Inn, one can still experience the warmth of hospitality for which Virginia is renowned.

PO Box 5307,
Charlottesville, VA 22905
•
Tel 804 296 2181
Fax 804 972 6024
Freephone in US
800 476 1988

General Manager:
Ms Sandie Greenwood

162 rooms including
11 one bedroom suites

Doubles $125 - $185 EP

Suites from $250
•
Tax 6.5%
•
Outdoor pool, tennis, conference facility, hot-air ballooning, massage, fitness center. Childrens' programme during Summer (nominal charge). Nearby: indoor pool, golf, horseriding.

Children Welcome
•
VS • MC • Amex • Diners

VIRGINIA

KESWICK HALL
CHARLOTTESVILLE

When Sir Bernard Ashley first saw Keswick, he knew that his long-cherished ambition of creating a fine estate in the tradition of English country life would be fulfilled. The former Villa Crawford, built in 1912 has been transformed into a very special Country House Hotel with forty-eight outstanding bedrooms and exquisite country areas.

Residents may also enjoy the private Keswick Club which offers an eighteen hole Arnold Palmer signature golf course and other exceptional leisure facilities. As with all Ashley House properties Keswick Hall provides unobtrusive service from staff who genuinely delight in making guests feel at home.

Great dishes are created by our Chefs from a combination of European classic recipes and the best of modern cooking using fresh produce of the highest quality. A fascinating collection of wines from both the old and new worlds enhances the menus.

701 Club Drive,
Keswick, VA 22947

•

Tel 804 979 3440
Fax 804 977 4171
Freephone in US
800 Ashley 1

•

General Manager:
Stephen Beaumont

•

48 rooms including
4 one-bedroom suites

•

Tax 6.5%

Doubles and suites
$195 - $645
B&B

•

Outdoor and indoor pools, tennis, golf, conference facilities, full spa facilities including saunas, steam, exercise room, massage and facials.
Nearby: horseriding.

•

Children over 8 welcome

•

VS • MC • Amex • Diners

177

VIRGINIA

L'AUBERGE PROVENCALE
WHITE POST

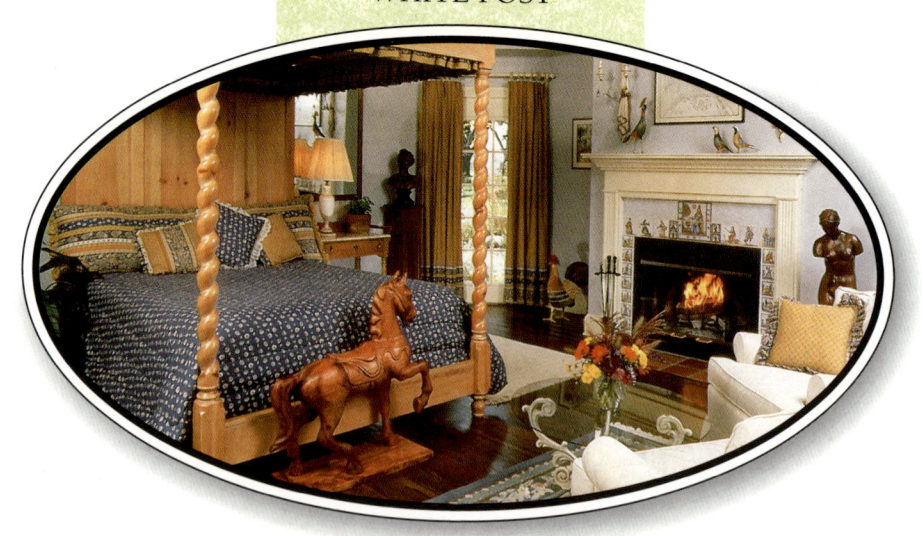

Set on 10 acres in the heart of Virginia Hunt country is the culinary treasure L'Auberge Provencale. With extensive flower, herb, vegetable gardens and orchard, this premier country inn offers both charm and sophistication. Award winning Chef/Owner Alain Borel has been nationally and internationally acclaimed for his food. Dining in our intimate and romantic Four Diamond restaurant decorated with antiques, original art and Provencale ambience is an experience not to be missed.

Rooms are individually decorated with french charm and gracious timelessness, some with fireplaces, and included in your rate is a full gourmet breakfast. Relax on our spacious terrace with a glass of wine or enjoy one of our wonderful picnics as you tour the beautiful Blue Ridge countryside. Go horseback riding, canoeing, hiking or wine tasting at local vineyards.

L'Auberge Provencale is the inn where great expectations are quietly met.

P.O. Box 119,
White Post,
VA 22663

•

Tel 540 837 1375
Fax 540 837 2004
Freephone in US
800 638 1702

•

Owners:
Alain & Celeste Borel

•

10 rooms including
1 one bedroom,
1 two bedroom suite

Doubles $145 - $195
B&B
Suites $195 - $220

•

Tax 4.5%

•

Conference facilities.
Nearby: swimming, tennis, golf, riding.

•

Children over 10 welcome

•

Non-smoking

•

VS • MC • Amex • Diners

VIRGINIA

MORRISON HOUSE
OLD TOWN ALEXANDRIA

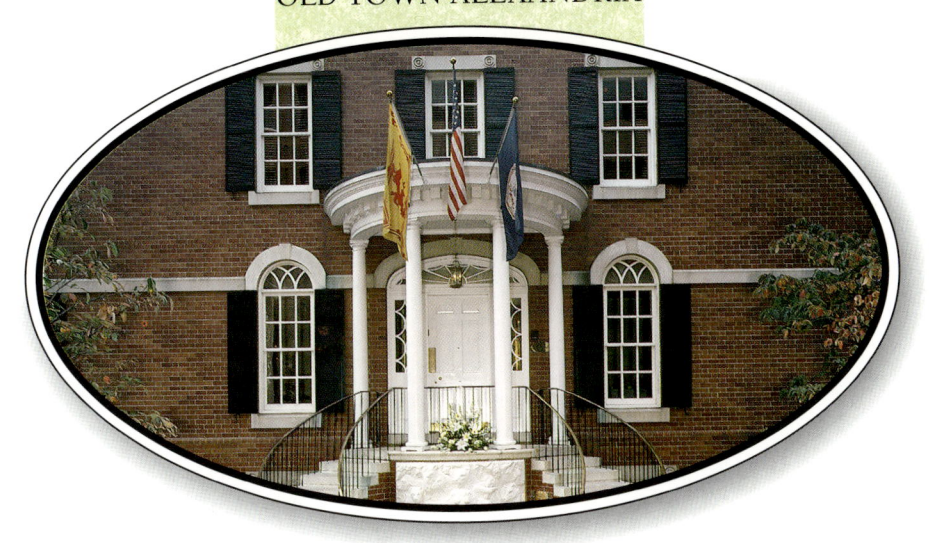

The award-winning, Four Star, Four Diamond rated Morrison House resembles an 18th-century manor house combining the personalised service and warm atmosphere of an inn with the amenities of a larger hotel. Classic Federal-style architecture is complemented by interior design featuring mahogany four poster beds and Italian marble baths. Thoughtful touches such as robes, welcoming cookies and turndown service with chocolate, contribute to your welcome with a selection of things you might have forgotten to pack, kept in stock by the housekeeping department. Secretarial services and baby-sitting are also available. Enjoy the Elysium Dining Room for fine dining or the Elysium Grill for a club atmosphere, both featuring delicious Mediterranean-inspired cuisine.

Located in historic Old Town Alexandria, Morrison House is an easy walk to many historic landmarks, quaint shops and a wide range of restaurants. Ten minutes away, just across the river, are all the attractions of Washington DC, with National and Dulles Airports within easy reach.

116 South Alfred Street,
Alexandria,
VA 22314

•

Tel 703 838 8000
Fax 703 684 6283
Freephone in US
800 367 0800

•

Hotel Manager:
Wanda McKeon

•

45 rooms including
3 one-bedroom suites

Doubles $150 - $295 EP
Suites $295

•

Tax 9.5%

•

Conference, meeting
space for up to 45 people

•

Children welcome

•

Parking $6 per day

•

VS • MC
Amex • Diners

VIRGINIA

STAUNTON HILL COUNTRY INN
BROOKNEAL

The history of the Staunton Hill Plantation is tied to the accomplishments and personalities of the Bruce family. Under the ownership of Charles Bruce, State Senator, philanthropist and intellectual, one of the most valuable libraries in North America was founded and in 1861 he organised, equipped and financed a Confederate artillery which drilled on a cleared field called "Waterloo at Staunton Hill". In 1933, William Adams Delano was commissioned to build the last portico and landscape the gardens.

Today, several cottages with guest rooms; tennis and racquetball courts, pool, open air hot tub and exercise room, have been added to the Plantation House as has an up to date Conference Centre and an adjacent Bistro restaurant.

David S. Bruce, the latest generation of the family, returned from the Far East to Staunton Hill to develop a magnificent gathering place which visitors and guests leave with regret and with memories of a unique blend of history, landscape and graciousness.

Rt 2, Box 244-B
Brookneal
VA 24528
•
Tel 804 376 4048
Fax 804 376 5929
•
Innkeeper:
Janet Bruce
•
20 rooms, 10 with
private bath
including 10 one bedroom
suites
3 cottages

Doubles $95 - $125 B&B
Suites & Cottages
$95 - $400
•
Tax 4.5% s.c. 15%
•
Outdoor pool., tennis,
conference facilities
Nearby: golf
•
Children over 16 welcome.
•
Non-smoking
•
VS • MC • Amex

VIRGINIA

TIDES INN
IRVINGTON

Mr & Mrs E.A. Stephens opened The Tides Inn in 1947 with forty six rooms, a dining room, a bottle club and a dream. Locals by birth, entrepreneurs by spirit, they built the inn as something of a hobby after the war - "two amateurs with much enthusiasm and probably too much energy!". Energy which eventually yielded one of the world's finest resorts - a tranquil haven with a grand family tradition, an unrivalled quality of warmth and a loyal, long-serving staff, dedicated to ensuring your enjoyment.

Arrive by boat and you will find the soft beaches of the Tides Inn on the Chesapeake Bay's western shore, eight miles up the Rappahannock on Carter's Creek. By car, it is a splendidly scenic drive of just over an hour from Williamsburg or Richmond - and a million miles from your everyday worries. Join us for a moonlight cruise aboard our exquisite private yacht, indulge in 45 holes of championship golf, enjoy award-winning cuisine, partake of the many activities available at the inn or simply sit back in a chair and contemplate the serenity of your surroundings.

Box 480, King Carter Drive,
Irvington, VA 22480
•
Tel 804 438 5000
Fax 804 438 5222
Freephone in US
800 843 3746
•
President & General
Manager:
G. Michael Thomas CHA
•
111 rooms & suites
•
Doubles $250 - $408 MAP
Suites $388 - $744

Tax 4.5% s.c. $15 per
person per day
•
Outdoor, saltwater heated
pool, tennis, golf, yachting,
small boat rentals, bicycles,
games room, beach,
conference facilities.
•
Children welcome,
childrens' programmes
available, free of charge
June - August
•
VS • MC
Amex • Diners

VIRGINIA

APPLEWOOD COLONIAL
WILLIAMSBURG

This delightful, four guest room, Flemish-bond brick home, located just four blocks from the historic area was built in 1929 by a construction manager overseeing the restoration of Colonial Williamsburg itself and features many eighteenth century details. Comfortable bedrooms have queen sized canopy or four-poster beds. A unique "apple" collection add to the colonial decor and a favourite in the parlour is the apple checker set. A basket of menus from favourite local restaurants helps with dining decisions. Delicious full breakfasts are served at a large mahogany pedestal table, giving you an ideal opportunity to meet and chat with other guests. Afternoon refreshments such as teas, sparkling cider, and homebaked cookies are set out in late afternoon.

605 Richmond Road,
Williamsburg,
VA 23185

Tel 804 757 0205
Fax 804 757 9405
Freephone in US
800 899 2785

Innkeepers:
Marty & Roger Jones
4 rooms including
1 one-bedroom suite

Doubles $75 - $100
Suite $125
B&B

Tax 8.5%
Free parking available
Children welcome

Non smoking
VS • MC

CHESTER HOUSE
FRONT ROYAL

This stately, Georgian style mansion on two acres, now part of Front Royal's Historic District, features architectural details seldom seen today outside of museum houses. Crystal chandeliers, oriental rugs, artwork and family antiques blend the old with the new for a touch of comfortable elegance. Spacious bedrooms with private baths overlook the secluded, century old English gardens.

Special touches include homemade cookies, beverages and snacks, fresh flowers, turn-down service, bedside mints, robes, fine hand ironed linens and outstanding hospitality. Walk to antique and craft shops, historic attractions, wineries and excellent restaurants. Enjoy hiking, horseriding and canoeing and fishing on the Shenandoah River. A short drive to Skyline Drive (one mile) and only seventy miles from Washington D.C.

43 Chester Street,
Front Royal,
VA 22630

Tel 540 635 3937
Fax as above
Freephone in US
800 621 0441

Innkeepers:
Ann & Bill Wilson
6 rooms, 4 with
private bath, including
1 one-bedroom suite

Doubles $65 - $110
B&B
Suite $135
Tax 10.5%

Free parking
Nearby: outdoor pool,
tennis, golf.

Children over
12 welcome
Restricted smoking
VS • MC • Amex

VIRGINIA

CLIFTON – THE COUNTRY INN
CHARLOTTESVILLE

Clifton – The Country Inn offers guests a gracious escape: a chance to slip away to a less hurried Jeffersonian life. Every room has its own wood-burning fireplace, with firewood freshly laid, ready for the strike of a match. Guests are also warmed by down comforters on each of the antique beds. Each private bathroom is as individual and unique as the rooms themselves.

Warmer weather calls for use of the clay tennis court, swimming pool with waterfall, and heated spa. A short walk through the woods brings you to a private lake where oversized innertubes are perfect for a lazy float.

A highlight of your visit will be chef Craig Hartman's dinner. A graduate of the Culinary Institute of America, chef Hartman has been honored by the James Beard Foundation and the Wine Spectator.

1296 Clifton Drive, Charlottesville, VA 22901	Tel 804 971 1800 Fax 804 971 7098 Innkeepers: Craig & Donna Hartman	14 rooms including 7 one bedroom suites	Doubles $165 - $205 B&B Suites $215 - $225	Tax 6.5% Outdoor pool, tennis, croquet, volleyball.	Well behaved children always welcome Non-smoking VS • MC

COLONIAL CAPITAL
WILLIAMSBURG

Warm hospitality awaits you in our AAA Three Diamond Bed & Breakfast just three blocks from the Colonial Williamsburg historic area.

Antiques, oriental rugs, cosy canopied beds and en suite baths blend charm, and elegance throughout this Colonial Revival (c. 1926) with modern comforts, gourmet breakfasts and afternoon tea and wine. Plantation parlour, screened porch, patio and deck await your enjoyment with friends old and new.

We're here to spoil you!

501 Richmond Road, Williamsburg, VA 23185	Tel 804 757 0233 Fax 804 253 7667 Freephone in US 800 776 0350	Owners/Hosts: Barbara & Phil Craig 5 rooms including 1 two-bedroom suite	Doubles $95 - $125, B&B Suite $135 - $145 Additional person $20	Tax 8.5% Lower tariffs Jan 1 - Mar 15 Children over 8 welcome	Free parking No smoking indoors VS • MC Amex • Discover

VIRGINIA

FREDERICK HOUSE
STAUNTON

Made up of several connected buildings and ideally located for shops and restaurants, the Frederick House consists of several connected townhouses, originally built between 1810 and 1910. The warm and hospitable atmosphere at the inn is fostered by Joe and Evy and their staff who are always willing to offer assistance to travellers, with knowledgeable recommendations on places to eat, walking tours or mountain hiking or biking tours.

Rooms are comfortably furnished with period antiques and offer tv, phone, air-conditioning, ceiling fans and robes. There is a delightful flower-filled backyard. Breakfast is served in the inn's Chumley's Tea-room and includes fresh fruit, home-made breads, apple raisin quiche, waffles and syrup. For a small extra charge, exercise facilities and indoor swimming are available at an adjacent athletic club.

28 North New Street,
Staunton, VA 24401
Tel 540 885 4220
Freephone in US
800 334 5575

Owners:
Joe & Evy Harman
14 rooms including
5 one-bedroom suites,
2 two-bedroom suites.

5 bedroom, 3 bath cottage, 6 apartments with kitchens.

Doubles $65 - $105
B&B
Cottages & apartments $700 - $1800 per week EP

Tax 8.5%
Indoor pool
Children welcome

Non-smoking
VS • MC
Amex • Diners

HENRY CLAY INN
ASHLAND

Rebuilt in 1992 after fire destroyed its predecessor, the Henry Clay Inn combines the splendour of the original Georgian Revival building with modern comforts, fifteen spacious guest rooms decorated with floral and striped fabrics and a level of personal service that is exceptional. Early risers enjoy coffee in the upstairs parlour while downstairs a spacious Victorian style parlour/lobby and an oak-bannistered staircase welcomes guests. Homemade continental breakfast is included in the rates and a delightful extra touch is the art gallery featuring the work of local talents.

For the travelling businessman all rooms are fully equipped with phones and computer modem connections. For leisure travellers, the Inn is conveniently located 15 miles north of Richmond and 85 miles south of DC, making it an ideal base location for sightseeing in the area.

114 North Railroad Avenue
Ashland, VA 23005
Tel 804 798 3100
Fax 804 752 7555

Freephone in US
800 343 4565
General Manager/Innkeeper:
Carol Martin

15 rooms including 1 one bedroom suite
Doubles $80 - $145
B&B

Suite $145
Tax 8.5%
Nearby: outdoor pool, tennis, golf, historic sites, amusement parks

Children welcome, does not meet the needs of babies.

Non-smoking
VS • MC • Amex

VIRGINIA

HOMESTAY
WILLIAMSBURG

Cosy and convenient is this Colonial Revival home, furnished with turn-of-the-century family antiques and full of country charm whilst within easy reach of all the historic attractions.

A Noah's Ark collection enchants guests as they discover pieces in unusual locations all over the house. Relax with a lemonade on the porch or take a leisurely browse through the gardens.

Breakfast may include orange pecan pancakes, Virginia spoonbread or a pineapple soufflé.

517 Richmond Road, Williamsburg, VA 23185	Tel 804 757 7468 Fax as above (call first) Freephone in US 800 836 7468	Innkeepers: Barbara & Jim Thomassen 3 rooms	Doubles $75 - $90 B&B Tax 8.5% Free parking	Children over 10 welcome Non-smoking VS • MC

HUMMINGBIRD INN
GOSHEN

From first view of white picket fence, unique Carpenter gothic facade, wrap-around two-storey verandas, and rose gardens, the Hummingbird Inn will be a case of love at first sight.
The original main room is now a welcoming rustic den, complete with open fireplace, and original pine flooring... a warm place to cosy up with a good book.
In contrast, the rest of the Inn reflects the early Victorian era. The 1853 solarium, white wicker chairs bathed in sunlight, provides a tranquil area for morning coffee or afternoon tea. Spacious air-conditioned rooms with sitting areas combine old-fashioned ambience with modern convenience.
From "skip-lunch" full country breakfasts to romantic four-course continental candlelight dinners (complimentary wine), dining is a special experience.
Goshen Pass, a spectacular rocky gorge, nearby historic Lexington and the beautiful Shenandoah Valley are among many area attractions.

P.O. Box 147, Goshen, VA 24439 - 0147	Tel 540 997 9065 Fax 540 997 0289 Freephone in US 800 397 3214	Innkeepers: Diana & Jeremy Robinson	5 rooms Doubles $70 - $95 B&B, $130 - $155 MAP (weekends only)	Tax 6.5% Children over 12 welcome	Non-smoking VS • MC Amex • Discover

VIRGINIA

INN AT GRISTMILL SQUARE
WARM SPRINGS

In the picturesque village of Warm Springs on a babbling brook is a restored gristmill, the centrepiece of the five carefully restored 19th century buildings that make up the romantic and welcoming Inn at Gristmill Square.

What was once the mill is now the Waterwheel Restaurant offering delectable dinners each evening and a small pub for a relaxing drink and chat. The old blacksmith's shop houses the inn office and two guest rooms together with a small gift shop while the hardware store houses seven rooms and the Steel House once a private home, four more.

On the premises are three tennis courts and an outdoor pool. The historic Warm Springs pools for relaxing and rejuvenating thermal mineral bathing are just a mile away. The McWilliams family are always happy to advise you on all the local activities.

| Box 359, Warm Springs, VA 24484 Tel 540 839 2231 Fax 540 839 5770 | Innkeepers: The McWilliams Family | 17 rooms including 1 two bedroom suite 1 apartment | Doubles $80 - $100 B&B $150 - $170 MAP. Suite/apartment $140 EP. | Outdoor pool, tennis, conference facility for 40. Nearby: golf, horseriding, fishing, hunting, hiking. | Tax 4.5% Children welcome VS • MC • Discover |

INN AT MEANDER PLANTATION
LOCUST DALE

Experience the charm and elegance of Colonial Virginia at this stately, 3-storey white mansion on 80 acres of rolling pasture and woodlands. The columned front porch and two level wrap-around back porches are favourite places to relish the quiet of nature and view spectacular Blue Ridge Mountains sunsets.

Inside, sun-drenched bedrooms welcome you with warmth and comfort, tastefully furnished with antiques and period reproductions, King or Queen beds and some fireplaces. Relish a bountiful plantation breakfast served in the formal dining room, a five-course gourmet dinner available with advance reservations or take-along picnic baskets.

Steeped in history, the Inn is near DC, several Civil War battlefields, Charlottesville and Thomas Jefferson's Monticello, as well as spectacular Skyline Drive and award-winning Virginia wineries.

| HCR5, Box 460A, Locust Dale, VA 22948 Tel & Fax 540 672 4912 | Freephone in US 800 385 4936 Innkeepers/Owners: Suzie Blanchard & Suzanne Thomas | 8 rooms including 2 one-bedroom suites, 2 two-bedroom suites 1 one-bedroom cottage with sofabed and kitchenette | Doubles $105 - $175 B&B Cottage $95 - $200 | Fishing Nearby: hiking, wineries | Tax 4.5% Children of all ages welcome VS • MC • Amex |

VIRGINIA

INN AT NARROW PASSAGE
WOODSTOCK

This historic inn has welcomed travellers since the 1740's. The large common room features gleaming pine floors, wing chairs and massive limestone fireplace with hearty, fireside breakfasts served in the panelled dining room. Many nearby fine restaurants offer choices for other meals.

Older guest rooms have wood floors, stencilling and colonial atmosphere, more recent additions are decorated in similar style, but open onto porches, with views of the Shenandoah River and the Mountains. Fully air-conditioned, many of the rooms also have working fireplaces.

Enjoy hiking, riding, canoeing and fishing, wineries, antique shops, battlefields, caverns and traditional festivals. Relax and stroll along the country road from the inn, crossing the river to the foot of the mountain with the swinging footbridge adding a little excitement!

PO Box 608, Woodstock, VA 22664 Tel 540 459 8000 Fax 540 459 8001	Freephone in US 800 459 8002 Innkeepers: Ellen & Ed Markel	12 rooms Doubles $85 - $110 B&B Tax 6.5%	Excellent fishing, small conference facilities	Nearby: outdoor pool, tennis, golf, riding, skiing.	Children welcome. Non-smoking VS • MC

LLEWELLYN LODGE AT LEXINGTON
LEXINGTON

This charming brick colonial, is just a short walk to the historic district and many fine restaurants. Ellen and John Roberts offer comfort and a warm friendly atmosphere with country charm and a touch of class. Each morning while Ellen whips up a fabulous breakfast, John, a native Lexingtonian, will share his knowledge of the surrounding areas and particularly his secret fishing "holes".

After a day of touring – the Shenandoah Valley, historic Lexington home of Stonewall Jackson, Robert E. Lee Chapel and Museum – you'll be ready to relax in the Lodge's comfortable living room or in the tv room. Snuggle down with a book or enjoy good conversation in front of the roaring fire in winter. Relax outside on the deck and sip some iced tea in the summer months.

603 South Main Street, Lexington, VA 24450	Tel 540 463 3235 Fax 540 464 3122 Freephone in US 800 882 1145	Innkeepers: John & Ellen Roberts	6 rooms Doubles $65 - $95 B&B Tax 7.5%	Nearby: outdoor pool, tennis, golf, horseriding, flyfishing, hiking and cycling – computerised routes and maps provided.	Children over 10 welcome Non-smoking VS • MC Amex • Diners

VIRGINIA

MANOR AT TAYLOR'S STORE
SMITH MOUNTAIN LAKE

The best of Virginia... historic ambience, unspoiled countryside, true Southern hospitality. This 120 acre estate in the foothills of the Blue Ridge Mountains offers relaxation, recreation and romance.

Enjoy private porches, fireplaces, hot tubs, exercise room, billiard room, guest kitchen, and large screen tv with movies. Built in 1820, the Manor has been renovated to maintain historic charm whilst offering modern comfort. Indulge in a "heart healthy" gourmet breakfast – crepes, pancakes, waffles, French toast, and other house specialities designed to be low-fat and high fibre to get the day off to a great start.

Explore and discover six spring-fed ponds for swimming, fishing and canoeing as well as hiking trails. Nearby Smith Mountain Lake provides additional recreational opportunities as does the Blue Ridge Parkway, only 20 minutes away.

Rt 1, Box 533,
Smith Mountain Lake,
VA 24184
Tel 540 721 3951
Fax 540 721 5243

Owners/Innkeepers:
Mary Lynn &
Lee Tucker

10 rooms including
5 one-bedroom suites
1 three bedroom
cottage
Tax 6.5%

Doubles $85 - $185
B&B
Suites/cottage $95 -
$195 (dependent on
no. of occupants)

Swimming, fishing,
canoeing, hiking.
Nearby: tennis, golf,
horseriding, sailing,
waterskiing.

Children welcome
in cottage
No smoking
in main house
VS • MC

THE OAKS
CHRISTIANSBURG

The warm hospitality and charm of Margaret and Tom Ray, comfortable elegance, romantic atmosphere and memorable breakfasts are the hallmark of this Four Diamond Victorian Inn.

Set on Christiansburg's highest hill in the beautiful mountain highlands of Southwest Virginia, the Oaks delights and welcomes leisure and business travellers from around the world. Surrounded by lawn, perennial gardens and 300 year old oak trees, the inn faces Main Street, once part of the Wilderness Trail blazed by American legends Daniel Boone and Davey Crockett.

A five hour drive from Washington, two miles from I-81 and only 26 miles from the Blue Ridge Parkway, perhaps America's most beautiful scenic highway, makes the Oaks a perfect stopover or destination. Relish the hospitality of small-town America.

311 East Main Street,
Christiansburg,
VA 24073

Tel 540 381 1500
Fax 540 382 1728
Freephone in US
800 336 6267

Owner/Innkeepers:
Margaret & Tom Ray
5 rooms

Doubles $115 - $150
B&B
Tax 8.5% s/c 10%
Meeting facilities for 12

Nearby: swimming,
tennis, golf, biking
and hiking, fishing
and boating.
Non-smoking

Children over
12 welcome
VS • MC
Amex • Discover

VIRGINIA

STEELES TAVERN MANOR
STEELES TAVERN

Seeking the serenity of the country and the splendour of the mountains? We invite you to spend a few nights. Each bedroom offers a queen or king sized bed along with antique furniture, comfortable sitting areas and modern conveniences such as televisions, video recorders and a video library. View the majestic Blue Ridge Mountains and our scenic pond from your private haven in the Dahlia room, turn back the hands of time in the Buttercup Room.

Breakfast is a special time at Steeles Tavern Manor with fine china, classical music excellent food and friendly conversation and what's a B&B without afternoon tea! Refreshments are served each day between 4 and 5 p.m. after a day spent golfing, birdwatching, hiking along our creek or fishing in our stocked pond (worms & rods provided). Plan a visit to Steeles Tavern Manor, take a step back to a quieter time.

Hwy 11, P.O. Box 39, Steeles Tavern, VA 24476	Tel 540 377 6644 Fax 540 377 5937 Owners/Innkeepers: Eileen & Bill Hoernlein	5 rooms including 2 one-bedroom suites	Doubles, Suites $95 - $140 B&B Tax 6.5%	Dinner available Friday and Saturday Children over 14 welcome	Non-smoking VS • MC

TRILLIUM HOUSE
NELLYSFORD

A country inn in the Devils Knob Village of Wintergreen (11,000 acres high in the Blue Ridge Mountains). Trillium House was designed and built in '83 as a small self-contained 12 room country hotel. Space and light have been cleverly combined to create in Trillium House a uniquely welcoming atmosphere year-round. All guest rooms have private baths with individually controlled heating and cooling. Relax alone or with other guests in the great room, garden room, tv room or the outstanding library.

The dining room looks out to professional bird feeding and the 17th hole of the Devils Knob golf course. Available to guests at preferred rates are two golf courses, four swimming pools, thirty tennis courts, 25 miles of mapped hiking trails, and downhill skiing in season. The entry gate to the Wintergreen Mountain Village is one mile from the Blue Ridge Parkway.

PO Box 280A, Nellysford, VA 22958	Tel 804 325 9126 Fax 804 325 1099 Freephone in US 800 325 9126	Innkeepers: Ed & Betty Dinwiddie 12 rooms including 2 one-bedroom suites	Doubles $90 - $105 B&B Suites $120 - $150 Tax 6.5%. Food and beverage tax 4%	Small conference facilities. Nearby: indoor and outdoor pools, tennis, golf, riding, fishing, hiking.	Well-behaved children always welcome Non-smoking VS • MC

WASHINGTON DC

GEORGE WASHINGTON UNIVERSITY INN

The George Washington University Inn (formerly The Inn at Foggy Bottom) is a newly renovated and upgraded boutique style hotel. We offer a charming and intimate atmosphere suitable for both the corporate and leisure traveller.

With the personalised and courteous service found only in smaller properties, we are ideally located on a quaint residential street of historic homes close to Georgetown, The Kennedy Center, The George Washington University and a mere two blocks from the Foggy Bottom Metro Rail Station.

Guest rooms are spacious and elegantly furnished. King size beds or two full size beds are available. Each guest room has a mini refrigerator, microwave, coffee maker, iron and ironing board. Fully equipped kitchenettes are also available. Guests will enjoy morning delivery of the Washington Post and evening turndown service with chocolates.

In addition there is a conference room available for meetings up to 35 people. A restaurant is located on the premises for guest convenience.

824 New Hampshire
Avenue NW,
Washington DC 20037
•
Tel 202 337 6620
Fax 202 337 2540
Freephone in US
800 426 2455
•
General Manager:
Steve Seeger
•
95 rooms including
31 one-bedroom suites
16 studios with kitchenettes

Doubles $105 - $155 EP
Suites and Studios
$125 - $195
•
Tax 13% + $1.50 occupancy
tax per room per night
•
Conference facilities
•
Children welcome
•
Non-smoking
rooms available
•
VS • MC • Amex • Diners

WASHINGTON DC

EMBASSY INN
WASHINGTON DC

The Embassy Inn is a unique and charming alternative to the larger DC hotels. Our guests enjoy the convenience and great location of a hotel with the atmosphere of a bed and breakfast inn. Rooms offer direct dial phones, cable tv, all private bathrooms and radio alarm clocks. Close to metro, White House, sights and restaurants, the Embassy Inn offers complimentary continental breakfast, newspaper, evening sherry and snacks to guests.

Built in 1910 as an apartment house, converted into a tourist hotel in 1919 and renovated in 1987, the Embassy Inn tries to maintain the intimate atmosphere of days gone by. At the same time we like to offer the conveniences of fax and copier service, valet dry cleaning and a 24 hour desk.

| 1627 16th St. NW, Washington DC 20009 | Tel 202 234 7800
Fax 202 234 3309
Freephone in US
800 423 9111 | General Manager:
Susan Stiles | 38 rooms
Doubles $79 - $110
B&B
Tax 13% | s/c $1.50 per night
On-street parking available
Children welcome | Non smoking rooms available
VS • MC
Amex • Diners |

NORMANDY INN
WASHINGTON DC

The Normandy Inn welcomes business travellers or sightseers with gracious old-world charm. This intimate 75-room hotel, in a cosmopolitan embassy neighbourhood, lies at the threshold of Washington's business and government districts. The Capital's famous sites, finest dining and fashionable shopping are within easy reach. Guest rooms, designed to create a comfortable retreat, are appointed with direct dial phone, cable tv, refrigerator, beverage maker and generous supply of bath amenities. The lounge is an inviting spot to rendezvous or relax, select a book from our library and settle by the fireplace with coffee and complimentary cookies. Each Tuesday, guests are invited to a complimentary wine and cheese reception. Continental breakfast is available. Whether business or pleasure brings you to Washington, you will find the Normandy Inn a delightful refuge.

| 2118 Wyoming Avenue, Washington DC | Tel 202 483 1350
Fax 202 387 8241
Freephone in US
800 424 3729 | General Manager:
Peter Hilary | 75 rooms
Doubles $79 - $113
EP
Tax 13%
Occupancy tax $1.50 | Parking available at $10 per day
Children welcome | Non-smoking rooms available
VS • MC • Amex
Diners • Discover |

WASHINGTON DC

WINDSOR INN
WASHINGTON DC

The Windsor Inn offers a variety of room options from suites to economical twin bed accommodations. We are located in the heart of Washington, close to metro, sights, the White House, and a variety of restaurants and unique shops. Our goal is to provide a comfortable, relaxed and homey atmosphere as well as great service and information on the many attractions of DC.

An expanded continental breakfast, newspapers and evening sherry are included in the rates. Rooms are equipped with private bathrooms, cable tv, movies and direct dial phones. Since we are small, we can give guests personalised attention and a secure environment in which to enjoy their stay.

If you enjoy the convenience of a hotel but the friendly charm of a bed and breakfast, then the Windsor Inn is ideal.

| 1842 16th St. NW, Washington DC 20009 | Tel 202 667 0300
Fax 202 667 4503
Freephone in US
800 423 9119 | General Manager:
Susan Stiles | 46 rooms
1 one-bedroom suite
Doubles $69 - $150
B&B | Tax 13%
s/c $1.50 per night
Children welcome | No smoking rooms available
VS • MC
Amex • Diners |

The WELCOME NEWS

*O*ur new, quarterly, full-colour newsletter for independent travellers to East Coast North America.
Packed full of interesting news and views, items of information, tempting places to stay plus seasonal special offers and some delicious innkeepers' recipes for you to try.
Just give us a call and we will
despatch a FREE copy to you straight away.

U.S. Welcome Ltd (U.K. Office)
Tel 01923 821469 Fax 01923 827157
100127.2706@compuserve.com
Toll free number in US & Canada 1-888-INN VISIT

WEST VIRGINIA

COUNTRY INN
BERKELEY SPRINGS

Nestled in the centre of the small historic town of Berkeley Springs, the 1832 Country Inn has continuously served the travelling public in a style befitting colonial days. Our motto "Retaining the Best of the Past", is practised each day.

A large lobby surrounded by antiques and fine art welcomes guests while the porches, rocking chairs and delightful gardens beckon them to spend some time relaxing and taking in the view. Dining is in two large and lovely dining rooms which feature live music at the weekends.

The Renaissance Spa sits high on the hill. Take advantage of the pure healthful spring water for which the town is named and enjoy whirlpool baths, massage, facials, manicure, pedicure and various other beauty treatments. Antique shops, park and theatre are only a short walk from the inn.

207 S. Washington Street,
Berkeley Springs, WV 25411

•

Tel 304 258 2210
Fax 304 258 3986
Freephone in US
800 822 6630

•

Innkeepers:
Jack & Alice Barker

•

70 rooms
(14 without bath en suite)
including 1 one bedroom,
1 two bedroom suite

Doubles $40 - $90 EP
Suites $105 - $145

•

Tax 6%

•

Spa facilities
Nearby: swimming,
golf, horseriding.

•

Children over
8 welcome

•

Non-smoking

•

VS • MC • Amex • Diners

WEST VIRGINIA

HILLBROOK INN
CHARLES TOWN

Gardens bursting with colour, a meandering stream, ducks on the pond, a hammock in the sun, the golden colours of autumn or the beauty of a winter storm when you are warm inside - Hillbrook is an inn for all seasons.

Built on a series of limestone ridges this small luxurious inn flows and blends into the landscape with cunningly contrived, imaginatively designed and decorated, cosy rooms all with delightful views, sitting areas and air-conditioning, some with working fireplaces.

Serving exceptional seven course dinners by candelight, a delicious three course prix-fixe lunch or a splendid high tea from November through April, Hillbrook offers guests a chance to delight both the palate and the eye.

Rt 2, Box 152,
Charles Town, WV 25414

•

Tel 304 725 4223
Fax 304 725 4455
Freephone in US
800 304 4223

•

Owner/Innkeeper:
Gretchen Carroll
Manager: Nadia Hill

•

6 rooms & suites

•

Doubles & suites
$198 - $400 MAP

Tax 3% room, 6% sales.
s.c. 15%

•

17 acres of gardens and
walking paths
Nearby: Harpers Ferry
National Park, golf,
riding.

•

Children over 12 welcome.

•

Non-smoking

•

VS • MC
Diners • Discover

SOUTHERN STATES

FLORIDA
1. Amelia Island Plantation — 196
2. Chalet Suzanne — 200
3. Darst Victorian Manor — 200
4. Elizabeth Pointe Lodge — 197
5. Heron House — 198
6. Hibiscus House — 201
7. Verona House — 201
8. Lakeside Inn — 199

GEORGIA
9. Glen-Ella Springs — 203
10. Little St. Simons Island — 202

NORTH CAROLINA
11. First Colony Inn — 204
12. Swag Country Inn — 205

SOUTH CAROLINA
13. Ashley Inn — 208
14. Cannonboro Inn — 208
15. Fulton Lane Inn — 206
16. Planters inn — 207

FLORIDA

AMELIA ISLAND PLANTATION
FERNANDINA BEACH

In deliberate and perfect harmony with nature... nestled between the beautiful marshes and estuaries of the Intracoastal Waterway and the Atlantic, the resort is an integral part of the island's ecosystem. Sandpipers forage the cool wet sand, the fragrance of bursting blossoms permeates the dense forests of ancient oaks. Spaciousness, privacy and peace are all pervading.

There are twenty three world-class tennis courts, health & fitness center, sportfishing, seven miles of nature walks, cycle paths and jogging trails and no less than 25 sparkling swimming pools. Choose a hotel room, a sumptuous penthouse suite or a fully equipped villa - most accommodations offer spectacular views of the ocean or maritime forests.

Choose the Amelia Inn Restaurant for oceanside dining or the Beach Club Sports Bar for more casual fare. At Amelia Island Plantation the natural beauty is breathtaking, the service warm and friendly and the pleasures endless.

PO Box 3000
Fernandina Beach
Fl 32034-3000
•
Tel 904 261 6161
Fax 904 277 5945
Freephone in US
800 874 6878
Cellet Travel Service Inc.
01564 79 4999
•
Resort Manager:
Jeff Johnson
•
462 rooms

including 130 one bedroom, 127 two bedroom & 78 three bedroom suites, & villas.
•
Doubles: $125 - $219 EP
Suites, & villas $146 - $530
•
Tax 9%
•
Outdoor & indoor pools, cycling, tennis, golf, conference facilities
Childrens' programmes
•
VS • MC • Amex

FLORIDA

ELIZABETH POINTE LODGE
AMELIA ISLAND

Rated amongst the 12 Best Waterfront Inns in America, focusing on individualised attention and located on the barrier island of Amelia with long stretches of often deserted beach, porches surround the main floor of this 1890s "Nantucket shingle". An abundance of rockers, sunshine and lemonade invite you to relax, whilst a full complimentary breakfast is served in a sunny room overlooking the ocean.

Although each of the guest rooms is different, making room hunting down the winding halls a pastime, they have in common fresh flowers, cable tv with movie channels, and oversized soaking tubs. Light lunch, dessert and room service are available all day. Complimentary wine and hors d'oeuvres are available at 6.00 p.m.

Sailing, fishing charters, tennis, golf, and horseback riding are nearby. Touring bikes, beach equipment and airport pickup are always available. Special tours, outings, and charters can be arranged to suit your adventure. The historic seaport of Fernandina is a short bike ride away for dining and shopping.

98 So. Fletcher Ave
Amelia Island
Florida 32034
•
Tel 904 277 4851
Fax 904 277 6500
Freephone in US
800 772 3359
•
Owner:
David J. Caples
•
25 rooms
including 1 one bedroom
suite, 1 two bedroom suite

Doubles $100 - $195
B&B
•
Tax 8%
•
Conference facilities
•
Children welcome.
•
Non-smoking
•
VS • MC
Amex

FLORIDA

HERON HOUSE
KEY WEST

In the heart of historic Key West, meticulously designed by gifted artists and craftsmen for the discerning traveller, a genuine sense of caring pervades every aspect of this very unique private retreat.

Don't expect a standard hotel room here, our style has been inspired by the informality of the Florida Keys' natural environment. With generous private decks and balconies, your private room merges with luxuriant tropical gardens. Interior and exterior spaces blend and flow together with ample use of natural materials such as teak, oak and cedar. A unique trademark is our handgrown rare orchids and we even have our own vintage champagne ready to put on ice.

The beach is just four blocks from the inn whilst for epicurean delights, entertainment, boutique shopping or a gallery, Duval Street is only one block away. Heron House is casual elegance presented in a warm relaxing atmosphere of luxury without pretence. Here you will always have the freedom to be yourself.

512 Simonton Street
Key West
FL 33040
•
Tel 305 294 9227
Fax 305 294 5692
Freephone in US
800 294 1644
•
Owner/General Manager:
Fred Geibelt
•
23 rooms
including 8 one bedroom
suites.

Doubles & Suites
$99 - $249 B&B
•
Tax 11.5 %.
•
Outdoor pool
Nearby: tennis, golf,
sailing, water skiing
•
Does not meet the
needs of children
•
VS • MC
Amex • Diners

FLORIDA

LAKESIDE INN
MOUNT DORA

Listed on the National Register of Historic Places, this vintage Victorian Inn has been a favourite destination for vacationers and diners alike for over one hundred years. Set on the shores of Lake Dora, surrounded by lush landscape of parks and trees, the inn is a charming centre piece in this quaint Florida town, reminiscent of a southern plantation with the ambience of a gentler era.

Guest rooms are exquisitely decorated offering a romantic atmosphere that includes such special touches as soft cotton robes, early morning coffee, continental breakfast and room service. Sunday Brunch on the huge front porch at the Inn is also an experience not to be missed. With its elegant Victorian decor and delectable American Regional cuisine, the Inn's Beauclaire Dining Room has won several awards and commendations whilst the Tremain's Lounge welcomes you to cosy fireside gatherings, friendly conversations and easy listening live entertainment. Enjoy the Lakeside experience, where, what once was.....still is!

100 N. Alexander St
Mount Dora
FL 32757

•

Tel 352 383 4101
Fax 352 735 2642
Freephone in US
800 556 5016

•

General Manager:
Tom Fultz

•

88 rooms
including 18 one
bedroom suites

Doubles $80 - $140 B&B
Suites $100 - $155

•

Tax 9%

•

Outdoor pool, tennis,
sailing, conference facilities
Nearby: golf, riding, water
skiing

•

Children welcome.

•

VS • MC • Amex
Diners • Discover

FLORIDA

CHALET SUZANNE COUNTRY INN
LAKE WALES

A 70-acre compound, nestled among orange groves, half an hour and a world away from Disney. From the moment guests walk through the wrought iron gates and see the unique towers, turrets and gables of Chalet Suzanne, they know they are in for a most unusual experience.

Guest rooms are individually decorated, fresh flowers are everywhere. Antiques, collectibles and potted greenery combine with oriental rugs and subtle colours to create a warm and cosy environment. Toiletries, hair-dryers, a decanter of sherry, fresh fruit and cable tv are a few of the in-room amenities.

Rated as one of the best restaurants in the US, five dining rooms overlook the lake. More than gourmet meals, more than comfort in a storybook setting, the Chalet Suzanne is rare balm for curing the ills of a busy world.

3800 Chalet Suzanne Drive, Lake Wales, FL 33853	Tel 941 676 6011 Fax 941 676 1814 Freephone in US 800 433 6011	Owner/Innkeepers Vita & Carl Hinshaw	30 rooms Doubles: $135 - $195 B&B Tax 10 %.	Outdoor pool, tennis courts, golf course, horseriding, sailing, water skiing, conference facilities,	private airfield. Children welcome. VS • MC • Amex Diners • Discover

DARST VICTORIAN MANOR
MOUNT DORA

Come to relax, shop or enjoy the sunset in our AAA Four Diamond Victorian inn overlooking beautiful Lake Dora and transport yourselves back to a time when every day was a peaceful one. Wake to freshly brewed coffee and a full gourmet breakfast each morning, later in the day relax and relish complimentary afternoon tea and desserts. In the evening, choose from the many acclaimed restaurants within easy walking distance.

Room choices include our Queen Victoria three room, lake-view, turret suite, Judi's Room, featuring a 1920s French Deco bed with canopy and a bay window sitting area or The Priscilla with dramatic black and rose colouring. After a relaxing bath or soothing shower, wrap yourself in a velour robe, as fresh flowers fill your room with fragrance, or work on a jigsaw puzzle in the homey atmosphere of the parlour.

495 Old Highway 441, Mount Dora, FL 32757	Tel 352 383 4050 Fax 352 383 7653 Owner/Innkeeper: Jim & Nanci Darst	6 rooms including 2 one bedroom suites.	Doubles $125 - $200 B&B Suites $180 - $200 Tax 9 %.	Outdoor pool open from early '97 Nearby: tennis, golf, riding, sailing, water skiing.	Children over 12 welcome. Non-smoking VS • MC • Amex

FLORIDA

HIBISCUS HOUSE
WEST PALM BEACH

Rated one of the ten best B&Bs in Florida and located in the historic district next to the Intracoastal Waterway. Hibiscus House provides easy access to the ocean and to the town of Palm Beach with its fabulous homes, excellent shopping and delightful restaurants.

Relax by our secluded heated pool and sip complimentary cocktails, enjoy the comfort of your room with air conditioning, paddle fans, tv and phones or step through French doors onto your private terrace to take in the beauty of the lush foliage.

A full two course breakfast is served each morning in the tropical gardens surrounding the pool or in the inn's formal dining room. We invite you to spend some time with us and enjoy tropical elegance at its best.

501 30th Street, West Palm Beach FL 33407 Tel 561 863 5633 Fax 561 863 5633	Freephone in US 800 203 4927 Owner: Raleigh Hill	7 rooms including 1 one bedroom suite. 1 two bedroom suite.	1 cottage with 2 bedrooms, 2 bathrooms & kitchen Doubles $65 - $125 B&B	Suites & cottage $120 - $160 Tax 10 %. Outdoor pool, tennis, sailing	Children over 12 welcome. Non-smoking VS • MC Amex • Diners

VERONA HOUSE
BROOKSVILLE

Verona House is a 1925 Sears and Roebuck catalogue house in historic downtown which, unlike most of Florida, boasts hills and picturesque oak-tree lined streets. This small town of 7,500 people offers a quiet get-away from the fast pace of city life and your hosts, Bob & Jan Boyd extend true southern hospitality, sharing with you the historical background of the area.

Four guest rooms are decorated in cherished pieces. Smoking is permitted on the porch but not indoors. Enjoy Jan's fresh baked casserole and delicious fruits for breakfast. Canoeing, horseback riding, golf and tennis are all nearby with major attractions such as Disneyworld, SeaWorld and Busch Gardens only an hour away.

201 So. Main Street Brooksville FL 34601 Tel 352 796 4001	Freephone in US 800 355 6717 Owners: Bob & Jan Boyd	4 rooms. 2 rooms with private bath 1 cottage	Doubles $45 - $80 B&B Cottage $90 - $100 Tax 8%.	Hot tub Nearby: tennis, golf, riding	Does not meet the needs of children. Non-smoking VS • MC • Amex

GEORGIA

LITTLE ST. SIMONS ISLAND
ST. SIMONS ISLAND

Your own private island awaits! A privately-owned 10,000 acre barrier island along the Georgia coast - paradise for nature lovers and outdoor enthusiasts, offering a wide variety of activities from its pristine beaches to ancient maritime forests and tidal creeks. The beauty of the landscape is punctuated by opportunities to observe the area's wildlife in this natural setting.

Accessible only by boat and accommodating just 24 overnight guests, gracious accommodations are set amongst the legendary moss-draped live oaks and shimmering marshes.

Culinary staff use nature's abundant regional offerings to create delicious cuisine home-style and brimming with flavours from the sea. Breakfast, lunch and dinner are served family-style in the main dining room or picnics are gladly prepared. During June to September, childrens' programmes available.

P.O. Box 21078,
St. Simons Island,
GA 31522
•
Tel 912 638 7472
Fax 912 634 1811
•
Resident Managers;
Debbie & Kevin McIntyre
•
12 rooms
2 four bedroom houses
•
Doubles $290 - $515 AP
Four bedroom houses
$1360 - $1860

Exclusive use of the island
$3150 - $4550
•
Tax 7% s.c. 15%
•
Outdoor pool, riding,
naturalist programmes,
birding, boating, canoeing,
angling, cycling, hiking,
conference facilities
•
Children over 6 welcome
Oct to May. All ages
June - Sept
•
Non-smoking
•
VS • MC

GEORGIA

GLEN-ELLA SPRINGS INN
TURNERVILLE

Down a gravel road at the edge of the Chatahoochee National Forest, just 90 miles north of Atlanta, lies one of the area's hidden surprises. Listed on the National Register, this 100-year old inn, the holder of several awards for restoration, is situated on 18 acres with swimming pool, lovely gardens, meadows and mountain streams.

Barrie and Bobby Aycock, their family and staff make every effort to welcome each guest and assist them in exploring the beautiful mountain areas of Northeast Georgia. Excellent hiking and whitewater rafting are nearby, while charming villages with fine folk art, antiques and craft shops provide more passive activities.

A bountiful breakfast is provided, with the inn's reputation for exceptional food attracting dinner guests from Atlanta and surrounding areas.

1789 Bear Gap Road, Turnerville GA 30523 Tel 706 754 7295 Fax 706 754 1560	Owners: Barrie & Bobby Aycock	16 rooms including 2 one bedroom suites.	Doubles $100 - $160 B&B Tax 11%	Outdoor pool, conference facilities, 18 acres of meadows, gardens, mountain stream	Nearby: tennis, golf, riding, water skiing Children over 6 welcome. VS • MC • Amex

FEEDBACK FEEDBACK FEEDBACK FEEDBACK
Your comments are valued!

Please write or call to tell us your opinion of the inns and hotels in which you stayed.

Were your expectations met? Was the welcome warm?
Did you feel you received good value for the money you spent?
Consumer feedback is a vital part of maintaining the standard of **U.S. Welcome Directories** and your input is of great value. As a small token of thanks, it will be our pleasure to send you a *complimentary copy* of our next book which will reach the bookshops in January 1998.

Please send letters, *no stamp required to:*
U.S. Welcome Directories Ltd.,
FREEPOST (HA4595)
Northwood,
England
HA6 3BR
Telephone : 01923-821469 (U.K.)   888-INN-VISIT (U.S.)

NORTH CAROLINA

FIRST COLONY INN
NAGS HEAD

Glorious beaches, refreshing ocean breezes, the uniquely calm and peaceful atmosphere of the Outer Banks and true southern hospitality at the historic First Colony Inn. Choose to lounge by the pool, follow the boardwalk to the gazebo on the ocean dune, visit numerous area attractions or simply relax in a rocking chair on the wrap-around verandah.

In 1988 your hosts, the Lawrence family, with their own roots deep in the area, took this "Grand Old Lady" ravaged by time and the encroaching Atlantic and, overcoming a myriad of obstacles, had the building cut into three sections and moved south. They then proceeded to return the inn to its former glory, scrupulously maintaining its character and history, whilst unobtrusively adding every modern convenience and comfort - heated towel rails, tv, phones, refrigerators, and in some rooms - kitchenettes, sitting rooms and private screened porches. This labour of love is now an internationally recognised, AAA Four Diamond Award winner and welcomes new generations to the old fashioned pleasures of the Outer Banks.

6720 S. Virginia Dare Trail,
Nags Head,
NC 27959
•
Tel 919 441 2343
Fax 919 441 9234
Freephone in US
800 368 9390
•
General Manager:
Camille Lawrence
•
26 rooms
including 6 one bedroom suites.
Plus 5 two or three bedroom cottages.

Doubles Summer
$100 - $250 B&B,
Cottages $450 - $800 EP
(weekly Sat-Sat)
•
Tax 10%
Outdoor pool, beaches.
Nearby: indoor pool, tennis, golf, riding, sailing, water skiing, diving, windsurfing, hang gliding, fishing
•
Children welcome.
Non-smoking
•
VS • MC
Amex • Discover

NORTH CAROLINA

SWAG COUNTRY INN
WAYNESVILLE

Made of hand-hewn logs and set on 250 acres, Swag Country Inn has its own private entrance to the 500,000 acre Great Smoky Mountains National Park. A consistent winner of the Mobil Four Star award, the inn offers a unique combination of handsewn quilts, antler chandeliers, rustic furniture, luxurious amenities and the great outdoors.

Each of the guest accommodations is different, some in log cabins, some featuring woodstoves, private porches and cathedral ceilings with thoughtful extras such as refrigerators, cofeemakers with grinders and terry cloth robes. Wake to a symphony of bird song and the sight of a Smoky Mountain sky at dawn, explore pristine waterfalls and stop for a delicious picnic lunch on a mountaintop. Spring invites romantics and nature enthusiasts to enjoy the wildflowers and birds that are beginning to migrate home. Summer is enchanting with lazy days by mountain streams and cool evening breezes. Fall is ablaze with colour, roaring fires and steamy saunas. Dining is sensational at the inn and the warmth of good conversation is part of every meal.

Join us, discover the beauty and simplicity of nature in ideal surroundings.

Route 2, Box 280-A
Waynesville, NC 28786
•
Tel 704 926 0430
Fax 704 926 2036
Freephone in US
800 789 7672
•
President/Innkeeper:
Deener Matthews
•
17 rooms
including 2 one bedroom
suites, 1 two bedroom suite.
3 cabins including 1 two
bedroom cabin

Doubles & Suites $190 -
$350 AP (rates are highest
at weekends)
Cabins $295 - $440
•
Tax 9% s.c. 15%
•
Outdoor pool, conference
facilities, racquet ball,
hiking
•
Children over 7 welcome.
•
Non-smoking
•
VS • MC • Discover

SOUTH CAROLINA

FULTON LANE INN
CHARLESTON

This romantic retreat is situated on a quiet pedestrian lane in the heart of Charleston's Historic District. The spirit of an antebellum Charleston summer home is beautifully recaptured - light filtering softly through louvered shades, fine woods, natural textures and soft pastels invite you to indulge in the simple pleasures of a more gracious time.

Spacious rooms and suites offer a full compliment of services including continental breakfast delivered on a silver tray, morning newspaper, wine and sherry in the lobby each evening and nightly turndown service with chocolates . Many rooms feature fireplaces, canopied beds, large whirlpool baths and cathedral ceilings. Across from Saks Fifth Avenue, the inn is within walking distance of Charleston's finest restaurants, antique shops and boutiques.

Other inns of Charleston include Kings Courtyard Inn, John Rutledge House Inn, Victoria House Inn and, opening early 1998, The Wentworth Mansion. Each different in architecture and style, but sharing a common link of gracious hospitality.

202 King Street Charleston
South Carolina SC 29401
•
Tel 803 720 2600
Fax 803 720 2940
Freephone in US
800 720 2688
•
Innkeeper: Randall Felkel
•
27 rooms
including 5 one bedroom suites
•
Doubles $105 - $210 B&B
Suites $180 - $255

Tax 12%
•
Conference facilities
Nearby: indoor pool,
tennis, golf, sailing
•
Parking $5.00 per day.
•
Children over 12 welcome.
•
Non-smoking
•
VS • MC • Amex
Diners • Discover

SOUTH CAROLINA

PLANTERS INN
CHARLESTON

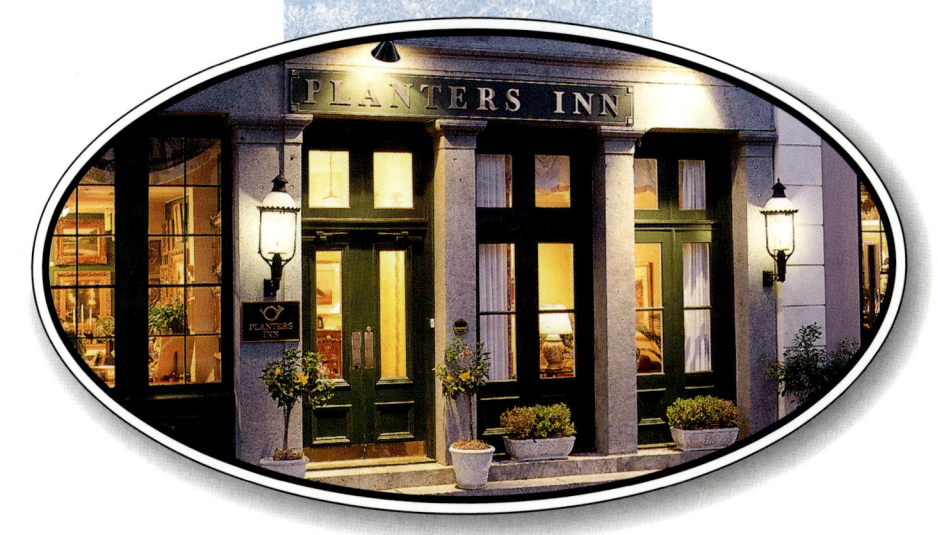

The heart and soul of historic Charleston, located at the entrance to the bustling City Market, the Planters Inn combines the care and charisma of an old world inn with the ambience and amenities of a full service hotel.

Elegant guest rooms and lavish suites are the most spacious in the city, boasting high ceilings, oversized marble baths and four poster Charleston Rice Beds. Each room is individually appointed some featuring working fireplaces and hardwood floors.

Included in your rates are breakfast delivered to your door and an afternoon wine and cheese reception. After an excellent meal at the Planters Café, fast becoming one of the most acclaimed restaurants in the city, retire to the comfort of your room to find your bed turned down with a chocolate and the following day's weather forecast.

Charleston's legends are only just beyond our lobby!

112 North Market Street
Charleston, SC 29401

Tel 803 722 2345
Fax 803 577 2125
Freephone in US
800 845 7082

General Manager:
Larry Spelts

41 rooms including
5 one-bedroom suites

Doubles $100 - $165
B&B

Tax 10%

Parking available

Conference facilities

Nearby: swimming,
golf, horseriding

Children welcome

31 rooms are
non-smoking

VS • MC • Amex • Diners

SOUTH CAROLINA

ASHLEY INN
CHARLESTON

This architectural treasure is tastefully furnished with antique four poster, pencil post and canopied rice beds. Private baths, air conditioning and cable tv add to your comfort. Warm hospitality and professional service are unmatched, let us assist with personal tours, restaurants and hints on all "must sees".

Sleep in until the aroma of fresh brewed coffee and sizzling bacon lures you to breakfast overlooking a beautiful Charleston garden. Guests rave over creations such as savoury sausage soufflé with fluffy zucchini and crunchy (yes crunchy!) french toast with hazelnut peach syrup.

To enhance your taste of gracious living, Southern style, enjoy afternoon tea, sumptuous home baked goods and evening sherry. Complimentary touring bikes offer the best way to see the city, hassle free!

201 Ashley Avenue, Charleston, SC 29403
Tel 803 723 1848
Fax 803 768 1230

Owners: Bud & Sally Allen

6 rooms including 1 one-bedroom suite
Doubles $69 - $115
B&B

Tax 10%
Parking available no charge

Smoking only on porches
Children over 10 welcome

VS • MC
Amex • Discover

CANNONBORO INN
CHARLESTON

With the true taste of southern hospitality, this c.1853 historic home skilfully combines old and new, offering six beautifully decorated bedrooms with antique and canopied beds but not forgetting air-conditioning and colour tvs. Known as Charleston's Gourmet Breakfast Place, the Cannonboro Inn is a place to be pampered.

Relish your delicious start to the day whilst relaxing in the columned piazza overlooking a low country garden and fountain. After breakfast you can tour nearby historic sites on complimentary bicycles, on foot or by horse-drawn carriage and enjoy beautiful Charleston, a city that will charm you with its slower more gracious pace.

At days end return to afternoon tea, sherry and sumptuous homebaked goods. This is what Charleston is all about – we look forward to seeing you.

184 Ashley Avenue, Charleston, SC 29403

Tel 803 723 8572
Fax 803 768 1230

Owners: Bud & Sally Allen

6 rooms
Doubles $69 - $115
B&B
Tax 10%

Parking available no charge
Smoking only on porches

Children over 10 welcome
VS • MC
Amex • Discover

NOTES

TASTERS

A TASTE OF THE REST

On the following pages are just a few of the wonderful choices that await when your travels take you further afield in North America.

ARKANSAS

EMPRESS OF LITTLE ROCK
Little Rock

Wonderfully ornate mansion featuring a 64 square foot glass skylight above a stunning walnut and chestnut staircase and a 3½ storey corner tower.

Tel 501 374 7966
Fax 501 375 4537
Innkeeper:
Sharon Welch-Blair

5 rooms, 2 mini-suites,
$85 - $125 B&B
Children over 10 welcome.
VS MC Amex

TASTERS

ARIZONA

SOUTHWEST INN AT SEDONA
Sedona

Luxurious AAA 4 Diamond award winner,. Large beautiful rooms, southwest decor. Fireplaces, private decks, magnificent red rock views. 2 hours, Grand Canyon, 2 hours north of Phoenix

Tel 520 282 3344
Fax 520 282 0267
Owners:
Joel & Sheila Gilgoff

28 suites.
$115 - $195 B&B
Children welcome.
VS MC Discover

BRITISH COLUMBIA

LABURNUM COTTAGE
North Vancouver

The warmest hostess in the Northwest - Delphine welcomes you to beautifully appointed rooms set in half an acre of gardens, surrounded by forest yet only 15 minutes from downtown Vancouver.

Tel / Fax 604 988 4877
Owner:
Delphine Masterton

4 rooms, 2 cottages,
$100 - $150 B&B
Children welcome.
VS MC

CALIFORNIA

CAMELLIA INN
Healdsburg

In the heart of the beautiful Sonoma wine country, near the Russian River. Spacious rooms with antiques, inlaid hardwood floors, specially chosen beds with heaped pillows.

Tel 707 433 8182
Fax 707 433 8130
Owners/Innkeepers:
Ray, Del and Lucy Lewand

9 rooms,
Doubles $70 - $135 B&B
Children welcome.
VS MC Amex

CALIFORNIA

CAMPBELL RANCH INN
Geyserville

35 acre ranch in the heart of the Sonoma County wine country. Rolling vineyards; an abundance of flowers; the warm welcome of an inn with the extra facilities of a professional tennis court and large swimming pool.

Tel 707 857 3476
Fax 707 857 3239
Owner/Innkeeper:
Mary Jane & Jerry Campbell

5 rooms, 1 two bedroom
cottage, $100 - $165 B&B
Children welcome.
VS MC Amex

CALIFORNIA

CHESHIRE CAT INN
Santa Barbara

Beautiful flower and fountain-filled patios and gardens, elegant suites & rooms in a southern Californian village by the sea.

Tel 805 569 1610
Fax 805 682 1876
Manger/Owner:
Christine Dunstan

14 rooms, suites, cottages
$100 - $270 B&B
Children welcome.
VS MC Amex

CALIFORNIA

GOOSE & TURRETS
Montara

In the seaside village of Montara, San Francisco Bay area, delightfully individual inn serving wonderfully creative four course breakfasts. 3 geese will welcome you to the inn.

Tel 415 728 5451
Fax 415 728 0141
Proprietor:
Emily Hoche-Mong

5 rooms,
$85 - $120 B&B
Children welcome.
VS MC Amex Discover

TASTERS

CALIFORNIA

THE INN AT UNION SQUARE
San Francisco

In the heart of San Francisco an elegant small hotel, carefully and individually furnished, as far from a chain hotel as it is possible to be. Complimentary breakfasts, afternoon tea and evening wine.

Tel 415 397 3510
Fax 415 989 0529
General Manager:
Brooks Bayly

30 rooms & suites,
$130 - $300 B&B
VS MC Amex Diners
Discover

CALIFORNIA

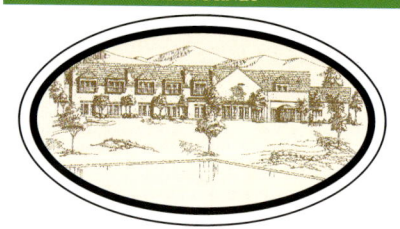

TWO ANGELS INN
La Quinta

After the style of a French chateau, this new inn, built to encompass every comfort is magnificently framed by the imposing Santa Rosa Mountains on one side and tranquil Lake La Quinta on the other.

Tel 619 564 7332
Owner/Innkeeper:
Hap & Holly Harris

11 rooms
Doubles $185 - $350 B&B
Children over 16 welcome.
VS MC Amex

COLORADO

ABRIENDO INN
Pueblo

Delightful choice of thoughtfully decorated and furnished rooms all with tv and phone in this conveniently situated, Foursquare architecturally styled inn in the centre of historic Pueblo.

Tel 719 544 2703
Fax 719 542 6544
Owner/Innkeeper:
Kerrelyn Trent

10 rooms,
$58 - $110 B&B
Children over 7 welcome.
VS MC Amex Diners

COLORADO

ALPINE INN
Telluride

A short walk to the ski slopes, no queues and the best view in North America. Visit in Summer to hike, horseride and taste the serenity that wildflowers, aspen trees and a truly welcoming inn can provide.

Tel 970 728 6282
Fax 970 728 3424
Owner: Denise Weaver
8 rooms, $70 - $135 B&B

2 cottages, sleep 4 - 6
$110 - $500 EP
Children over 10 welcome.
VS MC

COLORADO

CASTLE MARNE
Denver

An imposing historic mansion close to all of Denver's tourist attractions. Charming Victorian ambience, stained glass windows, games room, English garden and a full gourmet breakfast and afternoon tea.

Tel 303 331 0621
Fax 303 331 0623
Owners:
Diane & Jim Peiker

9 rooms & suites
$85 - $200 B&B
Children over 10 welcome.
VS MC Amex Diners

COLORADO

QUEEN ANNE INN
Denver

A delightful award-winning urban inn within easy reach of local attractions. Enjoy the grand oak staircase, the 35 foot open turret or treat yourself to a stay in the Aspen room with its unique mural and towering ceiling.

Tel 303 296 6666
Fax 303 296 2151
Owners/Innkeepers:
Tom King & Chris King

14 rooms & suites,
$85 - $165 B&B
Children over 12 welcome.
VS MC Amex

TASTERS

COLORADO

WOODLAND INN
Woodland Park

Cosy country inn in the foothills of majestic Pikes Peak. Surrounded by 12 private acres of aspens and firs but just minutes from Colorado Springs. Relax in the parlour and watch elk come to feed in winter and hummingbirds in summer.

Tel 719 687 8209
Fax 719 687 3112
Owners/Innkeepers:
Frank & Nancy O'Neil

7 rooms,
$50 - $80 B&B
Children welcome.
VS MC Amex

HAWAII

CHALET KILAUEA-THE INN AT VOLCANO
Volcano

A mile from the Hawaii Volcano National Park. Experience the comfort of a B&B or the freedom of your own vacation home. Whichever you choose, taste true Hawaiian hospitality.

Tel 808 967 7786
Fax 808 967 8660
Innkeepers:
Brian & Lisha Crawford

5 rooms, 3 suites,
5 vacation homes,
$135 - $295 B&B & EP
Children welcome.
VS MC Amex Diners

HAWAII

SHIPMAN HOUSE INN
Hilo

National Historic Register, Old Island Family, Orchids, Lily Ponds, Wide Verandahs, Fragrant Breezes, Waterfalls, Guest Cottage, Fresh Flowers. Add to this, a warm welcome from your hostess Barbara-Ann, and you have a perfect stay.

Tel 808 934 8002
Owner: Barbara-Ann Andersen

3 rooms, $130 B&B
Children over 15 welcome.
VS MC

MONTANA

BEAR CREEK LODGE
Victor

Nestled on 74 scenic acres in southwest Montana, this inn offers a truly unique experience and the opportunity to enjoy such activities as horseriding, hiking, fly fishing, rafting and white water rafting.

Tel 406 642 3750
Fax 406 642 6847
Owners:
Roland & Elizabeth Turney

8 rooms, $250 AP
off season $150 B&B
Children welcome by
prior arrangement.
VS MC Amex

OREGON

CHANNEL HOUSE
Depoe Bay

Perched on the rugged Oregon coastline with spectacular water views, watch migrating whales from the whirlpool on your own private deck, enjoy delicious breakfast amidst brass ships fittings and nautical antiques in the first floor serving room.

Tel 541 765 2140
Fax 541 765 2191
Owner/Innkeeper:
Vicki Mix & Carl Finseth

14 rooms & suites,
$135 - $200 B&B
Does not meet the needs
of children
Discover, Novus

OREGON

COLUMBIA GORGE HOTEL
Oregon

On the banks of the Columbia River which divides Oregon and Washington, stands the spectacular Columbia Gorge Hotel - one of the last of the truly romantic grand hotels. Enjoy fine dining, cosy rooms and a rose on your pillow at evening's end.

Tel 541 386 5566
Fax 541 387 5414
Owners:
Boyd & Hallo Graves

42 rooms,
$150 - $275 B&B
Children over 12 welcome.
VS MC Amex Diners

TASTERS

TENNESSEE

PEACOCK HILL COUNTRY INN
College Grove

Luxury country inn on a working cattle and horse farm. Rocking chairs on a front porch, black-eyed Susans and purple cone flowers nodding over brick walkways and only a short drive to Nashville and the Grand Old Opry.

Tel 615 368 7727
Fax 615 368 7933
Owners:
Walter & Anita Ogilvie

5 rooms, 1 log cabin
$95 - $125 B&B
Children welcome.
VS MC

TEXAS

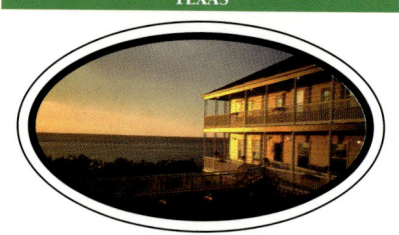

BROWN PELICAN INN
South Padre Island

Let gentle Gulf breezes caress you while the sun settles behind the Laguna Madre's sparkling blue waters on South Padre Island. Relax and be refreshed at the Brown Pelican Inn - a unique island experience.

Tel 210 761 2722
Fax 210 761 1273
Innkeeper:
Vicky Conway

8 rooms,
$70 - $115 B&B
Children over 12 welcome.
VS MC

TEXAS

MARIPOSA RANCH
Brenham

Working ranch with horse, cattle and emus and a caring hospitable welcome from Charles and Johnna with many thoughtful little touches to enhance your stay.

Tel / Fax 409 836 4737
Owners:
Charles & Johnna
Chamberlain

9 rooms & suites
$75 - $140 B&B
Children welcome.
VS MC

TEXAS

ROSEVINE INN
Tyler

A warm welcome at this Texan B&B inn with its white picket fence and cosy cheerful guest rooms. Helpful local knowledge willingly supplied by the Powells.

Tel 903 592 2221
Fax 903 593 9500
Owner/Innkeeper:
Bert & Rebecca Powell

7 rooms & suites,
$75 - $150 B&B
Children over 2 welcome.
VS MC Amex Diners

WASHINGTON

SHELBURNE INN
Seaview

Located between the Columbia River and the ocean on an unspoiled 28 mile stretch of Pacific Coast surrounded by stunning scenery complete with bird sanctuaries, lighthouses and panoramic vistas.

Tel 360 642 2442
Fax 360 642 8904
Owners:
Laurie Anderson & David
Campiche

15 rooms & suites,
$99 - $165 B&B
Children welcome.
VS MC Amex

WISCONSIN

MANSION HILL INN
Madison

Round-arched windows, ornate cornices. A spiral staircase leading to a panoramic city view, 24 hour valet service, breakfast in bed, an elegant option for a 4 Diamond stay in Madison.

Tel 608 255 3999
Fax 608 255 2217
Director of Hotel Operations:
Janna Wojtal

11 suites, $100 - $270 B&B
Children over 12 welcome.
Non-smoking
VS MC Amex

The Best of British Style

Recognised as the leading collection of privately owned hotels in Britain.

Pride of Britain

Is as much a part of Britain as her heritage.

Your stay at a Pride of Britain hotel will be a time to remember, as each is a home reflecting the individuality and sometimes eccentricity of its owners.

No matter where you may be travelling in Britain you will never be far from the warmth and welcome of a Pride of Britain hotel.

For your FREE copy of our Pocket Directory in the USA, call
ABERCROMBIE & KENT INT INC
Tel: 708 954 2944

or for RESERVATIONS
TOLL FREE 1-800 98 PRIDE

In the UK call
PRIDE OF BRITAIN (HOTLINE)
01264 736604

Ireland's Blue Book

A unique Association listing Ireland's most gracious Country Houses and gourmet Restaurants set amidst the quiet beauty of rural Ireland.

These properties are all owner managed and are renowned worldwide for all their high standards of traditional hospitality, elegant accommodation and superb cuisine.

IRELAND'S BLUE BOOK

Ask for the 'Blue Book'
at your
U.S. Welcome Hotel or Inn
or contact
Ireland's Blue Book,
Ardbraccan Glebe, Navan,
Co. Meath, Ireland.
Tel: 00-353-46-23416
Fax: 00-353-46-23292

The Portfolio Collection

Fine South African Country Houses and Private Game Reserves

The Country Places Collection in South Africa is one of a series of fine guides for the discerning traveller. Offering a selection of hand-picked Country Houses, Hotels and Private Game Reserves

Information and Reservations
The Portfolio Collection
Johannesburg, South Africa Tel +27 11 880 3414
Fax +27 11 788 4802
P O Box 52350, Saxonwold, 2132 Johannesburg
South Africa

E-Mail & Web Sites

	E-MAIL	WEB SITE
Alpine Inn	johnw@alpineinn.com	http://www.sni.net/telluride
Andrews Lodging	74232.116@compuserve.com	
Ardmore Inn	ArdmoreInn@aol.com	http://www.ArdmoreInn.com
Auberge Des Sablons	sablons@cite.net	
Barley Sheaf Farm,	barleysheaf@netreach.net	
Barrows House Inn	barhouse@vermontel.com	
Basin Harbor Club	res@bh-on-lc	http://www.bh-on-lc.com
Black Point Inn	bpi@nlis.com	
Blue Harbor House	balidog@midcoast.com	http://www.travelassist.com/reg/me105s.html
Blueberry Hill Inn	clarktg@vbi.champlain.edu	
Boston Harbor Hotel	sales@bhh.com	
Boulders		http://www.distinctiveinns.com/bldrs/index.html
Briars	briars@ils.net	http://www.ils.net/briars
Brown Pelican Inn	Vicky0515@aol.com	
Buttonwood Inn	button_w@moose.ncia.net	
Cambridge House	innach@aol.com	
Camellia Inn	DLewand@aol.com	
Captain Lord Mansion	captain@biddeford.com	
Captain's House Inn	capthous@capecod.net	http://www.distinctiveinns.com/cphse/index.html
Carnegie House	carnhouse@aol.com	
Castle Marne	themarne@ix.netcom.com	
Chalet Kilauea	bchawaii@aol.com	
Chalet Suzanne	chaletsuz@aol.com	
Channel House	CFinseth@newportnet.com	
Chatham Bars Inn	resrvcbi@chathambarsinn.com	
Cheshire Cat Inn	cheshire@cheshirecat.com	
Chester House	chesthse@rma.edu	
Chesterfield Inn	chtinn@sover.net	http://www.distinctiveinns.com/chstr/index.html
Churchill House Inn	rciatt@sover.net	http://www.pbpub.com/inntoinn/
Cliffside Inn	cliff@wsii.com	http://www.distinctiveinns.com/clfsd/index.html
Colby Hill Inn	infousw@colbyhillinn.com	http://www.colbyhillinn.com
Colonial Capital	ccbb@widomaker.com	http://www.ccbb.com
Colonnade		http://www.colonnadehotel.com
Columbia Gorge Hotel	cghotel@gorge.net	http://www.gorge.net/lodging/cghotel/
Copperfield Inn	copperfield@netheaven.com	http://www.mediausa.com/ny/cprfldin
Corner House	cornerhs@nantucket.net	http://www.cornerhousenantucket.com
Cornucopia of Dorset	cornucop@vermontel.com	http://www.cornucopiaofdorset.com
Cortina Inn	cortinal@aol.com	http://www.genghis.com/cortinainn.htm
Craftsman Inn	craftman@dreamscape.com	
Dan'l Webster Inn		http://media3.com/dan'lwebsterinn/~
Deerfield Inn	drfldinn@shaysnet.com	http://www.distinctiveinns.com/drfld/index.html
Ellis River House	76073.1435@compuserve.com	
Forest, A Country Inn	wguppy@aol.com	
Glen-Ella Springs	glenella@cyberhighway.com	
Golden Eagle Resort	stoweagle@aol.com	http://www.stoweinfo.com/saa/golden_eagle
Goose & Turrets	gooseandturrets@montara.com	http://www.montara.com/goose.html
Gorges Grant Hotel	gorgesgrant@ogunquit.com	
Greenville Inn	gvlinn@moosehead.net	
Hamilton House		http://www.madriver.com/lodging/hamilton.html
Hancock Inn	innkeeper@hancockin.mv.com	
Hawk Inn & Mountain Resort	hawkvermont@vermontel.com	
Heritage Plantation of Sandwich	museumcc@aol.com	
Heron House	heronkw@aol.com	http://www.fla-keys.com/heronhouse

E-Mail & Web Sites

Inn	Email	Website
Hummingbird Inn	hmgeird@cfw.com	
Inn at Essex	innessex@together.net	
Inn at Perry Cabin	perrycbn@friend.ly.net	http://www.perrycabin.com
Inn at Stockbridge	innkeeper@stockbridge.com	http://www.stockridge.com
Inn at the Brass Lantern	brasslntrn@aol.com	
Inn at Thorn Hill	thornhill@ncia.net	http://www.distinctiveinns.com/thhll/index.html
Inn at Union Square	inn@unionsquare.com	
Inn at West View Farm	westview@vermontel.com	http://www.vtweb.com/innatwestviewfarm
Jared Coffin House	jchouse@nantucket.net	http://www.nantucket.net/lodging/jchouse
John Carver Inn		http://media3.com/JohnCarverInn/
Keswick Hall	keswick@keswick.com	http://www.keswick.com/keswick.html
Lakeside Inn	lakeside@iag.net	
Landgrove Inn	vtinn@sover.net	
Lareau Farm Country Inn	Lareau@madriver.com	
Little Inn of Bayfield	littleinn@odyssey.on.ca.	http://www.odyssey.on.ca/littleinn
Little St. Simons Island	102063.467@compuserve.com	http://www.pactel.com.au/lssi
Llewellyn Lodge	lll@rockbridge.net	
Longfellow's Wayside Inn	innkeeper@wayside.org	http://www.wayside.org
Maine Stay Inn	mainstay@midcoast.com	http://www.distinctiveinns.com/mnsty/index.html
Maine Stay Inn & Cottages	copeland4@cybertours.com	
The Manor on Golden Pond		http://www.distinctiveinns.com/mngld/index.html
Middlebury Inn	midinnvt@sover.net	http://www.middleburyinn.com/vt
Mira Monte Inn & Suites	mburns@acadia.net	
Newcastle Inn	newcastinn@aol.com	http://www.distinctiveinns.com/ncstle/index.html
Notchland Inn	notchland@aol.com	
The Oaks		http://www.innbook.com
Old Tavern at Grafton	tavern@sover.net	
Olde Orchard Inn	inkeep1@aol.com	
Rabbit Hill Inn	rabbit.hill.Inn@connrivernet	http://www.distinctiveinns.com/rbthl/index.html
Resorts Ontario	escapes@resorts-ontario.com	http://www.resorts-ontario.com.
Ripplecove Inn	ripcove@multi-medias.ca	
Rose Inn	roseinn@clarityconnect.com	
Salem Inn	saleminn@earthlink.net	
Shelburne Inn	shelinn@aone.com	
Shelburne Museum		http://www.shelburnemuseum.com
Shipman House	bighouse@bigisland.com	
Shire Inn	shireinn@sover.net	
Siebeness Inn	siebenes@together.net	
Southwest Inn at Sedona	info@swinn.com	
Stage Neck Inn	stageneck@aol.com	http://www.stageneck.com
Steeles Tavern Manor	hoernlei@milo.cfw.com	
Sugar Hill Inn		http://www.musar.com/ traveler/sgnhlinn.html
Sugarloaf	info@sugarloaf.com	
Sugartree	sugartree@madriver.com	http://www.madriver.com/lodging/sugartree
Thorncroft Inn	kgb@tidc.net	
Tucker Hill Lodge	tuckhill@madriver.com	
Two Angels Inn	deuxanges@aol.com	
Vermont Inn	vtinn@aol.com	http://www.vermontinn.com
Village Country Inn	vcinn@sover.net	http://www.distinctiveinns.com/cntry/index.html
West Hill House	westhill@madriver.com	
West Mountain Inn	info@westmountaininn.com	
Wildflower Inn	wldflr@aol.com	
Windham Hill Inn	windham@sover.net	http://www.windhamhill.com
Woods	skivt@sover.net	

Index

	PAGE NOS.		
Abriendo Inn	212	Captain Lindsey House Inn	48
Alpine Inn	212	Captain Lord Mansion	39
Amelia Island Plantation	196	Captain Nickerson Inn	79
Andrews Lodging	46	Captain's House Inn of Chatham	60
Antrim 1844	152	Carnegie House	168
Applewood Colonial	182	Castle	136
Ardmore Inn	134	Castle Marne	212
Ashley Inn	208	Chalet Kilauea	213
Auberge des Sablons	20	Chalet Suzanne	200
Auberge Handfield	21	Channel House	213
Auberge Saint-Antoine	22	Charles Hotel	61
Bagley House	46	Chatham Bars Inn	62
Bailiwick Inn	174	Cheshire Cat Inn	211
Baladerry Inn	167	Chester House	182
Bar Harbor Hotel-Bluenose Inn	35	Chesterfield Inn	93
Barleysheaf Farm	167	Chimney Hill Farm	158
Barrows House	134	Churchill House Inn	136
Basin Harbor Club	117	Cliffside Inn	110
Bayview Hotel	36	Clifton	183
Bear Creek Lodge	213	Colby Hill Inn	101
Bed & Breakfast on the Point	111	Colonial Capital	183
Bee & Thistle Inn	25	Colonnade Hotel	63
Berkeley Hotel	175	Columbia Gorge Hotel	213
Bernards Inn	157	Copperfield Inn	159
Bird & Bottle	165	Corner House Inn	79
Black Point Inn	37	Cornucopia of Dorset	118
Blantyre	58	Cortina Inn	119
Block Island Resorts	109	Country Inn	193
Blue Harbor House	47	Craftsman Inn	160
Blue Hill Inn	47	Dan'l Webster Inn	64
Blueberry Hill Inn	135	Darst Victorian Manor	200
Boar's Head Inn	176	Deerfield Inn	65
Boston Harbor Hotel	59	Deerhill Inn	137
Boulders	26	Dexter's Inn & Tennis Club	102
Boxwood Inn	168	Diamond District Inn	80
Bradford Inn	78	Dockside Guest Quarters	48
Brandon Inn	135	Doneckers	169
Briars	17	Elizabeth Pointe Lodge	197
Brigadoon	30	Ellis River House	102
Brown Pelican	214	Embassy Inn	191
Buttonwood Inn	101	Empress of Little Rock	210
Cambridge House	78	Equinox	120
Camellia Inn	211	Evermay on the Delaware	169
Campbell Ranch Inn	211	First Colony Inn	204
Cannonboro Inn	208	Forest, A Country Inn	103
Captain Daniel Stone Inn	38	Four Columns Inn	121
		Foxglove	103

220

Index

Franconia Inn	104	Inn By The Sea	42
Frederick House	184	Inn of Exeter	96
French Manor	170	Inn on the Common	126
Fulton Lane Inn	206	Isaiah Hall	81
Gables	137	Isaiah Jones Homestead	82
Geneva-on-the-Lake	161	Jared Coffin House	67
George Washington University Inn	190	John Carver Inn	83
Glen-Ella Springs	203	Kennebunkport Inn	49
Golden Eagle Resort	122	Kent Manor Inn	155
Goose & Turrets	211	Keswick Hall	177
Gorges Grant Hotel	40	King's Cottage	171
Grandview	111	L'Auberge Provencale	178
Greenville Inn	49	Laburnum Cottage	211
Griswold Inn	30	Lakeside Inn	199
Halsey House	165	Landgrove Inn	140
Hamilton House	138	Larchwood Inn	112
Hancock Inn	104	Lareau Farm Country Inn	140
Harbor Court Hotel	153	Lawnmeer Inn	50
Harbor Light Inn	66	Lenox Hotel	68
Harraseeket Inn	41	Lighthouse Inn	83
Hawk Inn & Resort	123	Little Inn of Bayfield	18
Hawthorne Inn	80	Little St. Simon's Island	202
Henry Clay Inn	184	Llewellyn Lodge at Lexington	187
Heron House	198	Lodge at Moosehead Lake	50
Hibiscus House	201	Longfellow's Wayside Inn	84
Hillbrook Inn	194	Maine Stay Inn	51
Historic Inns of Annapolis	155	Maine Stay Inn & Cottages	51
Historic Smithton Inn	170	Manhattan East Suite Hotels	162
Homestay	185	Manor at Taylor's Store	188
Homestead Inn (Greenwich)	27	Manor House	31
Homestead Inn (New Milford)	31	Manor on Golden Pond	97
Hummingbird Inn	185	Mansion Hill Inn	214
Inn at Essex	124	Maple Leaf Inn	141
Inn at Gristmill Square	186	Mariposa Ranch	214
Inn at Meander Plantation	186	Marlborough	84
Inn at Millrace Pond	158	Mary Prentiss	85
Inns at Mills Falls & Bay Point	94	Middlebury Inn	141
Inn at Narrow Passage	187	Millcroft Inn	19
Inn at National Hall	28	Mira Monte Inn	52
Inn at Ormsby Hill	125	Morrison House	179
Inn at Perry Cabin	154	Mostly Hall	85
Inn at Stockbridge	81	Mountain Road Resort	127
Inn at the Brass Lantern	138	Mr. Mole	156
Inn at the Round Barn Farm	139	Newcastle Inn	52
Inn at Thorn Hill	95	New London Inn	105
Inn at Union Square	212	Normandy Inn	191
Inn at West View Farm	139	Norwich Inn & Spa	29

221

Index

Notchland Inn	105	Sugar Lodge	144
Oaks	188	Swag Country Inn	205
Ocean Edge Resort & Golf Club	69	Thorncroft Inn	74
Ocean Gate	53	Tides Inn	181
Ocean Point Inn	53	Trillium House	189
October Country Inn	142	Tucker Hill Lodge	145
Old Mystic Inn	32	Two Angels Inn	212
Old Tavern at Grafton	128	Vermont Inn	145
Olde Orchard Inn	106	Verona House	201
Onset Pointe Inn	86	Villa	112
Peacock Hill	214	Village Country Inn	146
Pineapple Hill	171	Village Green Inn	88
Planters Inn	207	Village House	107
Pleasant Bay Village Resort	86	Village Inn	89
Publick House Historic Inn	70	Wades Point Inn on the Bay	156
Quechee Bed & Breakfast	142	Waterville Estates Resort	100
Queen Anne Inn (Mass)	87	Weathervane Inn	89
Queen Anne Inn (Colorado)	212	Wedgewood Inn	90
Rabbit Hill Inn	129	Wedgwood Inn of New Hope	173
Red Lion Inn	72	West Hill House	146
Ripplecove Inn	23	West Mountain Inn	147
Riverwind Inn	32	Whalewalk Inn	75
Rocky Shores Inn & Cottages	87	White Hart Inn	33
Rose Inn	166	Wildflower Inn	90
Rosevine Inn	214	Windham Hill Inn	131
Roycroft Inn	163	Windsor Inn	192
Sagamore on Lake George	164	Woodland Inn	213
Salem Inn	73	Woods	147
Sedgwick Inn	166	Woodstock Inn & Resort	132
Settlers Inn	172	Yankee Clipper Inn	76
Sharon Inn	88	York Harbor Inn	54
Shelburne Inn	214		
Shipman House	213	**INDEX OF ADVERTISERS**	
Shire Inn	143		
Siebeness	143	Capital Region	148
Sise Inn	98	Distinctive Inns of New England	55
Snowvillage Inn	99	Heritage Plantation of Sandwich	82
Southwest Inn at Sedona	211	Old Sturbridge Village	71
Spruce Point Inn	43	Original Historic Inns of New England	113
Stage Neck Inn	44	Plimouth Plantation	77
Staunton Hill Country Inn	180	Shelburne Museum	133
Steeles Tavern Manor	189	Vermont State	116
Sterling Inn	172	Wexas	223
Sugarbush Inn & Resort	130	Pride of Britain	215
Sugarloaf	45	Ireland's Blue Book	216
Sugartree	144	Portfolio Collection	217
Sugar Hill Inn	106		

FREE 940-PAGE TRAVELLER'S HANDBOOK WHEN YOU JOIN

WEXAS

Est. 1970

Discount scheduled airfares worldwide

WEXAS International, the UK's Premier Travel Club, offers a range of membership publications and tailor-made travel services, including scheduled flights from a choice of UK airports to hundreds of destinations worldwide at special members-only fares. Business and leisure travellers alike can enjoy all the benefits and money-saving advantages of belonging to a large reputable travel organisation from just £39.58 a year (1997 subscription).

JOIN NOW

by calling the
WEXAS Membership Services Department on

0171-589 3315

INVESTOR IN PEOPLE | V2128 ABTA 91989 | IATA ACCREDITED AGENT | ATOL 2873

WEXAS International
45-49 Brompton Road, Knightsbridge, London SW3 1DE
Tel: 0171-589 3315 Fax: 0171-589 8418 email: mship@wexas.com

A FREE COPY OF ...
Welcome News

... INDISPENSABLE FOR INDEPENDENT TRAVELLERS !

New quarterly full-colour newsletter

Travel tips * News & views * Seasonal offers
Special purchases * Regional recipes * Plus lots more....

CALL TODAY FOR YOUR FREE COPY

Tel 01923 821469 (U.K. Office)   Fax 01923 827157
Toll free number in US & Canada 1-888-INN VISIT